Creating User Interfaces
by Demonstration

PERSPECTIVES IN COMPUTING, Vol. 22

**(Formerly "Notes and Reports in Computer Science
and Applied Mathematics")**

Creating User Interfaces by Demonstration

Brad A. Myers
Department of Computer Science
Carnegie-Mellon University
Pittsburgh, Pennsylvania

ACADEMIC PRESS, INC.
Harcourt Brace Jovanovich, Publishers

Boston San Diego New York
Berkeley London Sydney
Tokyo Toronto

QA
76
.9
U83
M83
1988

ACADEMIC PRESS, INC.
1250 Sixth Avenue, San Diego, CA 92101

United Kingdom Edition published by
ACADEMIC PRESS, INC. (LONDON) LTD.
24-28 Oval Road, London NW1 7DX

Library of Congress Cataloging-in-Publication Data
Myers, Brad A.
    Creating user interfaces by demonstration / Brad A. Myers.
        p. cm.—(Perspectives in computing; vol. 22)
    Bibliography: p.
    Includes index.
    ISBN 0-12-512305-1
    1. User interfaces (Computer systems) 2. Computer graphics.
I. Title. II. Series: Perspectives in computing (Boston, Mass.);
vol. 22.
QA76.9.U83M94 1988
004'.01'9—dc19   88-12641
                                                CIP

Dedicated to my wife
Bernita

Table of Contents

List of Figures

Preface

This book describes the design and implementation of Peridot, and the research that led to its development. Peridot is a new, experimental tool for creating interaction techniques, and could be a critical component of future comprehensive User Interface Management Systems (UIMSs). This work was performed as part of the author's PhD research at the University of Toronto, Toronto, Ontario, Canada.

Peridot makes two important contributions: First, it demonstrates that user interface designers can create complex, graphical, highly-interactive interfaces by demonstration rather than by programming. Second, Peridot shows that Visual Programming, Programming by Example, Constraints, and Plausible Inference can be successfully integrated into practical, useful and easy-to-use systems.

The interaction techniques created by Peridot include many used in direct manipulation-style interfaces. To specify an interface, the designer demonstrates how it should look and act by drawing the screen display that the end user will see, and then manipulating the mouse and other input devices to show what the end user will do. This is achieved by combining some ideas that have shown promise in previous research but have seemed impractical for actual use. These techniques are *Visual Programming*, where programs are specified in a two-dimensional fashion, *Programming by Example*, where programs are created using examples of input and output data, *Constraints*, where relationships among graphical objects and data are automatically maintained even if the objects and data change, and *Plausible Inference*, where the relationships are guessed based on contextual information.

Peridot stands for Programming by Example for Real-time Interface Design Obviating Typing, and is a working prototype that is able to create many types of interaction techniques, including most kinds of menus, property sheets, light buttons, radio buttons, scroll bars, two-dimensional scroll boxes, percent-done progress indicators, graphical potentiometers, sliders, iconic and title line controls for windows, and many others. Thus, Peridot can create almost all of the Apple Macintosh interface, as well as many new interfaces, such as those which use multiple input devices concurrently. Peridot also created its own user interface. Peridot provides extremely rapid prototyping, since interfaces can be created and edited very quickly and easily.

Acknowledgements

I would like to thank my primary advisor, William Buxton, and my "official" advisor, Professor Ronald Baecker, for their support and good ideas. I would also like to thank the other members of my committee: Professors Fred Lochovsky, Ric Holt, Dave Wortman, John Mylopoulos, Russ Greiner, and Neville Moray, and the external reviewer Professor James D. Foley from George Washington University, for their support and helpful comments. For help with this and other papers on Peridot, I would like to thank Peter Rowley, Ralph Hill, Bernita Myers, William Buxton, and Ronald Baecker.

This research would not have been possible without the generous donation of equipment, software, and support from Xerox Canada, Inc. who supplied us with the Lisp machines, printer, file server, and the Interlisp-D environment. This research was also partially funded by the Natural Sciences and Engineering Research Council (NSERC) of Canada.

On the personal side, I would especially like to thank my wife, Bernita Myers, for her continued support and encouragement, and my parents and grandparents who made my education possible. I would like to also thank my son, Ryan, whose birth date gave the name to my system (Peridot is the birthstone for August).

Chapter I
Introduction

Peridot is a new, experimental tool for creating interaction techniques, and could be a critical component of future comprehensive User Interface Management Systems (UIMSs). This book describes the design and implementation of Peridot, and the research that led to its development[1]. Peridot, which stands for Programming by Example for Real-time Interface Design Obviating Typing, allows the user interface designer to create graphical, dynamic, highly interactive user interfaces by demonstration without programming. It is implemented in Interlisp-D [Xerox 83] on a Xerox 1109 DandeTiger workstation. With Peridot, the designer *demonstrates* what the user interface should look like and how the end user will interact with it. This approach frees designers from having to do any programming in the conventional sense, and allows them to design the user interface in a very natural manner. The general strategy of Peridot is to allow the designer to *draw* the screen display that the end user will see, and to *perform* actions just as the end user would, such as moving a mouse, pressing its buttons, turning a knob, or toggling a switch. The results are immediately visible and executable on the screen and can be edited easily. Peridot produces parameterized procedures, like those found in interaction technique libraries such as the Apple Macintosh Toolbox. The designer gives examples of typical values for the parameters and Peridot automatically guesses (or *infers*) how they should be used in the general case. The procedures created by Peridot can be called from application programs and used as part of other user interfaces. Peridot created its own interface and can create almost all of the interaction techniques in the Macintosh Toolbox.

Peridot uses a new approach to UIMS design. It successfully integrates Visual Programming, Programming by Example, Constraints and Plausible Inference. These techniques have not been combined in previous systems.

---

[1] Previous papers about Peridot are [Myers 86a] [Myers 86b] [Myers 87a] [Myers 87b] [Myers 87c].

1.1. Definition of Terms

Before describing Peridot, it is necessary to define some basic terminology.

The *user interface (UI)* of a computer program is the part that presents displays and accepts input from the person using the program. The rest of the program is called the *application* or the *application semantics*. A comprehensive *User Interface Management System (UIMS)* is a tool that helps a programmer create and manage all aspects of user interfaces.

One important component of a UIMS is an *interaction technique library*. This contains a collection of interaction techniques with which the interface is created. An *interaction technique* is a way of using a physical input device (mouse, keyboard, tablet, rotary knob, etc.) to input a certain type of value (command, number, percent, location, name, etc.). Examples of interaction techniques are menus, graphical sliders, and on-screen "light buttons."

Other important parts of UIMSs are the *Dialogue Control Component*, which handles the sequencing of events and interaction techniques, and the *Analysis Component* which helps to study and evaluate the user interface after it has been created. Very few tools for creating user interfaces can be called comprehensive UIMSs since they do not address all of these aspects. Therefore, in this book, a tool will be called a UIMS even if it only addresses some of the components.

There are four different classes of people involved with any UIMS and it is important to have different names for them so there is no confusion. One person is the designer of the UIMS (e.g., me). This person will be called the *UIMS creator*. The next person is the designer of a user interface, and will use the UIMS. This person may be a programmer or a graphic artist, depending on the specification technique used by the UIMS, and will be called the *user interface designer* or just *designer* for short. Another person involved is the programmer that creates the application program which has as its front end the user interface created by the user interface designer. This person is the *application programmer*. The final person involved is the person who actually uses the final product. This person is the *end user* or just *user*. Note that although this classification discusses each role as a different person, in fact, there may be many people in each role or one person may perform multiple roles.

A *pointing device* is a piece of hardware that returns a two (or more) dimensional value. The user identifies locations on the screen by simply pointing to them with the pointing device. Examples of pointing devices are light-pens, electromagnetic tablets, touch-sensitive surfaces, and mechanical or optical "mice." Typically, a small picture, called a "cursor" or "tracking symbol," follows the movement of the pointing device on the screen. Pointing devices typically have one or more buttons associated with them that allow the user to signal that the current point is of interest. The Interlisp system supporting Peridot uses an optical mouse with two buttons, so the term "mouse" will be used in this book instead of the more general "pointing device." The cursor used in Peridot is a small arrow pointing to the upper-left.

The interfaces that Peridot can create make heavy use of mice or other graphical (non-keyboard) input devices, and some of these are classified as *direct manipulation* interfaces [Shneiderman 83] [Hutchins 86]. As defined by Shneiderman [83, p. 57], "the central ideas [are] visibility of the object of interest; rapid, reversible, incremental actions; and replacement of complex command language syntax by direct manipulation — hence the term 'direct manipulation.' " For example, to move an object, the user might select it with the mouse and drag it to a new location.

When the user performs any action on the computer (e.g. moving the mouse, issuing a command, selecting an object, etc.), the user interface will typically provide some sort of pictorial or textual response on the screen. For example, when the user moves the mouse over a menu, the item under the mouse might be shown in a different color. This is called *feedback*. When the application is involved in feedback, so that application-specific information is required to provide the appropriate feedback, this is called *semantic feedback* [Myers prep]. Semantic feedback can be distinguished from low-level *lexical feedback* in that the former denotes "message understood" rather than "message received" [Thomas 83, p. 13]. For example, an object being dragged might jump to "legal" points, where the application determines what is legal based on context. This is often called "gravity" and an advanced form is "Snap-Dragging" [Bier 86]. Another example where semantic feedback is required is a simulation of a bridge, where the mouse is used to pull on various parts to show the loading, and the graphics change based on the structural analysis. These types of feedback are sufficiently complicated that the UIMS cannot provide them locally without access to the application's data structures. This is closely related to issues of *semantic error checking* and *semantic default values* which involve the application in detecting and handling errors and calculating default values. Taken together, these techniques can be called *fine-grain* control. The alternative, called *coarse-grain* control, is when an application is only notified at large intervals (typically, when a command and all its arguments have been gathered).

In order to try a new approach to User Interface Management Systems, Peridot uses ideas from *Visual Programming* and *Example-Based Programming* with *Plausible Inferencing,* and *Constraints* [Myers 86a]. *Visual Programming (VP)* refers to any system that allows the user to specify a program in a two (or more) dimensional fashion. Conventional textual languages are not considered two dimensional since the compilers or interpreters process them as long, one-dimensional streams. Visual Programming includes conventional flow charts and graphical programming languages. It does not include systems that use conventional (linear) programming languages to define pictures. This eliminates most graphics editors, like Sketchpad [Sutherland 63]. In addition, systems that use graphics to illustrate a program after it has been written in a conventional language do not use Visual Programming; these are classified as *Program Visualization* systems.

Peridot also uses a limited form of *Inferencing.* To draw an inference is to come to believe a new fact based on other information [Charniak 85, p. 14]. In particular, Peridot uses *Plausible Inference,* also called *abduction,* where the system generates explanations or generalizations based on limited information. These are only guesses and can be incorrect. In this book, the more general term "inference" is used to mean "plausible inference."

Example-Based Programming (EBP) refers to systems that allow the programmer to use examples of input and output data during the programming process. Some of these systems try to guess or *infer* the program from examples of input and output or sample traces of execution. This is often called "automatic programming" or *Programming by Example (PBE)* and has generally been an area of Artificial Intelligence research. Another class of systems require the programmer to specify everything about the program (there is no inferencing involved), but the programmer can work out the program on a specific example. The system executes the programmer's commands normally, but remembers them for later re-use. Buxton [private communication] coined the phrase *Programming with Examples (PWE)* to more accurately describe these systems. Halbert [84] characterizes Programming with Examples as "Do What I Did" whereas inferential Programming by Example might be "Do What I Mean." Peridot uses inferencing, so it is a Programming-by-Example system.

An important component of Peridot is *constraints,* which are relationships among objects and data that must hold no matter how the objects are manipulated. There are two forms of constraints used in Peridot. *Graphical constraints* insure that relationships among graphical objects (rectangles, circles, strings, etc.) always hold. An example of a graphical constraint is that a string is centered inside a rectangle. *Data constraints* insure that a graphical object has a particular relationship to a data value. An example of a data constraint is that the diameter of a circle is the same as the value of a parameter to a procedure.

Peridot uses *active values* to control any parts of the interface that can change at run time. *Active values* are like parameters to procedures except that their values can change at any time while the interface is being displayed. Parameters, on the other hand, are assigned a particular value when the interface is instantiated and retain that same value. Typically, graphical objects will be tied to active values using data constraints, so the objects will be immediately updated when the active value changes.

1.2. Motivation for UIMSs

Creating a good user interface for a system is a difficult task, and the software to support the user interfaces is often large, complex, and difficult to debug and modify. The user interface for an application is usually a significant fraction of the code. One study found that the user interface portion was between 29% and 88% [Sutton 78]. In artificial intelligence applications, an informal poll found it was about 50% [Fox 86], which is supported by one AI project which reported 40% [Mittal 86]. Unfortunately, it is generally the case that as user interfaces become easier to use for the end user, they become more complex and harder to create for the UI designer. The easy-to-use direct manipulation interfaces popular with most modern systems are among the most difficult kinds to implement [Williams 83] [Smith 82]. Some reasons for this are that they provide (a) elaborate graphics, (b) multiple ways for giving the same command, (c) a "mode free" interface, where the user can give any command at virtually any time, and (d) semantic feedback inside inner loops of interaction techniques.

1.2.1. Rapid Prototyping

In addition to being difficult to create, there are no guidelines or design strategies that will insure that the resulting user interface will be learnable, easy to use, and "user-friendly." Consequently, the only reliable method for generating quality user interfaces is to test prototypes with actual end users and modify the design based on the users' comments [Buxton 80] [Swartout 82] [Mason 83] [Anderson 85]. As reported by Sheil [83] "complex interactive interfaces usually require extensive empirical testing to determine whether they are really effective and considerable redesign to make them so." This methodology is called "iterative design" and has been used in the creation of some of the best current user interfaces: the Xerox Star [Bewley 83], the Apple Lisa [Morgan 83], and the Olympic Messaging system [Boies 85]. A particularly compelling example is presented by Good [84] where a mail system with a conventional textual command interface was iteratively modified. In the final version, without any instruction, 76% of the commands that novices naturally generated performed the expected operation.

The conventional technique for creating these easy-to-use interfaces is to have the user interface designer draw pictures on paper ("story boards") for how the user interface will look and act. These designs are then handed to pro- grammers who laboriously code the interfaces by hand. There clearly are many problems with this approach. The interfaces are difficult and expensive to create and hard to modify. In addition, it is very difficult to get a sense for how the user interface will "feel" since the story boards do not capture the dynamic behavior of the user interface, which is the most important part [Mason 83].

Consequently, there is a great desire to make the creation of user interfaces easier and quicker, and to make them easier to modify once created. Rapid pro- totyping is the ability to create and modify mock-ups of user interfaces quickly and easily.

1.2.2. Advantages of UIMSs

To provide rapid prototyping, and also to make the final user interfaces cheaper and easier to create, a number of User Interface Management Systems [Thomas 83] [Olsen 84] [Pfaff 85] have been created. Some of these have been successful. For example, the Apple MacApp UIMS has been reported to reduce development time by a factor of four or five [Schmucker 86]. In general, the advantages of using UIMSs are (from [Olsen 84] and [Thomas 83]):

- Designs can be rapidly prototyped and implemented.

- The overall quality of the resulting interfaces should be higher since it will be easier to incorporate changes discovered through user testing.

- Interactive applications can be more quickly and economically maintained.

- Use of a UIMS provides a more consistent interface both within and across applications.

- Interface specifications can be represented, validated, and evaluated more easily.

- Distribution of functionality across systems and processors is facilitated.

- The proper roles of the various people involved in interface development are represented and supported throughout the evolution of the interface. In particular, professional user interface designers (sometimes called "User Interface Architects" [Foley 84a]), who may not be programmers, should be involved in the design process.

- The ability to have non-programmers rapidly modify interfaces should allow system designers and salesmen to try different interfaces on products in front of customers and end users, and immediately incorporate their suggestions.

- The separation of the management of user dialogues from the application and the graphics package should allow the use of various physical devices and interaction techniques.

- There should be a cost savings due to the reduced construction cost and the increased usability of the product.

- The reliability of the user interface should be higher. Since the code for the user interface is created automatically from a higher level specification, it should be easier to get bug-free user interfaces.

1.2.3. Tools for Creating Interaction Techniques

As discussed in sections 1.1 and 2.2.1, user interfaces can be broken down into different levels. Many UIMSs have addressed the higher levels of user interfaces: connecting together various interaction techniques to construct an interface. Very few current UIMSs create the interaction techniques themselves (see section 2.2). The motivation for this is that interaction techniques are created once and stored in a library, and then used many times in many different interfaces. Peridot, however, is aimed at creating the interaction techniques themselves, so it is appropriate to discuss why this level should be addressed.

When the interface for a new software system or product is being designed, one of the first decisions is to choose the style of the interface. If it is going to conform to an existing style (e.g. a new Apple Macintosh program is likely to use the Macintosh style), then the designers will probably use a library that supplies interaction techniques supporting that style (e.g. the Macintosh Toolbox [Apple 85]). However, if the new system will have its own style or if it will be an environment unto itself, then the designers will need to investigate what style of interaction techniques should be used. They will probably want to try a number of styles and test them with end users. The choices might include single versus multiple clicking, one, two, or three buttons on the mouse, use of function keys versus the mouse, using additional input devices such as touch tablets, etc. The software for these interaction techniques is often relatively complex and hard to build [Cardelli 85]. Therefore, it would be helpful to have a UIMS that makes it easier to create these interfaces for testing and rapid prototyping.

Another motivation is that vendors of commercial software generally want their products to have a unique "feel." This comes from the desire to differentiate their products and to avoid copyright violation problems. Clearly, it is most appropriate to have a different user interface on products where the end user will be using that one product exclusively, as opposed to using different products from different vendors on the same machine. There are many examples of this in computer publishing, CAD/CAM/CAE, etc. Most UIMSs and libraries of interaction techniques provide only one style and "feel" for the graphics and operations. A UIMS that provided the ability to change the graphics (e.g. add and remove drop shadows, change the style for highlighting, etc.), as well as changing the way that the interaction techniques work, would allow vendors to customize their interfaces with less effort.

A final motivation is that many of the innovations in user interface design are at the interaction technique level. A UIMS that supports creation of interaction techniques might therefore promote research in new forms of user interfaces.

1.3. Problems with Existing UIMSs

The concept of UIMSs have gained general acceptance in the research and business communities. This can be seen by the large number of papers on UIMSs that appear in recent SIGGRAPH and SIGCHI conferences. In practice, however, very few commercial UIMSs have been used to any large extent[2], but there are a rising number of UIMS products. Unfortunately, most user interfaces are still created by hand without the use of appropriate tools. Two reasons for this are that (1) current UIMSs are very hard to use and often require the user interface designer to learn a special purpose programming-like language, and (2) UIMSs typically are fairly limited in the types of interfaces that they can create with few able to create direct manipulation style interfaces [Myers 87b].

One avowed goal of UIMSs is to allow professional UI designers who are not programmers to create user interfaces. Most UIMSs, however, use a textual

---

[2]Exceptions apparently include ACT/1 [Mason 83] and Apollo's ADM [Schulert 85].

specification with a rigid syntax that is a form of programming language or is much like one. These are too complicated to be used by non-programmers [Buxton 83]. Olsen [87] reports that there is a great reluctance on the part of UI designers to use UIMSs for this reason, and Shneiderman [86] has called for a system in which direct manipulation techniques are used to create direct manipulation interfaces.

Unfortunately, it is hardest to make UIMSs that can create the modern, direct manipulation style of interfaces that are popular for most new systems. For example, very few UIMSs can create the interaction techniques used in direct manipulation interfaces or can support semantic feedback. In addition, few UIMSs provide appropriate mechanisms to handle multiple interaction techniques that are *available* at the same time (so the user can choose which one is desired), and also multiple interactions that are *operating* at the same time (such as different devices under each hand). Having multiple interactions available is a cornerstone of mode-free interfaces, and using multiple devices in parallel has been shown to increase users' efficiency and satisfaction with systems in some experiments [Buxton 86].

1.4. Goals for Peridot

In order to address these problems, a research project was formed to investigate new approaches to user interface design and specification. The result of this research was the Peridot User Interface Management System. The goals for this project were to make a UIMS that:

- Is able to create highly interactive interfaces. This includes:

  — creating interaction techniques themselves,

  — investigating new forms of interaction techniques,

  — supporting multiple interaction techniques available and operating at the same time, and

  — supporting semantic feedback, semantic error checking and semantic defaults that work at a sufficient speed.

- Is easy to use. Creating user interfaces should be almost as easy as using them. This includes:

  — demonstrating both the look (graphic displays) and available actions (based on input devices),

  — allowing the interface to be created without conventional programming,

— using direct manipulation techniques whenever appropriate,

— using automatic inferencing (guessing answers) whenever appropriate to eliminate some work for the designer,

— allowing all graphics and interactions to be easily edited, and

— making the interface visible at all times so changes are immediately apparent.

- Significantly shortens the time to develop these kinds of interfaces and thereby provides extremely rapid prototyping.

- Creates reasonably efficient code so that:

— the resulting interfaces can be used with actual application programs, and

— the professional UI designer designs *and implements* the interface.

1.5. Conceptual Design of Peridot

Peridot attempts to meet these goals by taking a new approach to UIMS design. It uses ideas from Visual Programming, Example-Based Programming, Constraints and Plausible Inferencing. These areas have never been integrated into a UIMS before. Peridot successfully combines these technologies by limiting the domain in which they are applied, and by choosing the parts that can be implemented efficiently.

Visual Programming contributes the idea of creating programs by drawing pictures. As discussed in section 2.3.3.1, most Visual Programming systems have attempted to address general purpose programming and have not been successful. Creating graphical user interfaces is a very appropriate domain in which to use Visual Programming since the result is inherently graphical.

From Example-Based Programming comes the idea of developing the procedure using examples of the data that it will process. In Peridot, this allows the user interface designer to see an actual example of the interface being created. If Example-Based Programming were not used then no picture of the interface could be displayed, and the designer would have to design the interface abstractly, as with most other systems. This would be much more difficult because it would be less concrete and direct. Peridot is more successful than other Example-Based Programming systems because it limits the domain in which examples are used, so it is always easy to understand what the examples mean. The ambiguity inherent in using examples is minimized since there are only a small number of possible ways to generalize from the examples. Also, automatic inferencing alleviates the problem of requiring the user to specify which of the possible generalizations should hold.

Two kinds of constraints are used in Peridot: graphical constraints and data constraints. Graphical constraints are used to define the relationships among graphical picture elements (rectangles, circles, text and icons). The relationships supported by Peridot are much more restrictive than constraints in other systems. In Peridot, all of the graphical constraints can be executed in constant time for each object and do not require any complex constraint satisfaction techniques. The constraints are one-directional and recursion is not allowed. The vast majority of the graphical constraints are one of two forms: that a position attribute of an object is centered with respect to another object, or that an attribute of one object is a constant offset from an attribute of another object. These simple forms are sufficient to handle almost all the relationships that realistically hold in user interfaces. Other kinds of relationships can be explicitly defined by the designer, if necessary.

Data constraints in Peridot are also uni-directional and efficiently implemented. Active values keep a list of the graphical objects that have data constraints with them and reevaluate the attributes of those objects when the value changes. This simple mechanism is used to handle all dynamic updating in Peridot.

Plausible inferencing is used in Peridot to alleviate the problem of specifying what the constraints should be, and for specifying how to generalize from the particular examples provided. The inferencing mechanism is very simple because the domain severely limits the number of reasonable possibilities. In addition, inferencing in Peridot is more successful than in previous systems because Peridot assumes that the guesses will occasionally be incorrect. Therefore, three strategies are used to protect against incorrect inferences: Peridot always asks the designer to confirm every inference, the results of each inference are always clearly and immediately visible or executable on the screen, and the inference can be undone if incorrect.

1.6. Contributions of Peridot

The primary contributions of Peridot are:

- Peridot demonstrates that Visual Programming, Programming by Example, Graphical and Data Constraints, and Plausible Inferencing can be efficiently and effectively applied in computer systems.

- Peridot shows that it is possible to have a non-programmer create graphical, highly interactive, direct manipulation interfaces. With Peridot, user interface specialists, graphic artists, psychologists, human factors experts, ergonomists, etc. will be able to design, modify, and implement user interfaces.

Other major contributions of Peridot are:

- As far as we know, Peridot is the first system to allow the dynamic, interactive behavior of user interfaces to be specified in a demonstrational manner without programming.

- As far as we know, Peridot is also the first system to create parameterized user interface procedures by demonstration without programming.

- Peridot demonstrates that it is possible to provide *extremely rapid prototyping*. It takes very little time to create interaction techniques from scratch. For example, a simple menu such as Figure 1.1 took me only 3 minutes, and the complex scroll mechanism of the Macintosh (Figure 9.5) took only 30 minutes. This is around a factor of 50 faster than programming these interfaces by hand (see section 15.4). In addition, when the designer edits an interface, the results are immediately visible, and when the designer changes the behavior of the mouse or other input devices, the new behavior can be executed immediately. For example, to change the color of the border of the menu of Figure 1.1 only takes 10 seconds, and to modify the strings to be centered instead of left justified takes 45 seconds.

- Peridot demonstrates that graphical constraints can be automatically inferred using a simple form of plausible inference, and that this will be helpful to users and appreciated by them.

- Peridot demonstrates that a limited form of graphical constraints, which is still highly useful, can implemented efficiently so that they can be used in actual systems.

Figure 1.1.
A simple menu that can be created in about 3 minutes in Peridot.

- Peridot demonstrates that active values with data constraints are an appropriate and useful communication mechanism for user interface construction. Active values provide a modular structure in which semantic feedback and fine grain control can be provided. Applications can be involved in providing feedback, error checking, and default values at a low level, which is still efficient. The application is insulated from details of the graphic presentation of the feedback and input techniques used to generate the values. Peridot also supports coarse-grain control, in which applications are not called until there is a substantial amount of work to be done.

- Peridot demonstrates that active values are an effective way to support concurrency for input and output. Multiple input devices can be active at the same time, and application programs can have multiple processes updating output objects at the same time.

- The interactions that Peridot supports are all based on three primitive mouse behaviors: choice, changing in a range, and changing freely. This suggests that there might be similar primitives with which other kinds of interfaces could be built, leading to a taxonomy of interaction techniques and user interfaces in general.

Some lower level contributions of Peridot are:

- The interface to Peridot is similar to that of MacDraw and other software designed for the general public which suggests that end users might be able to use Peridot to customize interfaces on programs they receive. Peridot has successfully been used by 5 non-programmers to edit and create interfaces (see section 14.3) which suggests that Peridot itself is easy to use.

- Peridot allows the user interface designer to choose among application (internal) control, UIMS (external) control, or parallel control [Tanner 85]. For application control, the interfaces can be constructed as a procedure library, or, for UIMS control, the interfaces can call application procedures when events happen. Since Peridot supports multiprocessing, parallel and mixed control are also possible.

- Peridot promotes structured design and creates well structured code. The designer creates functions with (optional) parameters and return values for each interaction technique and then combines these procedures into higher level structures. Many previous UIMSs have promoted unstructured programming with GOTOs and global variables, whereas Peridot uses iterations, conditionals, and parameterized functions. In addition, calls to application procedures from within Peridot are appropriately parameterized.

- Since user interfaces are created graphically and by demonstration in Peridot, it is much easier for the designer to visualize the resulting interfaces. This may increase the quality of the interfaces and will certainly make it easier for designers to create the interface they have in mind. Most other UIMSs require the designer to use a textual specification for the interface.

- Peridot easily deals with continuous operations, such as dragging, whereas many UIMSs only deal with discrete operations.

1.7. Overview of Book

Peridot uses a new approach to user interface design. It is based on the idea of presenting a computer-based story board of the interface, so the designer can present an example of the interface in action to the computer. Peridot is therefore an enhanced drawing package and it creates the actual interfaces when the original picture is drawn. In order to achieve this, Peridot uses ideas from other areas: Visual Programming, Programming By Example, Constraints, and active values, which are discussed in Chapter 2. Chapter 2 also discusses some existing UIMSs. Chapter 3 gives an overview of the design of Peridot and works through an extended example.

Chapter 4 discusses graphical constraints and the rule-based plausible inferencing that guesses them. All of the interfaces can be easily edited in various ways (Chapter 5) and the changes can be seen and run immediately.

Peridot also infers control structures: iterations through lists (such as the menu items in Figure 1.1), which are discussed in Chapter 6, and conditionals (for choices in iterations, such as the black rectangle in Figure 1.1, as well as making objects appear and disappear), which are discussed in Chapter 7. Using "active values," Peridot supports connection to the application program and semantic feedback. "Active values" (Chapter 8) are variables that can change at run time and have data constraints that cause the associated graphics to change immediately.

One of Peridot's important innovations is allowing the behavior of the mouse to be programmed by demonstration (Chapter 9) including support for selection, constrained or unconstrained dragging, exceptions and multiple-clicking.

Peridot also supports other input devices, such as a clock, sliders, and switches (Chapter 10). Peridot creates efficient code so that all interfaces can be used with actual application programs (Chapter 11).

Chapter 12 discusses the Programming by Example and Visual Programming aspects of Peridot and how these techniques have been used successfully.

Although ideas for design and implementation enhancements are contained in each chapter, the more global changes and ideas are discussed in Chapter 13.

Chapter 14 discusses the experience of implementing Peridot in Interlisp-D, and what the designers who used Peridot thought of it. Finally, Chapter 15 summarizes the book and reviews the contributions.

The appendices contain some auxiliary information. Appendix A shows pictures with brief descriptions of a variety of interfaces created using Peridot. Appendix B compares Peridot with Ralph Hill's Sassafras system [Hill 87a] [Hill 87b] [Hill 87c], which was created concurrently with Peridot, also at the University of Toronto. Appendix C lists the commands available to the designer, and Appendix D lists the rules used by Peridot to infer graphical constraints.

Chapter II

Related Research

2.1. Introduction

The design for Peridot was influenced by research in a number of areas. These include User Interface Management Systems (UIMSs), Visual Programming, and Programming By Example with inferencing, constraints, and active values. This chapter discusses related research in each of these areas.

2.2. User Interface Management Systems

2.2.1. Structure of UIMSs

There does not seem to be any general agreement about what should be called a User Interface Management System, beyond an idea that it is something that helps to build user interfaces. Section 1.1 defines a comprehensive UIMS as a tool that helps the programmer create and manage all parts of user interfaces. Figure 2.1 shows a model by Tanner and Buxton [Tanner 85] for the important parts of user interface design that should be handled by a UIMS[1]. Here the term "UIMS" will be used in a more general way for tools that create *any* part of the user interface. This will include tools, such as Peridot, for creating the interaction techniques in the library. Section 2.2.2 discusses these. Most UIMSs, however, are directed at "gluing" the interaction techniques together. These UIMSs are discussed in Section 2.2.3.

2.2.2. Interaction Technique Libraries and Builders

Most window systems, such as Sapphire [Myers 84] and the Apple Lisa [Williams 83] and Macintosh [Apple 85] come with a set of routines that application programs can use. These include menus of various types, scroll bars, etc. Using a library has the advantage that the final UI will look and act similarly to other UIs created using the same library, but clearly the styles of interaction are limited to those provided. In addition, the libraries themselves are often expensive to create: "The primitives never seem complex in principle,

---

[1] The figure is slightly modified from [Tanner 85]. The parts labeled "Interaction Technique" in the figure are called "Modules" in [Tanner 85].

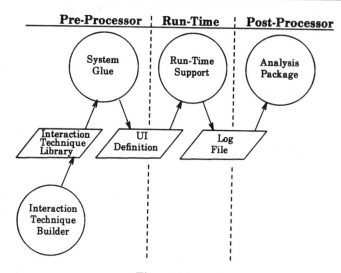

Figure 2.1.
Model for User Interface Management Systems (from [Tanner 85]).

but the programs that implement them are surprisingly intricate'' [Cardelli 85, p. 199].

A few UIMSs have been built to help create interaction techniques. Squeak [Cardelli 85] is a textual language for programming mouse interfaces that exploits concurrency. Squeak supports multiple devices active at the same time, and the primitive inputs are mouse button transitions, keyboard keys, incremental movements of the mouse or other devices, and clock timeouts. Squeak attempts to compile the program into a non-sequential state machine. Although it provides a compact notation for specifying complex, time-dependent interfaces, correct code is unfortunately still fairly difficult to write in Squeak. For example, the article presents a buggy attempt to handle mouse button double-clicking.

A new UIMS that allows interaction techniques to be specified textually using tables is Panther [Helfman 87]. Here, the designer specifies what action should happen in each region of the screen. Options deal with the highlighting style, procedures for drawing the picture in the region, and procedures to call when a button is pressed in the region. Panther supports menus, forms and sliders, but the entire specification must be created using typed-in numbers and procedure calls. Figure 2.2 shows an example of a Panther specification.

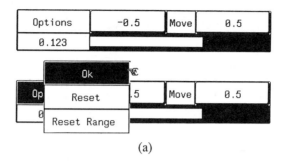

(a)

name	coordinates $x1,x2,y1,y2$				highlight style	draw flag	parent name	draw routine	selection routines		
OPTS {	1,	103,	1,	32,	1,	0,	BAR,	PANdbox("Options"),	BARpopup(POP),	0,	0 }
RANO {	104,	211,	1,	32,	1,	1,	BAR,	PANdran(RANO,0),	PANpickran(0,1),	0,	0 }
MOVE {	212,	253,	1,	32,	1,	0,	BAR,	PANdbox("Move"),	BARmoveparent(),	0,	0 }
RAN1 {	254,	360,	1,	32,	1,	1,	BAR,	PANdran(RAN1,1),	PANpickran(1,1),	0,	0 }
BARO {	104,	360,	38,	50,	2,	1,	BAR,	PANdbar(BARO,VALO),	PANupbar(0),	0,	0 }
VALO {	2,	102,	34,	55,	1,	1,	BAR,	PANdval(0),	PANpickval(0),	0,	0 }
OK {	1,	120,	1,	32,	1,	0,	POP,	PANdbox("Ok"),	BARok(),	0,	0 }
SET {	1,	120,	33,	65,	1,	0,	POP,	PANdbox("Reset"),	BARrset(),	0,	0 }
RSET {	1,	120,	66,	98,	1,	0,	POP,	PANdbox("Reset Range"),	BARranset(),	0,	0 }
BAR {	0,	361,	0,	57,	0,	0,	0,	PANdpic(0),	0,	0,	0 }
POP {	0,	121,	0,	99,	0,	0,	BAR,	PANdpic(0),	0,	0,	0 }

(b)

Figure 2.2.

Two interfaces (a) and their specification using an "input table" (b) in Panther [Helf-
man 87].

2.2.3. "Glue" Systems

Many (probably most) UIMSs concentrate on combining ("gluing") the
interaction techniques together after they have been created, since it is often
non-trivial to write the programs that coordinate the interaction techniques.
This is evidenced by the need for the MacApp system [Schmucker 86] to help
write programs that use the Macintosh Toolbox. These systems can be
classified into a number of groups: those that use state transition networks,
those that use grammars, those that use a pointing device to allow the designer
to place interaction techniques, those that use object-oriented techniques, and
others.

2.2.3.1. State Transition Networks

Newman implemented a simple UIMS using finite state machines in 1968
[Newman 68]. Many of the assumptions and techniques used in modern systems were present in Newman's: different languages for defining the user interface and the semantics (the semantic routines were coded in a normal

programming language), a table-driven syntax analyzer, and device indepen-
dence. Newman's system only handled textual input, but it was apparently the
first UIMS.

Jacob [83a] claims that defining a user interface using state transition
diagrams is better than using formal grammars because the time sequence is
explicit with diagrams. The specification can be created in a textual [Jacob 84]
or graphical [Jacob 85] manner. Figure 2.3 shows a diagram created with the
system. There are separate diagrams for the syntactic and lexical levels of the
interface, and, like all other UIMSs, the semantic level is coded in a conventional language. The diagrams can have potentially recursive calls to other
diagrams on arcs, so they are classified as a Recursive Transition Networks.
There is an interpreter for the specification that allows the designer to review
the user interface. The system cannot handle any graphical I/O, although the
text output can be directed to different "windows" on the screen. An important ability provided by the system is having the semantic level choose which
arc out of a node to use. This is required, for example, to determine whether a
password is correct and therefore accept a command, or whether to re-prompt
for another try at the password. The feedback from the semantic level seems to
be limited to choosing an arc, however, so the semantics cannot specify default
values, for example. The interface between the various levels is through a
plethora of global variables, and for all nodes there must be explicit arcs for
any possible erroneous inputs and any universal commands such as HELP and
UNDO [Jacob 84].

RAPID (RApid Prototyping of Interactive Dialogues) [Wasserman 82] is
another transition network system. The user interface part, RAPID/USE (User
Software Engineering), is just a small portion of a large system for supporting
software engineering. The user interface portion is very similar to Jacob's
except that it has more powerful output primitives.

State diagram UIMSs are most useful for creating user interfaces where a
large amount of syntactic parsing is necessary or when the user interface has a
large number of modes (each state is really a mode). However, most highly-
interactive systems attempt to be mostly "mode-free" [Tesler 81] so state
diagrams UIMSs have not been successful for them.

2.2.3.2. Grammars and Production Systems

Most grammar-based systems are based on parser generators used in compiler development. These are good for textual command languages. Syngraph
(SYNtax directed GRAPHics) [Olsen 83] is a system that generates user interface programs in Pascal from a description written in a formal grammar using

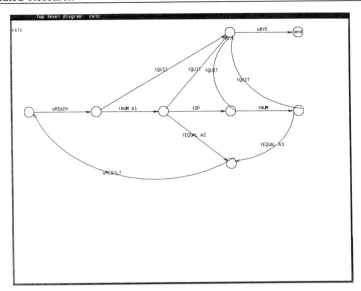

Figure 2.3.
State diagram description of a simple desk calculator [Jacob 85].

an extended BNF. The system handles prompting, echoing and errors. Syngraph provides menus and text input and also provides a few predefined interaction devices (locator, valuator, pick, etc.) with some limited ability for tracking. Syngraph concentrates on dealing with semantic error recovery, "Cancel" and "Undo" at the semantic level, and the problem of knowing what to select when multiple items are on the screen at the position of a "pick". Syngraph does not, however, provide semantic feedback or defaults since there is no way for application routines to affect the parsing.

Grammar-based UIMSs, like state diagram UIMSs, are not appropriate for specifying highly-interactive interfaces, since they are oriented to batch processing strings with a complex syntactic structure.

Hill's Event Response System (ERS) [Hill 87a] [Hill 87b] [Hill 87c] is a parallel language for programming user interfaces, which is an extension of grammars and production systems. The system is especially well suited for handling concurrent interfaces; for example, ones that use multiple input devices at the same time [Buxton 86], since it incorporates synchronization mechanisms. ERS can support direct manipulation interfaces since it facilitates efficient and frequent communication between the interaction techniques and the application program. Appendix B contains a detailed discussion of ERS and how it relates to Peridot.

2.2.3.3. Graphical Layout

The UIMSs described in this section all allow interaction techniques to be placed on the screen using a mouse. The interaction techniques must have been previously coded by hand in a conventional programming language, however. These UIMSs perform the "System Glue" function in Figure 2.1. Another common feature of these systems is that they organize the user interface as a hierarchy or network of mostly static "pages" or "frames." These contain interaction techniques and text that appear together, as well as commands that cause the system to erase the page and go to different pages. Two of these systems, Menulay and Trillium, are apparently the only UIMSs, other than Peridot, designed to be used by non-programmers.

Menulay[2] [Buxton 83] allows the designer to place text, graphical potentiometers, iconic pictures, light buttons, etc. on the screen and see exactly what the user will see when the application is run. The designer does not need to be a programmer to use Menulay. Each active item in the display is associated with a semantic routine which is invoked when the user selects that item with the pointing device. Like virtually all other UIMSs, the semantic routines are written in a conventional programming language. Menulay generates tables and code which link to its run-time support package that executes the user interface for the application. Menulay generated itself and it does support multiple input devices operating concurrently, so it is a fairly powerful system. However, it has a rigid table-driven structure, so the interaction between the semantic level and the user interface is limited. This prevents semantic feedback, defaults, selection, and error handling.

Trillium [Henderson 86], which is aimed at designing the user interface panels for copiers, is very similar to Menulay. One strong advantage Trillium has over Menulay is that the frames can be executed immediately as they are designed since it is interpreted rather than compiled. Trillium also separates the behavior of interactions from the graphic presentation and allows the designer to change the graphics (while keeping the same behavior) without programming. One weakness is that it has little support for frame-to-frame transitions, since this rarely is necessary for copiers.

GUIDE (Graphical User Interface Development Environment) [Granor 86] is a compiled system similar to Menulay. GUIDE provides more elaborate control for interaction techniques (called "tools"), including conditions for their

---

[2] "Menulay" is actually part of a larger group of programs sometimes called the "U of T UIMS." Menulay will be used here to refer to the entire set of programs, however.

display, and various ways to transfer to different pages (called "contexts"). Although the position of tools can be specified with the mouse, all parameters and control information must be entered using forms or menus.

The GRINS (GRaphical INteraction System) UIMS [Olsen 85a] combines a grammar processor (an "Interactive Push-Down Automaton") with a constraint-based "input-output linkage" system to handle semantic feedback. It incorporates a graphical editor that allows the interaction techniques (menus, icons, and text areas) to be placed using a mouse. The constraint-handling parts of GRINS are discussed in section 2.4.2.

RAPID/USE [Wasserman 82] (discussed in section 2.2.3.1) also allows interaction techniques to be placed using a mouse. Nevertheless, it supports only limited mouse-based interfaces.

2.2.3.4. Object-Oriented UIMSs

An important new class of UIMSs provides an object-oriented framework in which the user interface is programmed. These systems typically provide the higher-level "classes" that handle the default behavior and the designer provides specializations of these classes to deal with specific behavior desired in the user interface. This uses the inheritance mechanism built into the object-oriented languages [Goldberg 83].

These systems can handle highly-interactive, direct manipulation interfaces since there is a computational linkage between the input and the output which the application can modify to provide semantic processing. Although these systems make it much easier to create user interfaces, they are still programming environments, and are clearly inaccessible to non-programmers.

MacApp [Schmucker 86] is programmed in Object Pascal and makes it easier to create Macintosh programs. GWUIMS (George Washington User Interface Management System) [Sibert 86], which uses "Flavors" [Weinreb 80] in Franz Lisp, provides a classification of interface operations and objects that fit into each class. HIGGENS [Hudson 86] adds a structured data description that allows the UIMS to automatically manage the recalculation and redisplay of objects in an intelligent way when data changes. The structure is also used to support UNDO and REDO.

2.2.3.5. Others

There are many other UIMSs that have been created, and new ones are appearing all the time.

Tiger [Kasik 82] supports a sophisticated menu network. Flair [Wong 82] provides for a hierarchy of mostly static frames, like the systems in section 2.2.3.3. In Flair, however, the displays must be programmed textually using calls to CORE primitives.

Cousin [Hayes 85] and Domain Dialogue [Schulert 85] both allow the designer to specify forms containing menus, buttons, text input fields and graphic output areas using declarative, textual descriptions. The application programs then request and set the values of "variables" which the end users set and view using these forms.

2.3. Visual Programming and Example-Based Programming

In addition to previous UIMSs, Peridot was influenced by a number of Visual Programming and Example-Based Programming systems[3].

2.3.1. Definitions

Section 1.1 defines "Visual Programming" (VP) and "Example-Based Programming" (EBP). As a review, "Visual Programming" refers to systems that allow the specification of programs using graphics. Systems that use graphics to *illustrate* a program after it has been written in a conventional language are not classified as Visual Programming; these are called "Program Visualization" systems. "Example-Based Programming" (EBP) systems allow the use of examples of the data the program should process during the development of the program. Some Example-Based Programming systems use inferencing, and these are called "Programming *by* Example" (PBE) systems. Example-Based Programming systems that do not use inferencing are called "Programming *with* Example" (PWE) systems.

---

[3] I presented most of the ideas in this section in a previous paper [Myers 86a], but here the new term "Example Based Programming" is used instead of "Programming by Example" for the class of all programs that use examples. This is because "Programming by Example" is commonly used for programs that use both inferencing and examples. Also, this section includes a number of new systems that had not been reported at the time of the earlier paper.

Any programming language system may either be "interpreted" or "compiled." A "compiled" system has a large processing delay before statements can be run while they are converted into a lower-level representation in a batch fashion. An interpretive system allows statements to be executed when they are entered. This characterization is actually more of a continuum rather than a dichotomy since even interpretive languages like Lisp typically require groups of statements (such as an entire procedure) to be specified before they are executed.

The sections below discuss some important VP and EBP systems and place each in a taxonomy based on whether it is visual or not, uses examples or not, and is interpreted or compiled.

2.3.2. Advantages of Using Visual Programming and Example-Based Programming

Visual Programming, Program Visualization, and Example-Based Programming are very appealing ideas for a number of reasons. The human visual system and human visual information processing are clearly optimized for multi-dimensional data. Computer programs, however, are conventionally presented in a one-dimensional textual form, not utilizing the full power of the brain. Two-dimensional displays for programs, such as flowcharts and even the indenting of block structured programs, have long been known to be helpful aids in program understanding [Smith 77]. Recently, a number of Program Visualization systems [Myers 80 and 83][Baecker 81][Brown 84] have demonstrated that 2-D pictorial displays for data structures, such as those drawn by hand on blackboard, are very helpful. It seems clear that a more visual style of programming could be easier to understand and generate for humans. Smith [77] discusses at length these and other psychological motivations for using more visual displays for programs and data. Recently, there have been a special issue of *IEEE Computer* [Grafton 85] and a conference [IEEE 86] that were devoted entirely to visual computer languages.

It is also well known that people are much better at dealing with specific examples than with abstract ideas. A large amount of teaching is achieved by presenting important examples and having the students do specific problems. This helps them to understand the general principles. Example-Based Programming attempts to extend these ideas to programming. In its most ideal case, the programmer acts like the teacher and just gives examples to the computer, and the computer, like an intelligent pupil, intuits the abstraction that covers all the examples.

Programming-*with*-example systems require programmers to specify the abstraction, but allow them to work out the program on examples as an aid to getting the program correct. This is motivated by the observation that people make fewer errors when working out a problem on an example (or when directly manipulating data as when editing text or moving icons on the Macintosh [Williams 84]) as compared to performing the same operation in the abstract, as in conventional programming. The programmer does not need to try to keep in mind the large and complex state of the system at each point of the computation if it is displayed for him on the screen. This has been called "programming in debugging mode" [Smith 77]. In addition, these Example-Based Programming systems may allow the user to specify a program using the actual user interface of the system, which is presumably familiar [Attardi 82].

2.3.3. Problems With VP and EBP

Most Visual Programming and Example-Based Programming systems share a number of problems, some of which are listed below. Sections 12.2 and 12.3.3 discuss how Peridot addresses these issues.

2.3.3.1. Visual Programming

(1) Difficulty with large programs or large data: Almost all visual representations are physically larger than the text they replace, so there is often a problem that too little will fit on the screen. This problem is alleviated to some extent by scrolling and abstraction.

(2) Lack of functionality: Many VP systems work only in a limited domain.

(3) Inefficiency: Most VP systems run programs very slowly.

(4) Unstructured programs: Many VP systems promote unstructured programming practices (like GOTO). Many do not provide abstraction mechanisms (procedures, local variables, etc.) which are necessary for programs of a reasonable size.

(5) Static representations of programs that are hard to understand: For many VP systems, including flowcharts, the program begins to look like a maze of wires. Other systems simply use a normal linear computer language as the the static representation.

(6) No place for comments: An interesting point is that virtually no VP system provides a place for comments.

2.3.3.2. *Programming with Example*

Programming *with* Example systems that do not attempt to do inferencing have been somewhat successful. Most of these are VP systems, so they share the problems listed in the previous section. Some additional problems with these systems (from [Halbert 84]) include:

(1) Lack of static representation: These systems often have *no* user-understandable static representation for programs.

(2) Problem with editing programs: The lack of a static representation makes editing difficult. One alternative is to run a program from the beginning, but this may take a long time. Specifying a change for the middle of a program by example may not be possible, however, without running it from the beginning since the state of the world may not be set up correctly. Saving periodic snapshots of the system state may alleviate this problem, but there may be a great deal of information to save. In addition, a change may invalidate steps of the program that come afterwards.

(3) Problem with data description: It is often difficult to specify what the procedures should operate on: constants, user-specified data, or data found somewhere in the system qualified by its type, location, name, etc. Unless there is some explicit mechanism for the user to tell it, the system does not know *why* the user chose some particular data. Also, if the user specifies the same data item in two different places, is this a coincidence, or should the identical item be used in both places?

(4) Problem with control structure: When specifying a conditional by example, only one branch can be traveled. To go back and demonstrate the other branch, a different example must be given, and the system must be returned to the correct state for the "IF" statement to be re-evaluated. An additional problem is how to specify where in the program the conditionals and loops should be placed.

(5) Lack of functionality: Many systems only provide Programming with Example for a few data types and a small number of operations. As a patch, some provide escapes to conventional programming languages when PBE is insufficient.

(6) Avoiding the destruction of real data or other undesirable consequences: In an environment such as an office, where actions in the system may have external consequences, it may be undesirable for the system to actually perform certain actions while the program is being written.

2.3.3.3. Programming by Example

Programming by Example systems (with inferencing) have been relatively unsuccessful because it is:

(1) Hard to choose appropriate examples: An important problem with these systems is that the user provides no guidance about the structure of the program so each new example can radically change the program. The programmer often knows, for example, which values are variables and which are constants, or where conditionals should go, but there is no way to directly convey this information to these systems. Choosing the correct examples requires great skill, and it is often difficult to modify programs once they exist.

(2) Difficult to insure correct programs: The generated procedures are often "convoluted and unstructured" [Bauer 78, p. 131] and the user is never sure if the generated procedure is correct unless he reads the code and checks it explicitly. If this is required, however, most of the advantage of PBE is lost since the user must know how to program in order to check it. In fact, the central idea of this "inductive generalization" programming is directly opposed to the modern software-engineering idea that testing with a few examples can never guarantee that a program is correct. Clearly, generating a program from a few examples has the same problem.

2.3.4. Taxonomy of Programming Systems

Figure 2.4 shows a taxonomy of some programming systems divided into eight categories using the orthogonal criteria of:

- Visual Programming or not,

- Example-Based Programming or not, and

- Interpretive or Compiled.

Of course, a single system may have features that fit into various categories and some systems may be hard to classify, so this figure attempts to characterize the systems by their most prominent features. The systems shown in Figure 2.4 are only representative; there are many systems that have not been included. A recent conference [IEEE 86] contains discussions of many recent systems and references to others.

Not Example-Based Programming

	Compiled	Interpretive
Not VP	All Conventional Languages: Pascal, Fortran, etc.	LISP, APL, etc.
VP	Grail [Ellis 69] AMBIT/G/L [Christensen 68,71] Query by Example [Zloof 77, 81] FORMAL [Shu 85] GAL [Albizuri-Romero 84] FPL [Cunniff 86] IBGE [Taylor 86] MOPS-2 [Ae 86] OPAL [Musen 86] SchemaCode [Robillard 86]	Graphical Program Editor [Sutherland 66] PIGS [Pong 83 and 86] Pict [Glinert 84] PROGRAPH [Pietrzykowski 83,84] State Transition UIMS [Jacob 85] HI-VISUAL [Yoshimoto 86]

Example-Based Programming

	Compiled	Interpretive
Not VP	I/O pairs* [Shaw 75]	Tinker [Lieberman 82] Editing by Example* [Nix 85]
VP	[Bauer 78] traces*	AutoProgrammer* [Biermann 76b] Pygmalion [Smith 77] Graphical Thinglab [Borning 86] Smallstar [Halbert 81,84] Rehearsal World [Gould 84] Music System [Desain 86] Peridot* [Myers]

Figure 2.4.

Classification of programming systems by whether they are visual or not, whether they have Example-Based Programming or not, and whether they are compiled or interpretive. Starred systems (*) have inferencing (Programming *by* Example), and non-starred Example-Based Programming systems use Programming *with* Example.

2.3.4.1. Not EBP, Not VP, Compiled and Interpretive

These are the conventional textual, linear programming languages that are familiar to all programmers, such as Pascal, Fortran, and Ada for compiled and LISP and APL for interpretive.

2.3.4.2. Not EBP, VP, Compiled

One of the earliest "visual" representations for programs was the flowchart. Grail [Ellis 69] could compile programs directly from computerized flowcharts, but the contents of boxes were ordinary machine language statements. Cunniff [86] reports that "several years of experience" with FPL (First Programming Language), which is another flowchart programming language, have "shown that this language might be particularly well suited to helping novices learn programming" because it eliminates syntactic errors. GAL (see Figure 2.5) is similar except that it uses Nassi-Shneiderman flowcharts [Nassi 73] and is compiled into Pascal [Albizuri-Romero 84]. Other flowchart languages are IBGE [Taylor 86] for the Macintosh, and OPAL [Musen 86] which allows doctors to enter knowledge about cancer treatments into an expert system. OPAL handles iterations, conditionals and concurrency in an easy-to-understand manner. SchemaCode [Robillard 86] is another flowchart variant. It is aimed at promoting structured, top-down refinement for professional programmers.

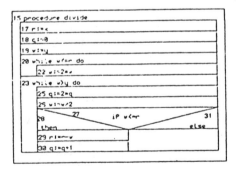

Figure 2.5.
A Nassi-Shneiderman flowchart program from GAL [Albizuri-Romero 84].

An early effort that did not use flowchart techniques was the AMBIT/G [Christensen 68] and AMBIT/L [Christensen 71] graphical languages. They supported symbolic manipulation programming using pictures. Both the programs and data were represented diagrammatically as directed graphs, and the programming operated by pattern matching. Fairly complicated algorithms, such as garbage collection, could be described graphically as local transformations on graphs[4].

You might think that a system called "Query by Example" would be a "Example-Based Programming" system, but in fact, according to this classification, it is not. Query by Example (QBE) [Zloof 77] allows users to specify queries on a relational database using two-dimensional tables (or forms), so it is classified as a Visual Programming system. The "examples" in QBE are what Zloof called variables. They are called "examples" because the user is supposed to give them names that refer to what the system might fill into that field, but they have no more meaning than variable names in most conventional languages. The ideas in QBE have been extended to mail and other non-database areas of office automation in Office by Example (OBE) [Zloof 81]. A related forms-based database language is FORMAL [Shu 85] which explicitly represents hierarchical structures.

The MOPS-2 system [Ae 86] uses "colored Petri nets" to allow parallel systems to be constructed and simulated in a visual manner.

2.3.4.3. Not EBP, VP, Interpretive

Probably the first Visual Programming system was William Sutherland's Graphical Program Editor [Sutherland 66] which represented programs somewhat like hardware logic diagrams that could be executed interpretively. Some systems for programming with flowcharts have been interpretive. PIGS [Pong 83] uses Nassi-Shneiderman flowcharts and has been extended to handle multi-processing in Pigsty/I-PIGS [Pong 86]. Pict [Glinert 84] uses conventional flowcharts, but is differentiated by its use of color pictures (icons) rather than text inside of the flowchart boxes (see Figure 2.6).

PROGRAPH [Pietrzykowski 83] is another interpretive VP system without EBP, but it is distinguished by supporting a functional data flow language. PROGRAPH attempts to overcome some of the problems of this type of language by using a graphical representation that is structured, as shown in Figure 2.7. Pietrzykowski [84] claims that this alleviates the problem of functional

---

[4] It is interesting to note that AMBIT/G, even though it was developed in 1969, used many of the "modern" user interface techniques, including iconic representations, gesture recognition, dynamic menus on the screen with selection using a pointing device, selection of icons by pointing, moded and mode-free styles of interaction, etc. [Rovner 69].

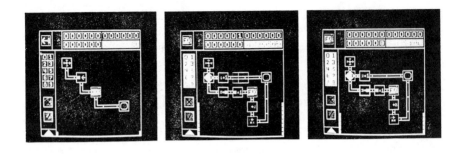

Figure 2.6.
Three frames from Pict [Glinert 84] showing an implementation of the factorial procedure. The original pictures were in color.

languages where "the conventional representation in the form of a linear script makes it almost unreadable." HI-VISUAL [Yoshimoto 86] also provides data flow programming, but it uses iconic pictures like Pict.

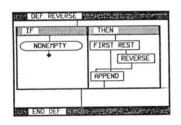

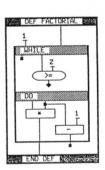

Figure 2.7.
Two procedures from PROGRAPH [Pietrzykowski 84].

Any of the UIMSs that allow the designer to specify the program graphically can also be classified as Visual Programming systems. For example [Jacob 85] (section 2.2.3.1) is an interpretive VP system without EBP.

2.3.4.4. *EBP, Not VP, Compiled*

Some systems have attempted to infer the entire program from one or more examples of what output is produced for a particular input. One program [Shaw 75] can infer simple recursive LISP programs from a single I/O pair, such as (A B C D) ==> (D D C C B B A A). This system is limited to simple list processing programs, and it is clear that systems such as this one cannot generate all programs, or even be likely to generate the correct program [Biermann 76a].

2.3.4.5. EBP, Not VP, Interpretive

Tinker [Lieberman 82] is a "pictorial" system that is not VP. The user chooses a concrete example, and the system executes Lisp statements on this example as the code is typed in. Although Tinker uses windows, menus, and other graphics in its user interface, it is not a VP system since the user presents all of the code to the system in the conventional, linear, textual manner. For conditionals, Tinker requires the user to give two examples: one that will travel down each branch. Tinker notices that two contradictory paths have been specified and prompts the user to type in a test to distinguish when each branch is desired.

A recent system that is based on ideas from I/O pairs is Editing by Example (EBE) [Nix 85]. Here, the system generates a small program that describes a sequence of editing operations. This program can then be run on any piece of text. The system compares two or more examples of the editing operations in order to deduce what are variables and what are constants. The correct programs usually can be generated given only two or three examples, and there are heuristics to generate programs from single examples. Like Peridot, EBE creates the programs from the *results* of the editing operations (the input and output), rather than *traces* of the execution, to allow the user more flexibility and the ability to correct small errors (typos) while giving the examples. EBE is seems to be relatively successful, chiefly because it limits the domain in which it performs inferencing.

2.3.4.6. EBP, VP, Compiled

Some inferencing systems that attempt to cover a wider class of programs than those that can be generated from I/O pairs have required the user to choose data structures and algorithms and then run through a computation on a number of examples. The systems attempt to infer where loops and conditionals should go to produce the shortest and most general program that will work for all of the examples. One such system is by Bauer [78], which also decides which values in the program should be constants and which should be variables. It is visual since the user can specify the program execution using graphical traces.

2.3.4.7. EBP, VP, Interpretive

Some of the most interesting systems fall into this final category. Except for AutoProgrammer [Biermann 76b], which is similar to Bauer's system, and Peridot, none attempt to do inferencing.

Pygmalion [Smith 77] was one of the seminal VP and EBP systems. It provides an iconic and "analogical" method for programming: concrete display images for data and programs, called icons, are manipulated to create programs. The emphasis is on "doing" pictorially, rather than "telling." Thinglab [Borning 79 and 81] was designed to allow the user to describe and run complex simulations easily. A VP interface to Thinglab is described in [Borning 86]. Here the user can define new constraints among objects by specifying them graphically (see Figure 2.8). Also, if a class of objects can be created by combining already existing objects, then it can be programmed by example in Thinglab.

Smallstar [Halbert 81 and 84] uses EBP to allow the end user to program a prototype version of the Star office workstation [Smith 82]. When programming, the user simply goes into program mode, performs the operations that are to be remembered, and then leaves program mode. The operations are executed in the actual user interface of the system, which the user already knows. Since the system does not use inferencing, the user must differentiate constants from variables and explicitly add control structures (loops and conditionals). This is done on a textual representation of the program created while the user is giving the example (see Figure 2.9). Halbert reports that Star users were able to create procedures for performing their office tasks with his system.

The goal of Rehearsal World [Gould 84] is to allow teachers who do not know how to program to create computerized lessons easily. Interactive graphics are heavily used to provide a "collaborative, evolutionary and exploratory" environment where programming is "quick, easy and fun." The metaphor presented to the user is a *theater*, where the screen is the *stage* and there are predefined *performers* that the user can *direct* to create a *play* (see Figure 2.10). The teacher developing the program sees at every point exactly what the student-user of the play will see. In addition, the teacher can have additional performers in the *wings* (so the student will not see them) that provide auxiliary functions such as flow control. Everything is made visible to the teachers, however, which allows their thinking to be concrete, rather than abstract as in conventional programming environments. When a new performer is needed, often its code can be created using examples, but when this is not possible, some Smalltalk code must be written. The static representation for all performers is Smalltalk code, which can be edited by those who know how.

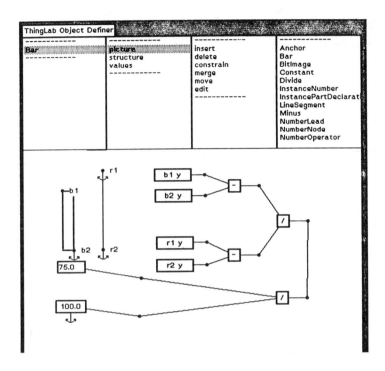

Figure 2.8.
Creating a constraint graphically in Thinglab [Borning 86] to keep the height of a bar proportional to the value of a register.

A different kind of system uses direct manipulation to configure icons and circuit diagrams to define sound processing systems [Desain 86]. This system is classified as Programming With Example because the resulting sound is continuously played while the circuit is being constructed.

The Peridot UIMS is also classified as an EBP, VP, Interpretive system, and it uses inferencing.

2.4. Dynamic Constraint Systems

Peridot uses *constraints*, which are relationships among objects and data that must hold no matter how the objects are manipulated. Constraint systems can be classified by whether the constraints are mainly among graphical objects or between graphical objects and data structures. Peridot uses graphical

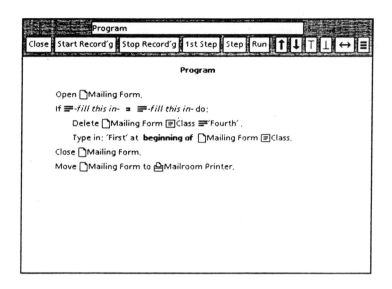

Figure 2.9.
Code generated by Smallstar based on the user's examples. This code must be edited
by the user to complete the program [Halbert 84].

constraints to link graphical objects together and data constraints to link objects
to active values.

2.4.1. Graphical Constraints

As defined in section 1.1, graphical constraints are when attributes of one
graphical object, such as its position or size, depend on attributes of another
graphical object.   The original drawing program using constraints was
Sketchpad [Sutherland 63] which allowed lines to be constrained to have certain
relationships to other lines (parallel, perpendicular, attached to, etc.). Thinglab
[Borning 79, 81 and 86] (section 2.3.4.7) extends Sketchpad to provide a general simulation environment. The constraints in Sketchpad and Thinglab are
bi-directional, which means that if two objects are attached by a constraint, then
either can be modified and the other will be updated appropriately. The user of
the original Thinglab had to supply hand-written code to calculate and enforce
the constraints. A new version of Thinglab, described in section 2.3.4.7, allows
some constraints to be entered graphically. The constraints are expressed in a
declarative fashion, and Thinglab generates and compiles code to solve the constraints at run time. The solver tries to find a path through the constraints that
will work in linear time, but it is willing to use relaxation if there are recursive

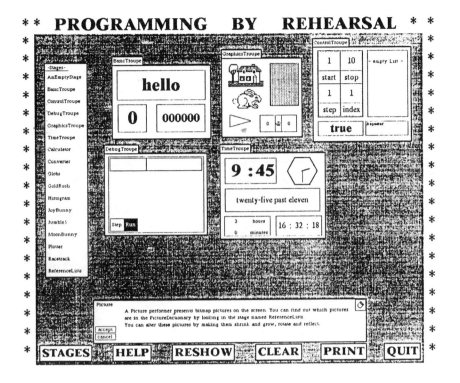

Figure 2.10.
A screen from Rehearsal World [Gould 84] showing the basic menu (on the left) and the standard set of "performers."

dependencies. Animus [Duisberg 86] extends Thinglab to also handle constraints about time, and therefore can support realistic animations of dynamic processes. The Alternate Reality Kit [Smith 86 and 87] allows realistic simulations of objects reacting to physical laws (like gravity) using a form of constraints.

Juno [Nelson 85] is a drawing package similar to Sketchpad, but it has many more capabilities. Juno creates a code representation which is always kept consistent with the drawing. The user can edit either and the other will be updated immediately. Like Peridot, the drawing operations are imperative commands, but the arguments to those operations are defined by declarative constraints. The drawing order is preserved so that objects can obscure one another as shown in Figure 2.11. Juno's constraints are less powerful than Thinglab's but can still handle quadratic expressions needed for parallelism and congruence. Juno has a direct manipulation interface for creating pictures in a WYSIWYG (What You See Is What You Get) fashion.

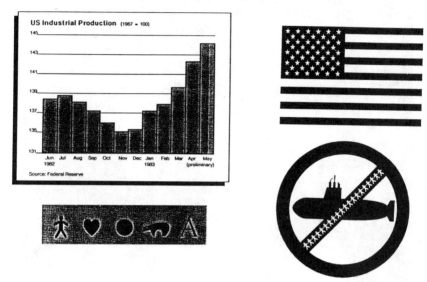

Figure 2.11.
Pictures created by Juno [Nelson 85]. The original pictures were in color.

The systems discussed above require the user to explicitly specify constraints. In contrast, the PED graphics editor [Pavlidis 85] infers constraints among hand drawn graphical objects in order to automatically "beautify" the figure. The relationships it tries to infer include equality of slope or length of sides, colinearity of sides, vertical and horizontal alignment, etc. In addition, PED infers "negative" constraints which specify such relationships as that two lines should not be made to overlap so that one disappears. The beautification step is run as a batch process, explicitly invoked by the user, after which PED displays the results.

2.4.2. Data Constraints

Another application of constraints is for monitoring dynamic processes, such as manufacturing operations. Graphical displays can be connected using constraints to the data which represents the process, and then the displays will be updated automatically when the data changes. Often, these constraints will be bi-directional so the displays can be modified by the user to control the process. The Steamer system [Stevens 83] supports computer-aided instruction of Navy steam engines using graphical simulations created out of a library of graphical objects. The Process Visualization System (PVS) [Foley 86] allows non-programmers to construct displays and establish relationships from the displays to underlying data. For example, the value of a datum might determine the color of a picture element, the position on the screen of a valuator, or the presence or absence of an icon. Displays in PVS are constructed out of graphical primitives (circles, polygons, text, lines, etc.), and any attributes (position, size, visibility, font, etc.) can be attached to data items. Much of the interface can be programmed graphically. For example, the user can point to extreme positions for an object that moves in a range.

When data values change in PVS, the associated picture is updated automatically. This might be supported by "triggers" or "alerters" in a data base [Buneman 79]. Other process monitoring systems (e.g. [Morse 84] [Honeywell 85]) have similar aims, but most only allow the placement of predefined icons (dials, gauges, valves, etc.).

```
Object Slider( Max,Min:Real;
    ! Max and Min define the range for the
    ! slider in the units of the application
      SliderVal:Real
    ! This returns the slider value
      ) =
    ! This display object is defined in a
    ! local coordinate system ranging from
    ! 0.0 to 1.0.
  Control YLoc: Real := 0.5;
    ! This is the slider location which is
    ! set by the dialogue manager.  This is
    ! defined in the coordinates of the
    ! slider object.
  Assert (YLoc <= 1.0) and (YLoc >= 0.0);
  Def SliderVal:=YLoc*(Max-Min)+Min;
    ! This is the value of the slider which
    ! the application can read.
  Line( (0.0,1.0),(0.0,0.0),Black);
    ! This is the slider range
  Def SliderTop:=YLoc+0.1;
      SliderBottom:=YLoc-0.1;
  Polygon( (0.1,SliderTop),(-0.1,SliderTop),
      (-0.1,SliderBottom),(0.1,SliderBottom),
      Black);
  Text( RealToString(SliderVal),
  (0.11,YLoc),0.0,0.1, Black);
EndObject;
```

Figure 2.12.
GRINS code for a graphical slider [Olsen 85a].

A closely related capability is available in GRINS [Olsen 85a] (section 2.2.3.3). It provides a constraint-based "input-output linkage" system to handle semantic feedback. The constraints are programmed textually in a straightforward manner. Graphics can depend on "Control" values and will be updated whenever the Control value changes. The GRINS specification for a slider is shown in Figure 2.12.

Similar uses of "Control" values, which are usually called *active values*, are found in some Artificial Intelligence simulation and control environments (e.g., Knowledge Engineering Environment (KEE) [Ramamoorthy 87] and LOOPS [Stefik 86]) and in some systems which provide parameterized "display lists" for updating pictures [Amanatides 83] [Bergman 76].

2.5. Chapter Summary

This chapter discusses work that is related to Peridot, which falls into four areas: UIMSs, Visual Programming, Programming by Example, and dynamic constraint systems.

Chapter III
Overview and Extended Example

3.1. Introduction

This chapter describes the basic structure of the Peridot UIMS and discusses how the various pieces fit together. These pieces are then discussed in detail in the following chapters. Each chapter presents both the user interface and the implementation aspects.

In order to demonstrate how easy it is to create interfaces using Peridot, this chapter ends with a detailed example of exactly how the designer would create a menu. Although this book attempts to give a good description of how the interface of Peridot works, it is much easier to tell from a videotape [Myers 87c] or a live demonstration.

3.2. Peridot's User Interface

3.2.1. Overview

When using Peridot, the designer sees three windows and a menu (see Figure 3.1). The menu, which is on the left, is used to give commands to Peridot. The window in the center shows what the user will see as a result of this procedure (the actual end-user interface), and the window at the bottom is used for messages and prompts. The window at the top is divided into two areas. The top area shows the name of the current procedure, the name of its arguments, and *examples* of typical values for those arguments. The bottom area shows the names and example values for the relevant active values.

For debugging Peridot itself (and for the very few designers that will be interested), the system can be configured to display the generated code in a fourth window (Figure 3.2). It is not necessary for the designer to view or use the code to perform any operations in Peridot.

The menu lists the commands that are used to control Peridot. All of the commands will be discussed in this and subsequent chapters, and a summary of all the commands is provided in Appendix C.

To the user interface designer, Peridot seems like a computerized picture drawing program like Apple's MacDraw [Williams 84]. To create a user interface, the designer draws graphical objects like rectangles, circles, text, etc. in

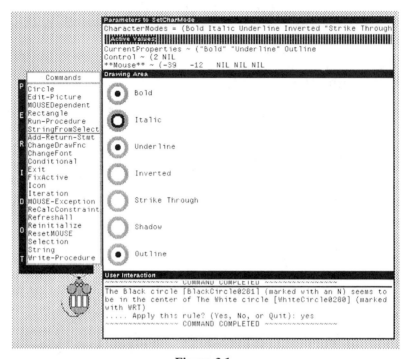

Figure 3.1.
The three Peridot windows (the parameter window at the top is divided into two parts)
and the Peridot command menu (on the left). The command menu is separated into
two portions by a line. The top portion contains the more common commands.

approximately the correct places. After each drawing operation, Peridot infers
how the new object relates to existing objects and asks the designer to confirm
the inference. If it is correct, the designer types "yes" and the constraint is
applied, which automatically "beautifies" the picture. If the inference is
incorrect, the designer types "no" and other guesses are tried. To edit the picture, the designer selects objects with the mouse and then gives one of the editing commands. To make parts of the picture move with the mouse or otherwise
depend on it, the "simulated mouse" icon is moved over the objects and the
MOUSEDependent command is given. Peridot then infers how the mouse
should control the graphics. The connection with the application programs is
achieved by attaching procedures to active values.

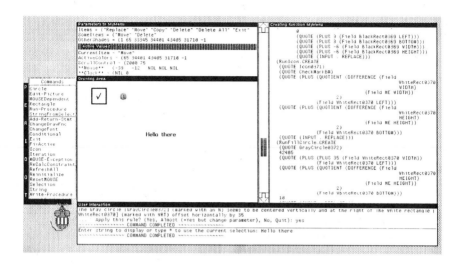

Figure 3.2.
The Peridot code display window on the right with its Peridot-created scroll bar. Normally, this window would not be visible to the designers.

3.2.2. Design Principles for Peridot's User Interface

One of the chief design goals of Peridot was that it should be easy to use. While this is an elusive goal and can depend a great deal on personal taste, it was the guiding factor in a number of decisions. There are many places where there was a choice of how to have the designer give some piece of information to the system: the designer could (1) type in the choice using the keyboard, (2) select the choice from a menu, or (3) demonstrate which is desired by doing some graphic operation and having Peridot infer the choice. The decision of whether to use menus or typing was made based on whether the designer will need to be looking at the prompt window to answer a question (in which case typing is used). If a parameter can be any number or string, then typing is also used to enter it. Otherwise, a menu containing all the choices is generated. The use of menus or typing will be called *specification*. The choice between specification and demonstration is much more interesting.

As discussed in section 2.3.2, demonstrational systems will often be easier to use. In general, however, it is much easier to implement the specification technique, and in some cases, demonstration may actually be harder for the designer to use. This happens when the designer knows how the system should act and believes that it would be much easier to simply specify the actions rather than laboriously demonstrate them. For example, to demonstrate *by example* whether an action should **toggle, set,** or **clear** a value, the designer must demonstrate the action twice: once over a value which was originally set (this will cause the value to be cleared for the function **toggle**, stay set for **set,** and cleared for **clear**) and once over a value which was originally cleared (this will cause the value to be set for the function **toggle**, cleared for **set,** and stay cleared for **clear**). To *specify* which should happen only requires the designer to chose one of **toggle, set,** or **clear,** which will probably be much quicker. In other cases, however, the number of possible choices is so large that it would be more difficult to use specification and then demonstration will be easier.

In order to make Peridot as easy to use as possible, the specification method is allowed whenever there are a small number of easily delineated choices. The demonstrational method is considered the primary method, however, since it is more novel and difficult to provide, and thus more interesting in a research context. In this book, the tradeoffs between demonstration and specification will be presented for many design issues.

Another design principle was for Peridot to try to guess as much information as possible and ask the designer for confirmation. Peridot is often able to infer the correct answers based on the current context, and in these cases it saves the designer from having to know what options are available and how to specify the desired one. When the guesses are incorrect, the designer can answer ''no'' to the confirmation, and Peridot will try other options or allow the designer to specify the answer. In general, this technique saves the designer considerable effort.

3.2.3. Graphical Primitives

When creating an interface, the designer can use rectangles, circles, text, and icons. Figure 3.3 shows examples of each of these. It should not be difficult to add straight and curved lines, polygons, etc. in the future if needed. There is a different graphical object type for each kind of primitive (rectangle, string, icon, and circle).

All graphical objects have various *attributes* which are under the control of the designer. The attributes are such things as position, size, color, string, font, picture, etc. For example, the rectangles and circles can be filled with various grey halftone shades, the text can use arbitrary fonts, and the icons can have any user-defined picture, which might be created using the Interlisp bitmap editor EDITBM. Figure 3.4 lists all the attributes for each type of object. The value for each attribute can be a constant, it can depend on the value of a parameter or active value (section 3.2.6), or it can depend on the value of an attribute of another graphical object (Chapter 4)[1].

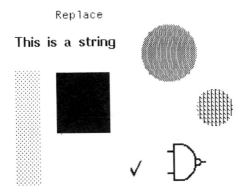

Figure 3.3.
Examples of all the graphic primitive objects in Peridot: strings, rectangles, circles, and icons.

Type	Value	Position&Size				Others	
Rectangles	COLOR	LEFT	BOTTOM	WIDTH	HEIGHT	Drawing Function	
Circles	COLOR	LEFT	BOTTOM	DIAMETER		Drawing Function	
Text	STRING	LEFT	BOTTOM			Drawing Function	Font
Icons	BITMAP	LEFT	BOTTOM			Drawing Function	

Figure 3.4.
The attributes that can be set for each graphic primitive.

The basic graphic primitives can be combined to construct more complex graphical objects. For example, by drawing a white rectangle on top of a grey rectangle, a border can be created, as shown in Figure 1.1. The ''Drawing Function'' attribute controls how these pictures are combined on the screen. The choices are REPLACE, PAINT (OR), INVERT (XOR), or ERASE (AND), and the source can be inverted before it is used (INVERT) or normal (INPUT). Figure 3.5 shows some examples of graphics drawn with various drawing functions.

---

[1] Currently, the Drawing Function and Font attributes can only be constant, but this restriction should be easy to remove.

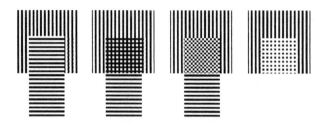

Figure 3.5.

Examples of graphics using the various drawing functions. The lower rectangle is drawn after the upper one using the functions REPLACE, PAINT (OR), INVERT (XOR), and ERASE (AND).

Since the picture is constructed by laying graphic objects on top of one another, the order in which the objects are drawn is important. The designer creates the picture from back to front; the most covered object is drawn first[2]. This is often called the "painter's algorithm."

To draw an object, the designer selects the object type (rectangle, string, circle, or icon) from the Peridot menu and then specifies each of the attributes.

The color for rectangles and strings is selected from a menu (see Figure 3.6). The <From Select> choice allows the color to depend on the value of a parameter or "active value" (section 3.2.6). The <Shade Editor> choice causes a small window to pop up which contains a graphical editor for defining the color (see Figure 3.7). Finally, the Other choice allows the color value to be typed in. Colors are specified using 16-bit integers, as described below in section 3.3.1. For icons, a menu appears with a set of predefined bitmaps, along with the choices <From Select>, <New Icon From Bitmap Editor>, and Other. For strings, the value can be typed or a parameter or active value can be selected that it should depend on.

The position and size attributes are specified by drawing the shape of the object using the mouse. A hair-line box follows the mouse to show the designer where the object will be. The Drawing Function and Font attributes use the global defaults which are set with the special Peridot commands ChangeDrawFnc and ChangeFont. All attributes can be edited in various ways after the object has been created (Chapter 5).

---

[2] Commands to change the drawing order of existing objects could be added. See section 13.2.4.

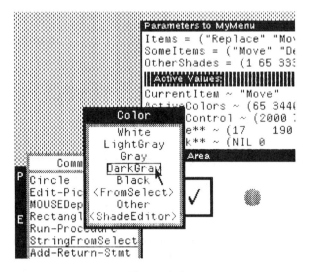

Figure 3.6.
The menu that pops up to allow the designer to choose a color for rectangles and circles. This menu was created using Peridot.

3.2.4. Selection

In order to refer to graphical objects after they have been created, or to refer to parameters or active values of the procedure, the designer can "select" them using the left mouse button. More than one thing can be selected at a time, and all selected objects are shown by having a pattern of dots and dashes move around their border like a movie marquee (Figure 3.8). This feedback technique was chosen because other popular ways to show the selection, such as reverse-video and underlining, would not be visible for certain objects. For example, the reverse-video of a black rectangle is a (possibly invisible) white rectangle. When the left button is pressed, Peridot only looks at objects that have not yet been selected so pressing with the left button multiple times will select all objects whose extent includes the mouse point (even if they are covered by other objects). The first one selected will be the topmost (last drawn) under the mouse. The designer presses the right button over objects to de-select them. Objects under the mouse are de-selected in the *same* order as they were selected to make it easier to select objects that are close together. For example, in Figure 3.9, pressing the left button over the grey rectangle causes it to be selected. Pressing in the same place again causes the black rectangle to be selected also. If the right button is then pressed without moving the mouse, the grey rectangle will be de-selected, leaving the black rectangle

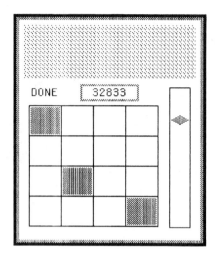

Figure 3.7.

If <Shade Editor> is chosen in the menu of Figure 3.6, then this window appears which allows the designer to choose a halftone grey shade. The individual squares at the bottom can be toggled (each represents a pixel), or the slider can be moved up and down. The slider chooses from 16 built-in grey shades ranging from white (at the top) to black (at the bottom). The resulting shade and its 16-bit representation are continuously displayed at the top. This editor was created using Peridot.

selected. Although this may sound complicated, it is a very natural way to select objects that would otherwise be impossible to point to. If an object is not covered, of course, the designer can simply point to it directly.

If the right button is pressed when the mouse is not over any objects, then all objects are de-selected. This feature was added based on results of user tests (see section 14.3.1) that showed that novices had trouble de-selecting objects.

For the parameters and active values of the interface, the designer can select the name (Figure 3.10a) which refers to the parameter or active value as a whole. If the value of the parameter or active value is a list, then the designer can select an individual element of the list (Figure 3.10b) to refer to only that element. If the value is not a list, selecting the value is the same as selecting the name (it refers to the value as a whole). Currently, Peridot does not support selecting sub-lists (i.e., if an element of the value list is a list itself, then the items of the lower level list cannot be selected individually).

Since selection is a primary operation for the designer, Peridot provides some auxiliary ways to set and clear the selection. The Deselect-all

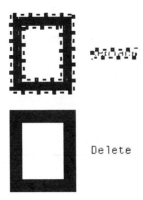

Figure 3.8.
The dots on the border of selected objects move around like a movie marquee, making it easy to identify what is selected. Here, there are 3 objects selected: the top black and white rectangles and the top string.

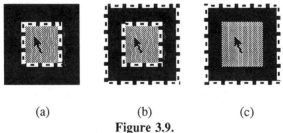

(a)   (b)   (c)

Figure 3.9.
With the mouse (represented by the arrow) over the grey rectangle, the first press with the left button selects the grey rectangle (a), the second press in the same place selects the black rectangle (b), and then pressing with the right button de-selects the grey rectangle leaving only the black rectangle selected (c). This feature would generally be used only when it would be difficult to point to the black rectangle directly.

command will de-select all objects at once, Select-In-Box, selects all of the objects inside a mouse-specified rectangular region, and DeSelect-In-Box works the same way for de-selecting. When the SelectByName command is given, a menu pops up containing all of the objects' names, values, and positions, as shown in Figure 3.11. The designer can then select or de-select objects from this menu.

(a)
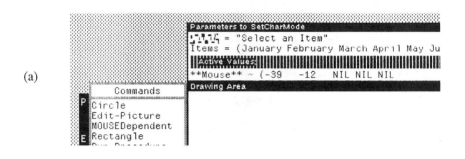

(b)

Figure 3.10.
In (a) the name of the parameter has been selected. In (b), the third element of the
list for the Items parameter has been selected.

3.2.5. Use of Inferencing

One of Peridot's important innovations is the application of inferencing to
user interface design. After each drawing or editing action, Peridot applies the
appropriate rules to see if any apply. Peridot uses inferencing in three ways:
(1) graphical constraints (Chapter 4), (2) control structures (Chapters 6 and 7),
and (3) mouse dependencies (Chapter 9). In each case, the inferencing method
is based on extremely simple condition-action rules [Charniak 85]. Each rule
has a test that determines if the relationship is appropriate (the *condition*), a
message which is used to ask the designer whether the rule should be applied,
and an *action* which causes the objects to conform to the rule. Because any
inferencing system will occasionally guess wrong, Peridot uses three strategies
to protect against incorrect inferences. First, Peridot always asks the designer if
guesses are correct, second, the results of the inferences can be immediately
seen and executed, and third, the inferences can be undone if they are in error.

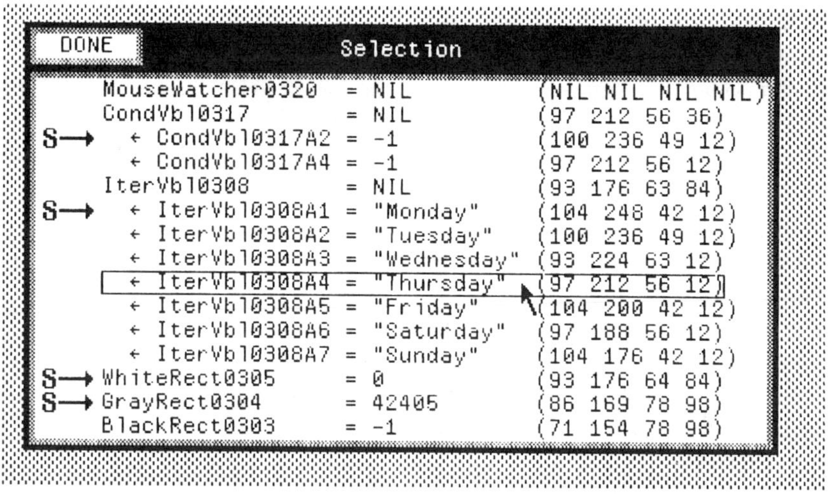

```
┌──────────────────────────────────────────────────────────┐
│  ┌────────┐                                                │
│  │  DONE  │               Selection                        │
│  └────────┘                                                │
│       MouseWatcher0320    = NIL        (NIL NIL NIL NIL)    │
│       CondVb10317         = NIL        (97 212 56 36)       │
│   S─→    ← CondVb10317A2  = -1         (100 236 49 12)      │
│          ← CondVb10317A4  = -1         (97 212 56 12)       │
│       IterVb10308         = NIL        (93 176 63 84)       │
│   S─→    ← IterVb10308A1  = "Monday"   (104 248 42 12)      │
│          ← IterVb10308A2  = "Tuesday"  (100 236 49 12)      │
│          ← IterVb10308A3  = "Wednesday"(93 224 63 12)       │
│        ┌─← IterVb10308A4  = "Thursday" (97 212 56 12)┐      │
│        └──────────────────────────────────────────┘ \      │
│          ← IterVb10308A5  = "Friday"    \(104 200 42 12)    │
│          ← IterVb10308A6  = "Saturday"  (97 188 56 12)      │
│          ← IterVb10308A7  = "Sunday"    (104 176 42 12)     │
│   S─→ WhiteRect0305       = 0          (93 176 64 84)       │
│   S─→ GrayRect0304        = 42405      (86 169 78 98)       │
│       BlackRect0303       = -1         (71 154 78 98)       │
└──────────────────────────────────────────────────────────┘
```

Figure 3.11.
A menu containing all objects' names, values and positions that the designer can use for changing the selection. The selected objects are marked by an s and arrow in the left margin. Whether objects are selected or not toggles if the mouse button is pressed over them. When the designer is finished, the mouse button is pressed over DONE. This menu was created using Peridot.

3.2.6. Data Constraints

Attributes of objects can be constant, they can depend on attributes of other graphical objects as graphical constraints, or they can depend on the values of parameters or active values as data constraints. The attributes all start off constant by default, but the LEFT, BOTTOM, WIDTH and HEIGHT attributes can be automatically inferred by Peridot to depend on those attributes of other objects (Chapter 4). These attributes can also be specified explicitly to depend on other objects (Chapter 5). In addition, attributes of objects can be specified to depend on the values of parameters and active values.

Some programming-by-example systems, such as [Bauer 78], try to guess when an attribute is constant and when it should depend on parameters, but Peridot requires that this be explicitly specified by the designer. This decision was made because it is much easier to simply point to a parameter than to have to type in the same value (which the system would then notice is the same as the parameter's). As an example, in Figure 3.10a, the designer selected the parameter Title and can then use the StringFromSelect command to draw a string using its value: "Select an Item:".

Using examples of a typical value for each parameter and active value is an important aid in making this process more direct and understandable. The main consideration about the examples is that the designer must be careful that they have the same types (list, string, number, etc.) that will be used at run time. This is because Peridot uses the type to infer how to reference the values and to determine other control information.

3.3. Peridot's Implementation

3.3.1. Implementation Environment

Peridot was implemented on a Xerox 1109 DandeTiger workstation using Interlisp-D [Xerox 83]. This section discusses the details of this environment focusing on the parts that are directly used by Peridot and which are important for understanding this book.

The workstation has 3.5 megabytes of memory, a 40 megabyte hard disk, and executes lisp at about 90% the speed of a VAX 11/780. The attached monitor is 1024 by 768 pixels with the longer dimension horizontal ("landscape"). Each pixel is one bit deep (monochrome). The attached mouse has two buttons, but the software simulates a three-button mouse by detecting a chord of the two buttons and returning that as the middle button.

The software that supports Peridot is the "Intermezzo" version of the Interlisp-D environment [Xerox 83] ("Interlisp" for short). This environment supports a dialect of the Lisp language which can be run interpreted or compiled, and Peridot makes use of both. Interlisp supports conventional Lisp constructs (lists, atoms, numbers, etc.). The garbage collector, which automatically deallocates lists, uses reference counts (each cell has a count of the number of times it is referenced). Unfortunately, this scheme does not work when there are cyclical structures (when an object refers to itself, the count never goes to zero), which occur often in Peridot.

Calls to functions in Interlisp can have fewer than the defined number of parameters and NIL will be used for the rest. Interlisp also has RECORDs of various types and an iteration statement which can take many forms. A typical example is:

```
(FOR <itervbl1> IN <list> AS
     <itervbl2> FROM <start_integer> TO <end_integer>
          BY <increment>
  DO <statements>)
```

(Note the use of AS to have two separate iteration variables.) Interlisp also has an IF statement which is similar to Pascal's. Its form is:

```
(IF <test1> THEN <statements1>
    ELSEIF <test2> THEN <statements2>
    ...
    ELSE <statementsN>)
```

Interlisp also supports multiple processes which share the same address space. Processes must explicitly yield to allow other processes to run (there is no time-slicing), and they can communicate through a number of shared-memory style mechanisms (monitors, condition-variables, "events", etc.). Processes can be added and deleted dynamically at run-time, and the process creation procedure looks like a procedure call:

```
(ADD.PROCESS <function name> <function arguments>)
```

Peridot uses multiple processes for handling the selection feedback (section 3.2.4), for handling multi-clicking (section 9.9), and for monitoring the input devices (Chapter 10).

One of the most important features of the Interlisp environment used by Peridot is its support for graphics. Interlisp provides multiple overlapping windows (although output can only be directed to uncovered windows) and each window retains a picture of what it covers, so the programmer does not need to worry about window refresh. Interlisp supports a number of drawing primitives in windows including RasterOp, rectangles and circles filled with halftoned grey shades, and lines and curves of varying thicknesses. The halftone grey shades are encoded as 16 bit numbers which represent a four by four block which is repeated over the area. Figures 3.12 shows the numbers which represent various shades. The designers generally do not deal with these numbers since they use the shade editor in Figure 3.7. Interlisp automatically orients the patterns so there is never a seam between two abutting areas with the same shade. A bitmap editor (EDITBM) creates and edits bitmaps of any size. This is the primary way "icons" (static, fixed-size pictures) in Peridot are created. Interlisp also supplies menu and scrolling window facilities which were used until Peridot could generate similar constructs.

| 1 | 32833 | 40997 | 42370 | 42405 | 42925 | 42941 | 61373 | 65527 |

Figure 3.12.
A number of rectangles of different halftone shades. Below each rectangle is the 16-bit value that represents the shade.

The origin of the coordinate system in each window is at the lower left. The default is for the origin to be (0,0) but any other values are allowed. Rectangles and REGIONs are defined in Interlisp-D by their lower left corner and a width and height, so a REGION list looks like (LEFT BOTTOM WIDTH HEIGHT).

Peridot does not use any object-oriented programming system or any tools to support rule-based control structures. In retrospect, it might have been wise to investigate the LOOPS system [Stefik 83] for Interlisp which supplies these features (see section 13.3.2).

3.3.2. Overview

Peridot's implementation is organized as a number of subsystems, each of which performs its own task. These subsystems correspond closely with the chapters in this book. As shown in Figure 3.13, some of the features are explicitly invoked using a command and others can either be explicitly invoked or will invoke themselves based on the designer's actions.

An important characteristic of this design is that the various features are mostly independent. It would be fairly easy, for example, to replace the graphical inferencing rules with a more sophisticated system, and this would have minimal impact on the rest of the system. The features are well-integrated as far as the designer is concerned, however, since they all have similar interfaces and work well together.

Underlying all of the modules are the basic data structures which represent the graphical objects, the graphical and data constraints, and the generated code. Section 13.6 discusses a different organization that might be used if Peridot were re-implemented in the future.

3.3.3. Object-Oriented Design

As an implementation strategy, Peridot uses an object-oriented design style to some extent. This is implemented as an Interlisp-D record with fixed fields. There is one type of record used for all objects, and this record contains data and procedures. Each graphical primitive is represented as an object. Each *type* of graphical primitive (rectangle, circle, etc.) has its own set of procedures in the object, and the data differentiates instances of the same type. The fields of the record are shown in Figure 3.14.

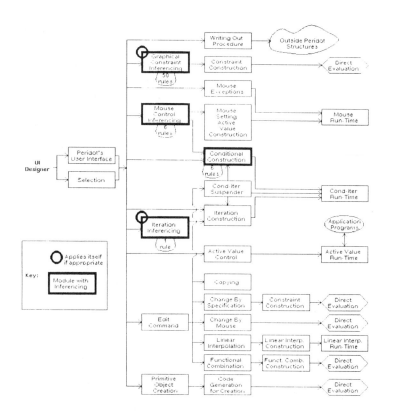

Figure 3.13.
Overview of Peridot's structure. The boxes with the circles watch the user's actions
and invoke themselves when appropriate.

3.3.3.1. Object Fields

The most interesting fields are DisplayedREGION, SavedREGION, VAL,
and VALReference. When an object is displayed, the DisplayedREGION
field holds the actual numbers for the position of the object. For example, (34
56 78 90) to indicate that an object is at LEFT=34, BOTTOM=56, WIDTH=78,
and HEIGHT=90. The region for one object will often depend on the region for
another. For example, the LEFT of the grey rectangle in Figure 3.9 depends on
the LEFT of the black rectangle, offset by 15 pixels. The BOTTOM, WIDTH,
and HEIGHT of the grey rectangle similarly depend on the black one. This relationship information implements the graphical constraints and is kept in the

Field	Type	Usage
MYNAME	LITATOM	The unique name given to this object
MYTYPE	Enumerated Type	The type of the graphical primitive (Rectangle, Icon, Iteration, etc.)
MYWINDOW	WINDOW	The window that this object is drawn in
INSIDEPFN	FUNCTION	When passed a point, returns T if the point is inside this object
BECOMESELECTEDFN	FUNCTION	Makes this object be selected
DRAWFN	FUNCTION	Draws this object in its window
ERASEFN	FUNCTION	Erases this object
DESELECTFN	FUNCTION	Causes this object to no longer be selected
DisplayedREGION	REGION numbers	Contains the numeric LEFT, BOTTOM, WIDTH and HEIGHT for this object if it is displayed
SavedREGION	REGION expressions	Contains four expressions to calculate the DisplayedREGION field
RegBackRef	REGION expressions	If any other objects refer to this one's SavedREGION, this field contains the reverse references
DrawFnc	Pair of Enumerated Types	Contains the Drawing Function to use when the object is drawn
VAL	Anything	The current value (color, string, or bitmap) for this object
VALReference	Expression	Expression to calculate VAL
ActiveP	BOOLEAN	Is this an active value?
VALBackRef	LITATOM	If this is an active value, then the reverse of all references to this object's VAL
OtherInfo	Type-specific	Extra information needed by the type
ArgumentP	BOOLEAN	Is this an argument to the procedure?
SubObjs	List of objects	If this object is an iteration or conditional, this lists the sub-objects
Statement	POINTER	Pointer to the statement in the procedure for this object
RefIterVal	Pair of NUMBER, value	If a sub-object of an iteration or conditional, then the loop index and loop value for this object

Figure 3.14.
Fields for the object record used in Peridot.

SavedREGION field, which contains four expressions to calculate the numbers in the DisplayedREGION field. This use of constraints to control graphical relationships is explained further in Chapter 4. For icons and strings, the WIDTH and HEIGHT parts of SavedREGION are automatically set with expressions to calculate the width and height of the picture.

In a similar way, the VAL field contains the current value used for the object (the color, string, or bitmap) and the VALReference field contains an expression to calculate that value. For example, if a string object is supposed to use the value of a parameter, the VALReference field of the string object would contain a reference to the parameter rather than a constant. Therefore, when the procedure is called with a different value for the parameter, the new value will be used. If the designer had selected Title as in Figure 3.10a and specified that the string should use its value, the VALReference field will simply contain Title. If the designer had referred to the third element of a list contained in the parameter Items (Figure 3.10b), the reference would be[3] (Index Items 3).

If any part of the SavedREGION or VALReference fields should be a constant, it will simply contain that literal value[4]. Section 4.2.5 presents the expressions used when referring to other objects (graphical constraints), and Chapter 8 discusses the expressions used to refer to active values (data constraints).

Another field of objects is the name of the instance (MYNAME). Each instance is given a unique name created by appending a number to a string name. The string name is based on the type and value of the object, and the number is guaranteed to be different for every object. The names are used primarily to allow one object to refer to another, but they are also used to ask the user about objects, so more intuitive string names would be appropriate.

3.3.3.2. Special Object Types

Some special objects are implemented using the same record type as the graphic primitives. These are *iterations, conditionals, active values* and *MouseWatchers*, which are explained in Chapters 6, 7, 8, and 9 respectively. Also, if Peridot supported the use of previously created interfaces as components in new interfaces (see section 13.2.1), the previous interfaces would be implemented as a special type of object. This uniform structure allows many operations to be independent of the type of their operands.

---

[3] Index is a function that returns a particular element from a list.

[4] Actually, the VALReference field might contain the constant quoted if the value does not evaluate (EVAL) to itself. For example the string "Delete all" EVALs to itself, so the VAL-Reference would just contain "Delete all". However, the atom Delete does not, so for it, the VALReference would contain (QUOTE Delete). Of course, this is handled automatically by Peridot and is not seen by the designer.

3.3.4. Code Generation

As the designer is creating an interface, Peridot generates a procedure that applications can call to use the interface. This code is basically a sequence of object creation statements with appropriate parameters. As the designer edits the interface graphically, the code is always kept consistent. The code being generated by Peridot is (optionally) displayed in a separate Peridot window (Figure 3.2). Currently, this code is presented in Interlisp-D. For example, to create a black rectangle at a fixed place, the code that would be generated might be:

```
(CreateRectangle
       `BlackRect0012        /* this object's name
       -1                    /* the color (black)
       34 56 78 90           /* the region
       `(INPUT . REPLACE))   /* the Drawing Function
```

The code is much more complicated when there are constraints, as can be seen in Figure 3.2. A more readable form could be designed for future use (see section 13.2.6). The displayed code and the picture are kept consistent, so if the picture is edited, the code is updated[5]. The code itself cannot be edited by the designer, although this might be a useful extension.

3.4. Detailed example

The best way to demonstrate how designers use Peridot is with an example. Unfortunately, a textual description of the process makes it seem very long and complex, which is really not the case. The videotape presentation [Myers 87c] or a live demonstration gives a much better feeling for how easy it is to create interfaces using Peridot.

This section presents the sequence of operations that a designer might perform to create a procedure which displays a menu of strings, where the string to use is selected by the mouse. Some of the strings are "illegal" and cannot be selected. These strings will be shown in grey. The procedure will accept a list of strings to display and a list of which of those strings cannot be selected. The procedure will return which string was selected or NIL if none are. The background graphics for the menu will include a drop shadow and a border around

---

[5] Actually, although the code is always kept consistent, it takes an annoyingly long amount of time to refresh the *display* of the code. Therefore, Peridot has a mode that simply greys out the code display when it is no longer current. Pressing a mouse button on the code will cause it to be redisplayed. This saves a lot of time, and is somewhat like the feature of spreadsheet programs that allow the user to specify whether the spreadsheet is updated after every change or only on user-request.

all the strings, and these will adjust their size to just fit around all the strings. The operation of the menu is similar to those in the Apple Macintosh [Williams 84]. An application program could use this menu as a pop-up menu, a pull-down menu or a fixed menu.

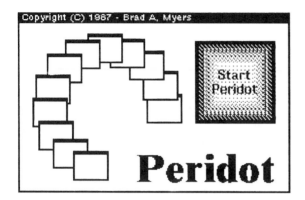

First, the designer presses with any button inside the Peridot logo window (Figure 3.15a). This causes the Start Peridot button in this window to disappear and the Peridot parameter prompting window to appear.

Figure 3.15a.

Figure 3.15b.

In this window (Figure 3.15b), the designer is prompted to type the name of the procedure, and so PopMenu is typed. Next, the designer is prompted to supply the number of parameters for the procedure: 2, the name for each parameter: Items and IllegalItems, and an example value for each: for Items the list ("Replace" "Move" "Copy" "Delete" "Delete All" "Abort" "Undo" "Exit"), and for IllegalItems the list ("Delete" "Delete All"). Next, the designer is asked the number of active values desired: 1, and the name for it: ReturnValue. Finally, the designer supplies an example value for the active value: "Copy".

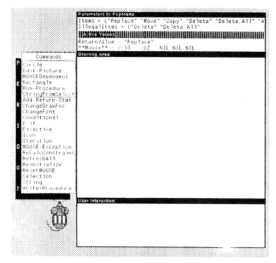

Figure 3.15c.

Peridot automatically adds an active value for the mouse input device: **Mouse** and finally creates the standard Peridot windows (Figure 3.15c).

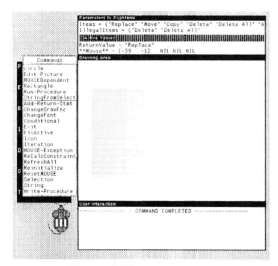

Figure 3.15d.

PopMenu will have a grey drop shadow, so the designer selects Rect from the Peridot command menu and then selects Grey from the subsequent color menu. The designer then draws this rectangle using the mouse. Peridot uses an Interlisp-D routine which displays hairlines to show the extent during the placement of the rectangle. The result is shown in Figure 3.15d.

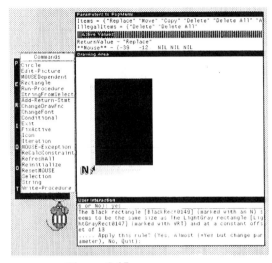

Next the designer draws a black rectangle approximately the same size as the grey rectangle and offset towards the upper right. Peridot then runs its rules to check whether this new rectangle has some relationship to the previous rectangle and discovers that it seems to be the same size and slightly offset and prints a message in the prompt window asking if this is correct (Figure 3.15e).

Figure 3.15e.

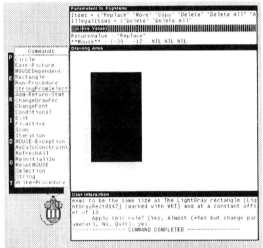

The designer types y for "yes" and the system immediately redisplays the black rectangle exactly the same size as the grey rectangle and offset by exactly 13 pixels (Figure 3.15f).

Figure 3.15f.

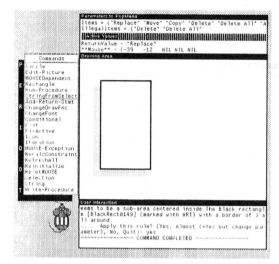

Next the designer draws a white rectangle nested inside the black one, and Peridot notices its relationship to the black rectangle and asks if it should be evenly nested. After the designer types y, the picture is adjusted to be exact (Figure 3.15g).

Figure 3.15g.

Figure 3.15h.

Next, the designer uses the ChangeFont command to change the font to be BIG-FONT and selects the first string of the parameter Items ("Replace"). The String-FromSelect command is then given, and a box the size of the string follows the mouse until the button is pressed, which the designer does at the top of the white rectangle (Figure 3.15h). Peridot correctly infers that the string should be centered at the top of the white rectangle. Peridot makes this assumption because the string was placed approximately centered in the box, as shown in Figure 3.15h. If the string had been placed at the left of the box instead, then Peridot would have asked if the string should be left-justified.

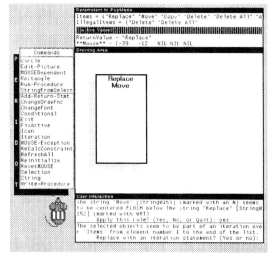

Next, the designer selects the second string of the parameter Items ("Move") and gives the StringFromSelect command again. This time, the designer places the string under the first, and Peridot infers that it should be centered below (Figure 3.15i).

Figure 3.15i.

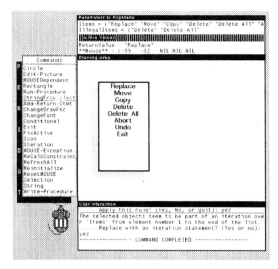

At this point, Peridot notices that the first two elements of a list (Items) have been used in graphics, and asks the designer in the prompt window if the rest of the items in the list should be displayed in the same manner. The designer confirms this, and Peridot displays the rest of the list (Figure 3.15j).

Figure 3.15j.

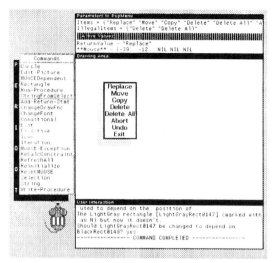

Figure 3.15k.

The designer selects the white rectangle and gives the Peridot Edit-Picture command and uses the mouse to adjust its size to be approximately the size of the strings. The system then asks if constraints should be checked for the white rectangle in its new position, and the designer types y. Peridot asks if the rectangle should be adjusted to fit exactly around all the strings, which is correct. Peridot then asks if the sizes of the black and grey rectangles should be adjusted based on the white rectangle, which is also correct. The final result is shown in Figure 3.15k.

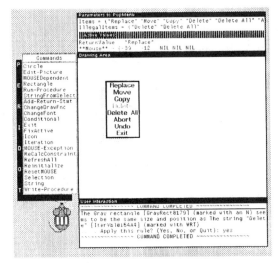

Figure 3.15l.

Now the designer wants to specify that the illegal items should be shown in grey. The Drawing Function is changed to ERASE using the ChangeDrawFnc command, and a grey rectangle is drawn over the string "Delete". Peridot infers that the rectangle should be the same size as the string (Figure 3.15l).

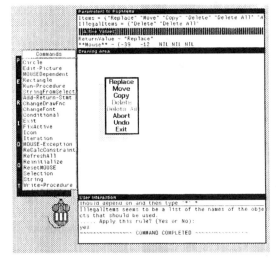

Figure 3.15m.

Next, the designer selects the grey rectangle and gives the Peridot Conditional command. The system ask which parameter or active value the condition should depend on, and the designer selects IllegalItems. Based on the type of the example value for IllegalItems, Peridot guesses that this is a list of the names of the items that should be used, which is correct. The grey rectangle then is immediately displayed over all the strings in the current value of IllegalItems (Figure 3.15m).

This completes the presentation aspects of PopMenu. It should be remembered that the code being generated does not depend on the specific example values for the parameters; any list of strings will work correctly for them, and the IllegalItems list could even be empty.

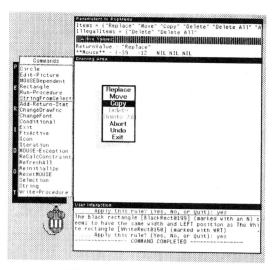

The designer wants an inverted rectangle to appear over the items when the mouse is moved over Pop-Menu. The Drawing Function is therefore changed to IN-VERT, and a black rectangle is drawn. Peridot infers that this rectangle is the same height and y position as the string "Copy" and the same width and x position as the white rectangle (Figure 3.15n).

Figure 3.15n.

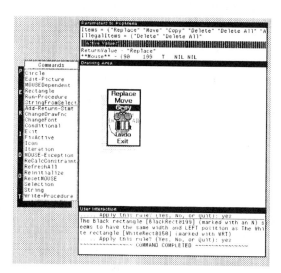

The designer then uses an icon, called the "simulated mouse," to demonstrate that the black rectangle is dependent on the mouse. The designer presses the real mouse's button over the simulated mouse's left button to show that this button should be pressed, and then positions the simulated mouse over the new rectangle by dragging it by its "nose" (Figure 3.15o).

Figure 3.15o.

The designer then gives the MOUSEDependent command. Based on the position of the simulated mouse, Peridot infers that the black rectangle should choose one of the items of the iteration, and it asks which active value should be set, proposing ReturnValue as the likely choice. The designer types * to confirm the use of `ReturnValue`, and Peridot uses the type of its example value (a single string) to guess that only one item is allowed to be selected at a time and that the active value should be set with the name of the string that the mouse is over. Peridot then generalizes from the specific example and asks if the operation should work when the mouse is over any of the strings in the iteration, and if the operation should happen continuously while the mouse left button is held down, both of which are correct. Finally, the system asks if a different value should be used for `ReturnValue` when the mouse goes off of the strings, and the designer types in `NIL`, since nothing should be highlighted when the end user moves the mouse outside the menu.

Now this piece of the interaction is complete and the designer can try it with the real or the simulated mouse. To prevent `ReturnValue` from being set with any `IllegalItems`, the designer selects the grey rectangle over "Delete" and gives the Peridot command `MOUSE-Exception`. Peridot confirms that this exception refers to the previously created interaction, and then the inverting rectangle will no longer show up over "Delete" or "Delete All". Finally, the designer selects the `ReturnValue` active value, gives the `Add-Return-Stmt` command, and specifies that the procedure should return when the interaction is complete (which is when the mouse button is released).

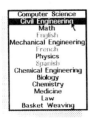

The `PopMenu` procedure is now complete. The designer can exercise it further and edit any part, or it can be written out and used by an application program. Figure 3.15p shows `PopMenu` being used by an application program with different values for the parameters.

Figure 3.15p.

If this description seems convoluted and complex, then it gives first-hand evidence for how inappropriate story boards and the associated static, textual specification are for defining user interfaces, and how much better Peridot's dynamic, example-based technique is. Although the textual description of the designer's actions is rather long, clumsy, and tedious, only about twelve actions had to be performed to create this procedure (plus confirming Peridot's guesses). Creating `PopMenu` from scratch only took me 4 minutes, which is significantly shorter than it would take to code this complex interaction technique by hand. As described in section 15.4, in an informal experiment, it took expert programmers an average of over 3 hours to program this exact menu, either from scratch or by modifying existing code. This experiment used a variety of hardware and software environments. If these numbers are accurate, then Peridot is a factor of around 50 faster than hand coding.

3.5. Extensions to the Graphic Primitives

As mentioned above, it would be desirable for Peridot to support straight and curved lines. This would allow Peridot to create circular dials and gauges where a rotating line is used as the indicator. Some other graphic primitives would make the interfaces created with Peridot look prettier, without increasing the functionality. These include rectangles with curved edges, rectangles with diagonal edges, and possibly curved lines (splines).

Other important extensions mentioned in this chapter are the ability to read in previously created interfaces and use them as components of new interfaces, having the Drawing Function and the Font depend on active values and parameters, editing the drawing order, having a designer-readable representation of the code, and better string names for objects. Most of these extensions are discussed further in later chapters.

3.6. Chapter Summary

This chapter presents an overview of Peridot's user interface and implementation. The basic graphic primitives supported by Peridot (rectangles, circles, text, and icons) and their attributes (value, position, size, drawing function, and font) are presented. The value for each attribute can be a constant, or it can be connected using a constraint to the value of an attribute of another graphical object, or to the value of a parameter or active value. Objects, parameters, and active values can be selected and de-selected using the mouse.

The implementation of Peridot uses an object-oriented style, and inferencing is performed using condition-action rules. The code generated for the interface is in Interlisp-D and can be displayed in a window.

The chapter concludes with a detailed example of using Peridot to create a menu of strings.

Chapter IV
Graphical Constraints and Inferencing

4.1. Introduction

Two of Peridot's important innovations are that it automatically infers relationships among the graphical objects, and that it generates efficiently-implemented constraints to insure that the relationships hold even if the objects move or change size. An example of a relationship that might be inferred is that a string is centered at the top of a rectangle. A constraint is established so the string will stay at the top even if the rectangle is moved or otherwise edited.

In order to create parameterized procedures, Peridot needs to have graphical constraints. If the picture being created for the interface was simply a static background that never changed size, it would not be necessary for the system to notice the relationships. For example, the displays in previous UIMSs such as Menulay [Buxton 83] and Trillium [Henderson 86] are mostly static frames, and the interaction objects used do not affect the overall size or shape of the display. In Peridot, however, the pictures usually depend on the parameters and active values for the procedure. For example, in the example of Figure 3.15, the size of the rectangles around the menu depend on the number of items in the menu and the width of the largest item. In order to make this parameterization work, Peridot must know how various objects depend on the parts that can change. As far as we know, this facility has never been provided before in a UIMS.

Another benefit of the graphical constraints is that they allow the designer to draw the picture quickly and sloppily and then have Peridot automatically "beautify" it by enforcing the graphical constraints. This benefit was unintended in Peridot, but it is an important motivation in drawing packages like Sketchpad [Sutherland 63] and Juno [Nelson 85] that support graphical constraints.

Peridot attempts to automatically guess what these constraints should be using a form of *Plausible Inference*, which is essentially pattern matching.

It would be possible instead to require the designer to specify how an object relates to other objects in the picture, but this would be very hard to use due to the large number of possibilities. Currently in Peridot, there are around 50 relationships that might hold between two objects, and there may be many objects in the scene that an object might be related to. Also, most of the relationships are parameterized (for example, the amount of space between nested rectangles). For the designer to understand the 50 choices and pick the correct one would be a tremendous burden.

Therefore, Peridot attempts to automatically infer the relationships among objects. As mentioned in section 3.2.3, the relationships inferred only deal with the size and position attributes (LEFT, BOTTOM, WIDTH and HEIGHT) of the graphical objects; the other attributes are constant or explicitly specified to depend on other objects.

4.2. Rules

Each graphical constraint that can be inferred is represented in Peridot as a simple *condition-action rule*. Appendix D lists the full set of rules currently used in Peridot. The operation of these object-object rules is described below.

4.2.1. Rule Structure

Each rule is composed of 7 parts:

(1) the rule's name, used for debugging,

(2) a list of the attributes set by this rule,

(3) a test that determines if the rule should be applied (the condition),

(4) a message that is used to ask the designer whether the rule should be applied if the test succeeds,

(5) the number of parameters of the rule that the designer can specify,

(6) an action which causes the objects to conform to the rule, and

(7) a list of the attributes *not* set by this rule.

Since the rules are currently expressed in Interlisp-D, the designer will not be able to add new rules. However, it is very easy for an Interlisp-D programmer to modify the rule set.

An example of a rule is shown in Figure 4.1. This rule tests to see if a rectangle (R2) is centered horizontally within another rectangle (R1).

(1) The name of the rule is Rect-Centered-X,

(2) the rule specifies the LEFT and WIDTH of the rectangle,

(3) the test is the code in the (AND ...),

(4) the message is in the (CONCAT ...),

(5) there is one parameter, called DIFF, which is the number of pixels on each side of the inner rectangle. This effectively controls the width of the inner rectangle,

(6) the action is the GENCHANGEREGION call, which changes the SavedRE-GION field of R2 as follows:

```
R2.SavedREGION.LEFT := R1.SavedREGION.LEFT + DIFF
R2.SavedREGION.BOTTOM is unchanged
    (NIL passed to GENCHANGEREGION)
R2.SavedREGION.WIDTH := R1.SavedREGION.WIDTH +
                (-(DIFF+DIFF))
R2.SavedREGION.HEIGHT is unchanged
```

(7) Finally, the rule does not specify the BOTTOM and HEIGHT attributes of the rectangle.

```
(Rect-Centered-X (LEFT WIDTH)
        (AND (SUBREGIONP (fetch DisplayedREGION of R1)
                         (fetch DisplayedREGION of R2))
             (SomeLessBySameAmt (fetch DisplayedREGION of R1)
                                (fetch DisplayedREGION of R2)
                                (QUOTE (T NIL T NIL)))
             (SETQ DIFF (QUOTIENT (DIFFERENCE (fetch WIDTH
                                                      of (fetch DisplayedREGION
                                                                of R1))
                                              (fetch WIDTH
                                                     of (fetch DisplayedREGION
                                                               of R2)))
                                  2)))
        ((CONCAT (GetGoodName R2 (QUOTE N))
                 " seems to be inside "
                 (GetGoodName R1 (QUOTE WRT))
                 " with a border of " DIFF " on the left and right")
         1)
        (GENCHANGEREGION R2 R1 DIFF NIL (MINUS (PLUS DIFF DIFF))
                         NIL)
        (BOTTOM HEIGHT))
```

Figure 4.1.
The actual Interlisp code for the Peridot rule to see if a rectangle is centered horizontally inside another rectangle.

Since the rules specify very low level relationships (e.g. that a string should be centered inside a box), there appear to be only a small number of rules required to handle existing interfaces. In an informal survey of a number of Direct Manipulation interfaces, and experience with using Peridot on a wide variety of interfaces by a number of designers (see Appendix A), about 50 rules seemed to be sufficient. These are listed in Appendix D.

4.2.2. Conflict Resolution Strategy

In order to allow for human imprecision, some leeway must be given to the designer as to the placement and size of objects, and the drawings need not be exact. For example, the designer may want one box to be inside another box with a border of 3 pixels all around, but actually draw it with a border of 5 on one side and 2 on another. Therefore the tests in Peridot for whether to apply a particular rule have thresholds of applicability[1]. The thresholds currently used by Peridot are somewhat arbitrary and have been chosen experimentally. Most of the thresholds are based on a constant offset (e.g. the width of one rectangle is within 5 pixels of the width of another), but some are proportional (e.g. the width is within 10 percent of the width of the other). As discussed in section 4.6.1, more experimenting is necessary to get better thresholds.

Unfortunately, one result of using thresholds for the rules is that the same drawing will often pass more than one test. Therefore, the rules must be ordered so the most likely rules are tested first. This ordering, sometimes called a *conflict resolution strategy*, is based on restrictiveness (the most demanding tests are first) and on a heuristically determined likelihood of their being appropriate. This ordering is further discussed in the next section.

There is a different set of rules for each pair of types of object (i.e., there is one set for rectangles with respect to rectangles, one set for rectangles with respect to strings, one set for strings with respect to rectangles, etc.). This is because different types have different attributes that can be specified (it is not possible to change the width or height of strings, for example) and because some rules are more appropriate to a certain pair of types. For example, it is much more likely for a text string to be centered at the top of a rectangle than for another rectangle to be, or for a rectangle to be centered at the top of a string.

4.2.3. Order for Objects and Rules

When an object is created, Peridot immediately tries to find another object that it relates to, as shown in the example of section 3.4. Applying the rules immediately when objects are created seems to be more successful and less annoying than applying them in a batched fashion as is done by picture beautifiers such as [Pavlidis 85]. The context of knowing the previously created object provides heuristics that help insure that the rule is correct. Also, since only one object is "beautified" at a time (the newly drawn one) and since the

---

[1] In Figure 4.1 the threshold is built into the SomeLessBySameAmt procedure.

result of the rule is immediately apparent (the object is redrawn after the rule is applied), it is very easy for the designer to verify that the rule was correct. In addition, the rule's message is in plain English and (hopefully) adequately explains what the rule will do. The designer can also use a command to have the rules re-evaluated for an existing object, as explained in section 5.8.

Most of the rules in Peridot relate one object to a single existing object. The exceptions are the special rules that makes the size of a rectangle be the sum of the sizes of all the objects inside of it. These special rules are discussed in section 4.5.

Peridot searches for the object that the new object should relate to in two passes. First, it searches through all objects using only those rules that constrain *all* of the size and position attributes of the new object, and if that does not work, then it searches through all objects applying the rules that constrain *some* of the attributes. Any attributes that are not constrained by any rules stay constant. The order for searching through the objects is: (1) any explicitly selected objects (this allows the designer to give Peridot a hint about which other object the new one should relate to), (2) the previous object that was created (this is the one that usually works when objects are being newly created), and (3) the objects in the vicinity of the new object. The system stops searching when an object and a rule are found that completely specifies all of the attributes of the new object.

Occasionally some of an object's attributes may depend on one object and other attributes depend on a different object. For example in Figure 4.2, the highlight bar has the same height and y value as the string, but the same width and x as the surrounding box. Therefore, Peridot will continue applying rules even after a rule succeeds if some of the attributes of the object are not specified. In this case, the rules that are applied subsequently are only those that cover the remaining attributes of the object.

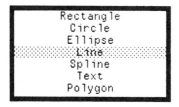

Figure 4.2.
The grey rectangle is the same height and y position as the string Line and the same width and x position as the white rectangle.

Usually, the first object tested is the correct one to apply rules to and the first rule whose test succeeds covers all of the properties of the object. Even when multiple comparisons are required, however, the rule checking occurs without any noticeable delay.

If the desired relationship is not found by Peridot, either the appropriate rule's test did not succeed, or Peridot does not have a rule for the desired relationship. In the first case, then the designer has drawn the object too sloppily and must redraw it. Peridot could provide the list of rules in a menu and allow the designer to pick the rule to apply, but this has not proven necessary. If this were added, the designer would select the two objects to apply the rules to, and the menu would use the rule's message to describe the rule. In this case, the test portion of the rule would be ignored. In the second case, where no appropriate rule exists, the designer can explicitly specify the relationship using the editing commands described in Chapter 5.

4.2.4. Asking the Designer

When a rule's test succeeds, Peridot queries the designer whether to apply the rule using the rule's message. The rule from Figure 4.1 will produce a message something like:

```
The white rectangle [WhiteRect0061] (marked with an N)
seems to be inside the black rectangle [BlackRect0059]
(marked with WRT) with a border of 10 on the left and right.
..... Apply this rule?
    (Yes, Almost (=Yes but change parameter), No, Quit):
```

Figures 3.15c-o show actual messages from rules in the bottom window. Since the objects that the message refers to are sometimes not obvious, Peridot shows two blinking arrows that point to the two objects named in the rule. The arrow for the new object has an ''N'' and the other object has a ''WRT'' (for ''with respect to''). The internal names (such as WhiteRect0061) are included since they are always guaranteed to be unique and sometimes can be helpful.

If the system has guessed wrong, the designer types n for ''no'' and the system will continue processing the rules in order to try to find a different rule that applies. If the designer believes that not only is this rule incorrect, but that there is no point in trying other rules, then q for ''quit'' can be typed. If the rule is entirely correct, the designer types y for ''yes.'' Sometimes the rule is correct, but the designer wants to use different values for the parameters. For example, the system may decide that a rectangle is inside another rectangle with a border of 10 pixels all around, but the designer may want to use 15 pixels instead. In this case, the designer types a for ''almost,'' and Peridot will prompt for the new values for each parameter:

New value for parameter 1 (old = 10) or * for no change:

A * can be typed in place of a new value for any parameter to have it keep its original value, or the designer can type the desired new value (e.g. 15).

The proposed values for the parameters of the rules are calculated by taking the average of all the distances involved (e.g. if a rectangle is nested on 4 sides inside another rectangle, then Peridot uses the average of the four distances between the two rectangles).

One concern is that the designer will be annoyed by having to answer the questions of many rules after every drawing operation. This does not seem to be the case. Although the primary motivation for having the rules is that Peridot needs to know the relationships, an unexpected side benefit is that it makes it very easy to generate pretty pictures since the rules neaten the drawings. The designers seem to be willing to answer the questions to allow them to draw the picture fairly quickly and sloppily and let the system neaten it up. Also, the system rarely asks more than one or two questions for each object.

4.2.5. Enforcing Rules

The action part of the rules insures that the relationship will hold between the two objects. It is not sufficient to simply calculate the numbers that make the relationship hold for the current configuration, since the relationship should be maintained even if the objects are modified. Therefore, Peridot generates an expression that will calculate the relationship. This expression is then saved in the appropriate element of the SavedREGION field of the new object. From the rule of Figure 4.1, the resulting expression for the LEFT field of the new rectangle (Rect0061) might be:

(PLUS 10 (Field Rect0059 LEFT))

where 10 was a parameter to the rule that was confirmed by the designer, Rect0059 is the other object, and the function Field is used to get the value of attributes of objects.

4.3. Reversing Relationships

When an object is created, its relationships to other objects is calculated and stored, as described in the previous section. This relationship is unidirectional. For example, in Figure 4.3a, the LEFT of the grey rectangle depends on the LEFT of black rectangle but not vice versa. This means that if the designer edits the black rectangle such that its LEFT field changes, the grey rectangle will move with it automatically, but what should happen if the designer edits the LEFT field of the grey rectangle? In conventional constraint systems like Thinglab [Borning 79] or Juno [Nelson 85], the black rectangle would change because all constraints are bi-directional. In Peridot, however, experience shows that this form of edit is usually performed because the designer is not happy with the relationship between the two objects. For example, the distance between the rectangles might be made smaller. In this case, Peridot will infer the new constraint and leave the black rectangle unchanged.

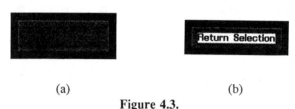

(a)   (b)

Figure 4.3.

Originally (a), the grey rectangle depends on the black rectangle. When the grey rectangle is later made to depend on the string (b), the black rectangle is made to depend on the grey rectangle; reversing the constraint.

On the other hand, sometimes the original constraint should still be in effect. For example, in Figure 4.3a, the WIDTH of the grey rectangle originally depended on the WIDTH of the black rectangle (because the grey rectangle was drawn after the black rectangle and the rules make later objects depend on earlier ones). However, after the string was added, the system inferred that the WIDTH of the grey rectangle should instead depend on the WIDTH of the longest string. This uses the rule Rect-Offset-Around-String which leaves a constant size border around the string. Now, the rectangles will adjust to fit around any size string. When this rule is applied, the relationship of the grey rectangle to the black one is lost. In order to retain this relationship, Peridot could re-run the rules to check for relationships of the black rectangle with respect to the grey rectangle, but to eliminate this inefficiency, Peridot saves the reverse of all relationships for use in these occasions. When the relationship of the grey rectangle to the string is specified, Peridot will ask whether to reverse the relationship from before and make the the black rectangle depend on the grey one (Figure 4.3b). This process is applied recursively, so if the black rectangle formerly depended on some other object (as in Figure 3.15 where the black rectangle depended on the grey rectangle which is the shadow), this relationship would be reversed also. Unfortunately, there does not seem to be any automatic way for Peridot to tell whether the relationships should be reversed, so the designer must always be asked.

As shown in the previous section, the relationships among rules are expressed symbolically and include references to attributes of other objects. It would therefore require a symbolic expression manipulation package to be able to convert the expression to the reverse relationship. Therefore, Peridot always generates the reverse expression when it generates the forward expression. This reverse expression is saved in the RegBackRef field of the other object.

It must be emphasized that the reverse of the relationships is only saved while inside Peridot for use if an object is edited. The *evaluation* of the relationships always uses a one pass algorithm which does not use the reverse relationships, as explained in the next section.

4.4. Implementing the Constraints

The dependencies of an object's attributes are often cascaded. For example, the LEFT position of the white rectangle in Figure 3.15 depends on the LEFT position of the black rectangle, which, in turn, depends on the LEFT position of the grey rectangle.

In addition, the dependencies may go forward in the drawing order as well as backwards. Normally, when an object is drawn, it depends only on objects drawn previously, so the numerical values of their attributes are available. However, if a relationship has been reversed or the user explicitly edits an attribute to depend on some object, an object may be drawn before the object it depends on is drawn. For example, the width of the grey rectangle depends on the width of the string in Figure 4.3, but the rectangle is drawn before the string. The drawing order of objects cannot be changed, however, since newer objects can obscure older objects. Therefore, the calculation order must be different from the drawing order.

Fortunately, it is easy to handle these cases with an efficient, recursive, one-pass algorithm. The Field function, which returns attributes of objects, uses the value of the attribute if it has been calculated, and if not, evaluates the appropriate reference field. This may recursively call Field, but no attribute will ever be evaluated more than once. Field also insures that attributes do not use themselves recursively by marking attributes as INPROGRESS. In pseudo-Lisp, the code for Field is:

```
(DEFUN Field (obj fld)
  (if obj.fld then
      (if (EQ obj.fld `INPROGRESS) then (ERROR "Recursive")
       else obj.fld)
   else
      (SETQ obj.fld `INPROGRESS)
      (SETQ obj.fld (EVAL obj.fldREFERENCE))
```

The time-complexity of this algorithm is clearly constant per object (linear in the number of objects) and usually does not require any more time than if the relationships had been hand coded.

As can be seen from the code listing in Figure 3.2, the parameters to each object creation procedure contain references to other attributes. Clearly, if any of these were *forward* references, they could not be evaluated when the object was created since the referent object has not been created yet. Therefore, as discussed in Chapter 11, when running the procedure outside of Peridot, all the objects are created before any of the attributes are evaluated. This is why the parameters to the procedure must be quoted; otherwise they would be evaluated as the object was being created.

4.5. Special Rules

The algorithm presented in the previous section works well for all the relationships used in Peridot except one. The special rules that allow the size of a rectangle to be just big enough to fit all the objects inside of it are difficult to implement. The straightforward way would be to simply calculate the display regions for all enclosed objects first and then calculate the rectangle width and height. Unfortunately, this may use the rectangle's width attribute before it is calculated, for example, if one of the enclosed objects is centered inside of the rectangle (as is the case for the strings inside the white rectangle in Figure 3.15).

Currently, there is only one rule for this case and it uses special purpose code to avoid this problem. The rule, which is used for menus of strings, makes the rectangle be the width of the widest string and the height of the sum of the heights of the strings. This will clearly not work for other cases, such as Figure 4.4, where a more general size calculation algorithm is needed.

A more general mechanism might run two passes through the evaluation. It would first use a dummy value for the size of the outer rectangle to calculate the sizes of all enclosed rectangles. These sizes would then be used to calculate the correct size for the outer rectangle, and then the enclosed objects would be recalculated so their positions would be correct. This would probably not be difficult to add and would not be too inefficient. Alternatively, more general constraint-solving techniques [Sutherland 63] [Borning 79] [Nelson 85] could be used.

4.6. Extensions

In addition to providing a more general algorithm for making rectangles become the size of their enclosed objects, there are a number of other extensions that would make the handling of object-object constraints better.

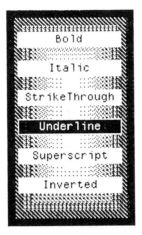

Figure 4.4.
A fancy menu in which a more complex size calculation is needed for the outer rectangle.

4.6.1. Adjusting the Thresholds and Ordering

Currently some of the thresholds of the rules are much too loose, so the rule fires even when no human would think that the rule could apply. Some fine tuning could easily adjust this problem to eliminate some extra rules that the designer has to say ''no'' to.

A more global change is to change the order that other objects in the vicinity are tested, especially when objects are being edited. Currently, the system always starts from the most recently created object and works backwards, and this may try objects that were created after the object being edited. Since most of the rules are set up to apply to objects that were created before the object being edited, it would probably be better to start with the object just before the object being edited, work backwards to the beginning of the list, and then wrap around back to the original object again.

4.6.2. Using a Best-Fit Algorithm

The rule application technique was chosen for its simplicity, and it is fairly successful. However, a more intelligent algorithm might reduce the number of rules the designer has to type ''no'' to. Instead of a boolean test, each rule would have an error measure, and the algorithm would check all rules and then ask the designer first about the rule with the lowest error. For example, in Figure 4.5, Peridot's current first-fit algorithm will ask the designer if the rectangle should be the same size as the string `Replace` before it asks about the string `Move` (since objects are checked in reverse drawing order). The proposed best-fit algorithm would notice that the rectangle is closer to `Move` and would ask about this string first. It is conceivable, but not likely, that a more clever algorithm would guess wrong so seldom that the prompt messages and questions could be eliminated.

Figure 4.5.
When calculating the black rectangle's relationships, Peridot asks about the wrong string (`Replace`) before asking about the correct string (`Move`).

It should be emphasized that this extension only complicates the rule structure a little. Typical AI systems have many other features, including backtracking, forward and backward chaining, and explanation facilities to discuss why a rule was asked, that would still be unnecessary in Peridot. On the other hand, if a full-fledged "Expert System" was desired for Peridot, the rule inferencing mechanism is a separable piece and a sophisticated inferencing system could be easily integrated with the rest of Peridot without affecting other mechanisms.

4.6.3. Adjusting the Rule Ordering

Currently, the order for applying the rules is hard-wired into the Lisp code. This order should be adjusted to help eliminate some cases where incorrect rules are asked. No matter what the ordering is, however, there will always be cases where incorrect rules will pass. For example, it is not possible to make the thresholds small enough to accurately distinguish between a string centered, left-justified, and right-justified under another string. Therefore, all of these rules are likely to be asked. If the designer always prefers one over another, then the preferred one should be first in the rule list. Therefore, it would be desirable to provide some way for the designer to specify the rule ordering.

Another possibility is for the system to try to guess what the rule ordering should be based on the designer's answers to the rules' questions. If the designer repeated answered "no" to one rule and "yes" to the next, the system might propose that the rule order be switched.

4.6.4. Easier Addition of New Rules

Currently, new rules can only be added by programming them in Lisp. Since the rules have a fairly simple structure and usually only involve simple arithmetic, it is conceivable that they could be specified in a way that would be accessible to a non-programmer. Then new rules could be added by the designer if common situations occurred frequently that were not covered by existing rules.

A more AI-ish approach to this idea would be to have the system try to infer the rules from the actual drawings, so the system would learn about the appropriate relationships in the user interfaces. This is probably not possible without considerable progress in the research on machine learning.

4.6.5. Eliminating Prompt Messages

Some people have proposed that rather than prompt for each rule, Peridot should just apply the rule and provide an UNDO command which would undo the rule and try another. If the system is almost always correct in its guesses, this might be easier to use. However, there are a number of problems with it. First, the current algorithm does guess wrong occasionally, and due to the necessity to provide thresholds to allow for human imprecision, it is unlikely that any future algorithm will choose perfectly. However, the visible modifications to the picture as a result of the choice of a wrong rule may not be significantly different from the correct rule, so the designer is unlikely to notice the error. Even if a message about the rule being used were to be displayed, if no question is asked, the designer would probably ignore the message. Previous programming by example systems had this problem, which contributed to their lack of success [Biermann 76a] [Bauer 78].

4.6.6. New Object Types

Another issue with rules is that currently there is a set of rules for every pair of graphical object types. Clearly, there is a concern that as the number of different types is increased (adding lines, curved lines, polygons, etc.), there will be a geometric expansion of the number of rule sets necessary. If the new objects operate like existing objects, then they can share rules (for example, icons and strings currently use the same rule sets). If the new objects relate differently than existing objects, then it is appropriate to create new rule sets. These extra rules will not affect the speed of rule application or the number of rules that have to be applied for a particular object, however. This is because the only rules that are applied between two objects are those that are appropriate for the types of the objects, and the number of rules for each pair of types is not likely to increase. In addition, few radically different types of objects are needed for user interfaces. The main important additions would be lines and polygons. Other popular shapes, such as rounded edge rectangles and ellipses, can share existing rules.

A related issue is how to handle new object types that are not adequately described by a rectangular region and a single value. A line's start and end can be defined by a rectangle, but if the width of the line can be specified, along with a color or dot-dash pattern, then a single value field will not be sufficient. For a polygon, a single value field for the color is sufficient, but more data is needed to define the shape. Clearly, the data structures used for objects will have to be changed, but the basic strategy used by Peridot should still be appropriate.

4.6.7. New Language for Expressing Constraints

The graphical constraints are currently expressed in Interlisp code, and they are kept in two places: in the `SavedREGION` field of objects and in the generated code for the procedure. It is a difficult problem to keep these consistent. As described in section 4.3, the reverse of the rules must be generated since calculating the reverse from the relationship is difficult. Currently, the reverse is only stored for one attribute. Some relationships, however, such as "center," depend on multiple attributes of objects:

```
Rect0023.LEFT := Rect0021.LEFT +
              ((Rect0021.WIDTH-Rect0023.WIDTH)/2)
```

All of these problems might be solved by inventing an intermediate language for the procedures which would be re-executed to generate the pictures (eliminating the need for the `SavedREGION` field) as is done in Juno [Nelson 85]. The language might be simpler to manipulate so a "reverser" for relationships could be provided. In addition, the language might be understandable to the designer (unlike the Interlisp code generated now), which would be an added advantage (see section 13.2.6).

4.6.8. Implementation Enhancements

The data structures that describe the forward and backwards relationships for attributes are complicated and difficult to maintain. In addition, since they have circular dependencies, the Interlisp-D garbage collector will not work with them. It might actually be easier to manage these data structures in a Pascal-like language with explicit de-allocation.

Another interesting area to explore would be to make the handling of rules and object editing (when rules are applied) work in a more object-oriented manner. This might alleviate some of the above problems and would certainly make the code more modular.

4.7. Chapter Summary

This chapter discusses two features of Peridot: the use of efficient graphical constraints to enforce relationships among graphical objects, and the rule-based inferencing which automatically determines which constraints should apply. Using inferencing, rather than requiring the relationships to be explicitly specified, has the advantage that the designer needs much less knowledge. This is because the designer does not have to know how to choose which of the 50 possible relationships to apply and what the parameters to those relationships are. An important side benefit is that these rules automatically "beautify" the picture.

Peridot will infer relationships among objects no matter how they are created. Therefore, the same rules will be applied whether an object is created from scratch, by copying some other object, or by transforming an existing object. Since Peridot generalizes from the *results* of the operations, and not *traces* of the actions like many previous Programming by Example systems, it provides much more flexibility to the designers and allows user interfaces to be easily edited. For example, if the designer makes an error when drawing an object or wants to change an existing object, he can simply correct it and Peridot will automatically apply the rules to the new version.

Peridot attempts to infer the LEFT, BOTTOM, WIDTH and HEIGHT attributes of an object by searching through all other existing objects in a particular order and applying the rules' tests. When a test succeeds, the designer is asked if the rule should be applied. If so, the relationship is enforced and the reverse relationship is saved in case it is needed later as the designer edits the picture. When the relationship is evaluated, a simple, constant-time algorithm is used that handles forward or backward dependencies.

A special rule is used to allow the size of a rectangle to be the sum of the sizes of objects inside of it, but the existing algorithm is very limited. Generalizing this algorithm, providing a more intelligent algorithm for applying the rules, making the addition of new rules easier, and handling new graphical object types could be added to Peridot in the future.

Chapter V

Editing Graphics

5.1. Introduction

Since Peridot is designed to be a prototyping tool, it is imperative that it support easy editing of all of the parts of the interface. This chapter discusses a number of different ways that the graphics can be edited. These include: erasing, copying, using the mouse, typing new values, changing the dependencies with active values, parameters, or other objects, and special features to allow an attribute to vary in a range (linear interpolation) or as a functional combination. The following chapters on iterations, conditionals, active values and input device handling discuss how those structures are edited.

All of the editing commands are available in a submenu that appears when the `Edit-Picture` command is given. In general, after each edit operation is performed, the code is updated and the picture is redrawn so that the designer always has an accurate view of the interface.

5.2. Erasing

One of the simplest editing operations is to erase an object. This removes the object from the screen, its code from the procedure, and deallocates any associated resources. The only complexity is that any attributes of other objects that referred to the object being erased must be changed to be constants based on the current value of the attribute. In addition, any back reference pointers to the erased object must be removed. Keeping track of these types of references is a major implementation difficulty in Peridot.

5.3. Copying

A set of objects can be selected and copied to a new place (the copy command makes use of the ability to have more than one object selected at a time). When the copy command is invoked, Peridot presents a menu which lets the designer specify what attributes in the copies will be changed with the mouse: nothing, LEFT, BOTTOM, or position (which is LEFT *and* BOTTOM)[1]. It is often

---

[1] Copy could be extended to allow the size of the copied objects to be changed also, but this is not usually desired, and the designer can always change the size of the new objects after the copy.

useful for copied objects to be aligned with the originals, either in x or y, in which case it is faster to just move the other dimension. If the designer selects "nothing," then the new objects appear directly on top of the old objects. Otherwise, the copy command calculates the bounding rectangle around all of the selected objects and lets the user place the objects with the mouse in either x or y or both.

As an example, suppose the black and white rectangles and the text string in Figure 5.1a were selected and the copy command given. The designer then selects BOTTOM from the menu to specify that the new copies should have different y values but the same x values as the corresponding old versions. Peridot then draws a dotted box the size of the bounding region around all the objects to allow the user to position the copies (Figure 5.1b). The box will only move up and down since it is constrained to have the same LEFT as the original. Then, Peridot creates new objects of the same type as the originals (two rectangles and a string) and copies the originals' fields into the copies. The names for the new objects are derived from the names of the corresponding old objects. For example, if the original black rectangle was named Black0122, the corresponding copy might be named Black0122Copy0132.

The major complication of the copy command is that relationships of the various objects copied must be modified so that they are constant or depend on the new copies rather than on the originals. This allows the copies to be in a new position even if the position of the originals was based on some other objects. Each field of the copied objects is modified so that (1) if it was a constant, it becomes the appropriate constant for the new position, (2) if it referred to one of the original objects, it now refers to the corresponding copied object instead, or (3) if it referred to some other object and if it was one of the fields that the user specified that would change (BOTTOM in this case), then it becomes a constant for the new position instead. In the example, due to case (2), the BOTTOM field of White0123Copy0156 would refer to Black0122Copy0155 (instead of Black0122), but, due to case (3), the BOTTOM of Black0122Copy0155 would be constant rather than referring to the BOTTOM of Grey0121 as the original (Black0122) does. The result is shown in Figure 5.1c.

After the copy, the new objects can be edited using the other editing commands and this will not effect the original objects (Figure 5.1d).

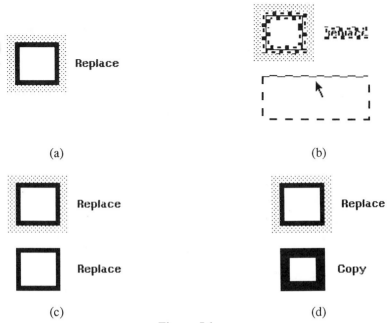

(a)   (b)

(c)   (d)

Figure 5.1.
The three phases of a copy command: (a) the original objects, (b) three of the objects
are selected and a dotted box the size of the selected ones follows the mouse up and
down, (c) the selected objects are copied below the originals. In (d), the copied objects have been modified without affecting the originals.

5.4. Changing Attributes with the Mouse

One of the most common ways to edit an object is to change its attributes
using the mouse. (Currently, only one object's attributes can be edited at a
time. After that object is edited, however, any objects that depend on it will be
automatically updated.) After the ChangePropByMouse command is given, a
menu pops up containing the attributes of the selected object that can change.
For rectangles, this menu is shown in Figure 5.2. For strings and icons, WIDTH
and HEIGHT are not listed, and for circles, they are replaced by DIAMETER.
After the attributes are selected, Peridot creates a hair-line box that follows the
mouse, allowing the designer to specify whatever has been chosen.

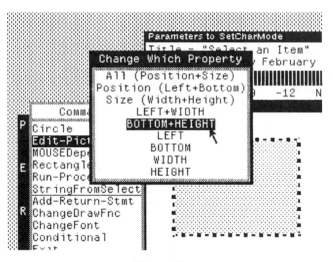

Figure 5.2.
This menu pops up to allow the designer to select which attributes of a rectangle to modify with the mouse.

5.5. Changing Attributes by Specification

Another common way to change an attribute is to explicitly specify a new value. Peridot allows the designer to type a new constant value for the attribute, or to select a parameter, active value, or other object that it should depend on. When the ChangePropBySpec command is given, a menu pops up containing the changeable attributes for the selected object (again, only one object can be selected for this command). This includes the size and position attributes, along with COLOR, STRING, or BITMAP for the VALUE field (depending on the type of the object), DRAWING FUNCTION, and, if the object is a string, FONT. If DRAWING FUNCTION or FONT is selected, a menu pops up which allows the designer to select the desired value. If one of the other attributes is selected, then Peridot prints a message in the prompt window showing the attribute's current value and asking for a new value, which the designer can type. If the color is being edited, then the designer can choose the new color from the color choice menu (Figure 3.6). Similarly, the icon menu will appear if the designer is editing the bitmap of an icon.

Alternatively, the designer can select another object for the attribute to depend on, and then type "*". The "*" is needed because it may take multiple selection actions to get the desired object, as explained in section 3.2.4. There-fore, without the "*", Peridot would not know when the designer is finished selecting. Parameters, active values and graphic objects are all selected in the same way. If another graphic object is selected and the attribute being changed is a position or size, then Peridot provides two ways for the constraints to be calculated. One provides a constant offset for the two values and allows the designer to confirm or change this offset. When prompting for the new constant, Peridot prints out the current value for the attribute. As an example, the left of one rectangle might be constrained to be 10 pixels less than the left of another rectangle. An expression is generated to keep the original object at that constant offset from the other object. The second way to specify the relationship for the attribute is with an arithmetic expression. The designer types in an expression using $ to represent the other object's attribute. For example, if the selected attribute was WIDTH, then the designer would type ($/3) to make the width of the first object be one-third the width of the other. The ability to provide even more general expressions, possibly involving multiple attributes, would be an appropriate extension (see section 13.2.3).

Each of these relationships is represented as a graphical constraint so the object will maintain the relationship even if the other object is modified.

5.6. Linear Interpolation

One of the more interesting ways to edit an attribute of an object is to make it vary in a range depending on any numerical value. This is a very common operation in user interfaces. For example, the diamond indicator moves from one end to another in a graphical potentiometer or slider (Figure 5.3a), the height of a percent-done progress indicator [Myers 85] varies from 0 to the height of the indicator (Figure 5.3b), and the indicator in a scroll bar moves up and down inside its box (Figure 5.3c). Peridot allows these to be specified in a demonstrational, direct manipulation manner.

First, the designer draws the object so that it represents one graphical extreme. For example, with the scroll bar, this might be shown by having the indicator box at the bottom (Figure 5.4a). The designer selects the indicator and gives the ChangeByLinearInterp command which causes Peridot to save a copy of its attributes. Then the designer can perform as many editing steps on the objects as desired; as usual, Peridot infers from the *results* of the edits, rather than a *trace* of what edits were performed. In this example, the indicator box would be moved using the mouse to the top of the box (Figure 5.4b). When the designer gives the ChangeByLinearInterp command again, Peridot notices that it has already saved the previous state of the object, so it confirms that a linear interpolation operation is desired between the old and new states of the object. Then, Peridot asks, for each attribute that changes (in this

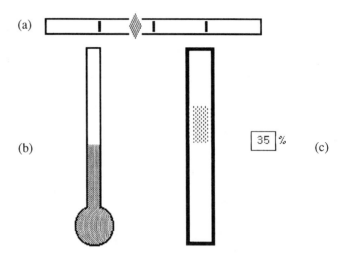

Figure 5.3.
Three interaction techniques created using linear interpolations. (a) Slider, (b) percent-done progress indicator [Myers 85], and (c) scroll bar.

case only the BOTTOM attribute changes), whether that attribute should be changed to be a linear interpolation.

Next, Peridot prompts the designer to select a parameter or active value that this should depend on, or to type a constant number for the current value for the interpolation (in Figure 5.4, the active value ScrollPercent is selected). The designer is then prompted to provide numerical values that correspond to the two graphical extremes. For Figure 5.4, this would be 0 for (b) and 100 for (a). The indicator then immediately jumps to the position that is the appropriate amount of the way between the two graphical extremes. In Figure 5.4c, ScrollPercent (the controlling value) is 20, so the indicator jumps to be 20% of the way from the top (20 in a range from 0 to 100). If the linear interpolation depends on an active value, as it does here, then Peridot sets up a data constraint so that when the active value changes, the indicator will move (see Chapters 8 and 9). When the active value changes, the linear interpolation will be updated immediately, as shown in Figure 5.4d.

It must be emphasized that the graphics used for the indicator is entirely arbitrary and can be any collection of objects. Peridot infers the relationship of the indicator objects to the static objects (in Figure 5.4, the relationship of the grey rectangle to the white rectangle) in each of the extreme graphical positions.

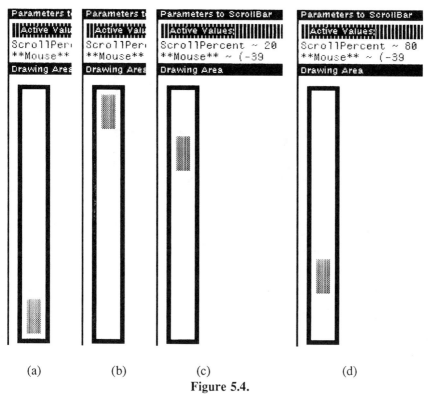

    (a)   (b)   (c)   (d)

Figure 5.4.

Snapshots during the demonstration of the graphical extremes for a linear interpolation (a-c). If the controlling value (ScrollPercent) changes, the indicator will change also (d).

The linear interpolation is calculated between these expressions, rather than the constants. In the example, the interpolation for the BOTTOM field of GreyRect0101 would be something like:

```
(LinearInterp ScrollPercent                    /* control value
             0                                   /* min of control
             100                                 /* max of control
             (White.TOP-GreyRect0101.HEIGHT-10) /* min of graphics
             (White.BOTTOM+10))                  /* max of graphics
```

Note that the graphical extremes are expressions instead of numbers. This means that the indicator will be shown properly no matter how the background graphics might change (Figure 5.5).

Figure 5.5.
When the graphics of Figure 5.4 are edited, the linear interpolation object changes automatically so it stays at the correct proportional position.

Different attributes of objects can be tied with linear interpolations to different parameters or active values, and they will operate independently. For example, the height of the scroll bar can be tied to a different active value to show the percent of the file that is being seen (Figure 5.6). Similarly, a two-dimensional scroll area can be made by attaching linear interpolations to the LEFT and BOTTOM positions of the indicator. This might be useful for a spreadsheet program, map, or picture (see Figure 5.7).

The important property of linear interpolations is that they allow application programs to deal in their own units (between the minimum and maximum values of the controlling parameter) and have the graphics updated appropriately. Therefore, the application is totally independent of the graphical representation of the value.

If an attribute depends on a linear interpolation, and the attribute is edited using the ChangePropBySpec command (section 5.5), then Peridot gives the designer the choice of providing a new value for the linear interpolation control, or removing the linear interpolation and using the new value directly. The former is useful for making tic marks as in Figure 5.3a, where the marks have values 25, 50 and 75 out of 100, and the linear interpolation is from one end of the white rectangle to the other.

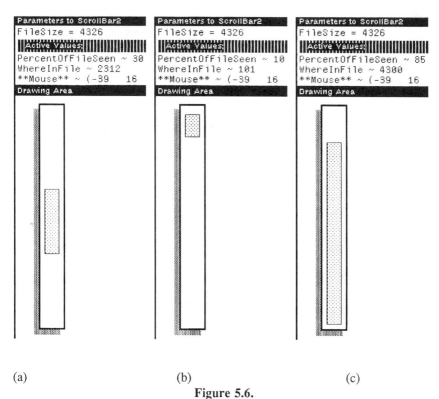

(a)   (b)   (c)

Figure 5.6.

Scroll bar in which the height is proportional to the percent of the file visible
(PercentOfFileSeen) and the position independently shows what part of the file is
visible (WhereInFile).

5.7. Functional Combination

Another way to edit an attribute of an object is to make it be the result of
having a function applied to two values for that attribute. This works similarly
to linear interpolation: the designer makes the attribute have one value and
gives the ChangePropByFunctionalCombination command, and then edits
the attribute to be the other value and gives this command again. Then the
designer chooses which function to apply to the old and new values of the attribute. The typical functions to use are MAX, MIN or PLUS. For example, in
Figure 5.8, the width of the white rectangle is first defined to be the width of
the widest string in the iteration using the object-object rules (as in the example
of Figure 3.15k), and this value for the width is saved using the

 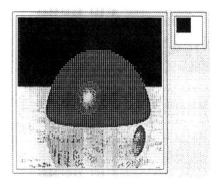

Figure 5.7.
Two views of a two-dimensional scroll area. The small black box in the upper right represents the part of the picture that can be seen in the large window. The user can point to this box with the mouse and move it in two dimensions. This is implemented as two independent linear interpolations.

ChangePropByFunctionalCombination command. Then the width of the white rectangle is modified to be the width of the title string, and the command is given again. The designer chooses MAX as the function, and then the width of the white string will as wide as the maximum of the widest string and the title line. Another example where this command was used is the object selection menu (Figure 3.11). Here, the size of the white rectangle was defined to be the sum (PLUS) of the width of the widest string and the width of the "S" icon used to mark the selection.

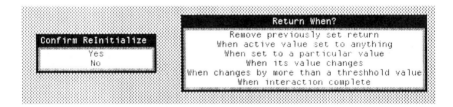

Figure 5.8.
Two menus displayed by the *same* menu procedure with different arguments for the strings to be displayed and the title. Using a functional combination, this menu is defined to have its width be the maximum of the width of the widest string in the menu and the width of the title.

5.8. Recalculating Relationships

Another way to edit an object is to request that its relationships to other objects be recalculated using the `ReCalcConstraint` command. This runs the rules that would have been run if the object had just been newly created. This command is useful for changing the parameter of the constraint that is currently in force. In addition, of course, an entirely different relationship might now apply due to objects that have been newly created or moved. An example of this is seen in Figure 4.3 where the grey rectangle was changed to depend on the strings inside of it, rather than on the black rectangle.

When the `ReCalcConstraint` command is given, the designer can select other objects to give Peridot a hint about with which objects the constraints should be. This is useful if there are a large number of objects in a small area and the designer wants to avoid answering "no" to a number of inappropriate constraints before the correct one is found.

5.9. After Editing

After an attribute is changed using the mouse, Peridot asks the designer if it should check for new relationships based on the attribute's new value. For example, after the grey rectangle in Figure 5.4a is moved with the mouse to the top of the white rectangle (Figure 5.4b), Peridot asks if it should check for new relationships. The designer says "yes," and Peridot infers that the gray rectangle's TOP now is offset by 10 from the top of the white rectangle. If the designer had answered "no," then the attribute would be simply set to the constant value returned from the mouse.

After any kind of edit, Peridot checks to see if there are previous relationships that need to be reversed (section 4.3). An important exception to this is when the new relationship is with the same object that the old relationship was with. In this case, the old relationship clearly cannot be reversed since this will cause a recursive dependency. Therefore, Peridot checks, and if the new dependency is to the same object as the old one, then it does not ask whether to reverse the constraints.

Of course, after any kind of edit, Peridot calculates and sets any back references that are needed, clears all old ones that have been removed, updates the code, and then redisplays the picture.

5.10. Extensions

The expressions supplied for ChangePropBySpec and ChangePropBy-
FunctionalCombination allow the designer a fair degree of flexibility in
defining constraints explicitly. There are still some relationships that are hard
to specify, however, and more general expressions might be helpful, as discussed in section 13.2.3.

A useful extension to ChangePropBySpec would be to allow the relationship with another graphic object to depend on an offset from the top or right of
the objects, rather than just the left and bottom. Regions in Interlisp and Peridot are defined by their left and bottom and width and height. Therefore it is
more difficult to refer to the top and right. Peridot should eliminate this asym-
metry and allow the explicit specification to be on either side. The designer
would have to be queried to disambiguate how the object should change to
enforce the constraint. For example, if the right side depends on an object and
that object moves in x, this constraint can be maintained either by changing the
width or the left of the object. Alternatively, Peridot could infer from the positions of the two objects what side is closest, and propose this to the designer.
Of course, confirmation would be required and the offset between the two
objects could be modified.

It might be nice to combine the ChangePropBySpec and ChangeProp-
ByMouse commands into some sort of property sheet style interface. For
example, a property sheet might pop up and the designer could select certain
fields and then type in new values, or use the mouse to modify those fields or
specify what they should depend on.

One important editing operation that is currently not supported is changing
the drawing order for objects. This is called "Top" and "Bottom" in window
managers. Section 13.2.4 discusses this extension.

All of the editing operations are easily reversible except for EraseSelection. It would be very useful to have some kind of "undo" so that objects
erased by accident could be retrieved. Of course, for convenience and consistency, the undo should work for the other operations also.

Currently, the implementation of the Copy command does not distinguish
how the original objects were created. If they came from an iteration or conditional, it will usually be better to copy the entire iteration or conditional, rather
than copying the individual elements. This is not yet supported, however.

After an edit, Peridot needs to redraw the picture. Currently, it simply
redraws all the objects. It would be better for Peridot to calculate which objects

need to be redrawn, but this is not an easy task. Since an object obscures the objects it covers, all objects that overlap the object's old or new place would need to be redisplayed (along with any objects that these overlap). In addition, any objects that have dependencies on the modified parts of the changing object should be redrawn, along with any objects they overlap. [Olsen 85b] discusses a similar algorithm to calculate the minimum set of objects that need to be redrawn. The complexity of this algorithm, coupled with the facts that often every object is affected anyway and redrawing is fairly quick, suggests that redrawing all objects is acceptable.

5.11. Chapter Summary

Since Peridot aims to make rapid prototyping of user interfaces extremely fast and easy, it is important to provide flexible editing of graphical objects. Therefore, graphical objects can be erased, or their attributes can be changed using the mouse or by typing in new values or pointing to parameters, active values or other objects to refer to. A group of objects can be copied, and Peridot will automatically fix any relationships so the copied objects refer to the correct objects in the copy rather than to the original. Peridot provides linear interpolations which are useful for implementing scroll bars, sliders, percent-done progress indicators, and any other quantities that vary within a range. The designer demonstrates the graphical extremes, and types the numerical value that each extreme corresponds to, and Peridot enforces the relationship so that the application program can deal in its own units independent of the graphical representation. Similarly, the functional combination command allows the attribute to be any function of the two graphical extremes. The designer can also explicitly specify that the constraints on an object should be recalculated. After an object is edited, Peridot updates its internal data structures and adjusts the code and picture display, so that the designer always sees the results of the editing immediately.

The many different ways to edit objects provide the designer with a great deal of flexibility. If the automatic object-object rules do not find the correct relationship, it is almost always possible to specify the constraint without programming, using the editing commands described in this chapter.

The same result can often be achieved in multiple ways. For example, to change the white circle in Figure 5.9 to be nested inside the grey circle with 5 pixels all around instead of 10, the designer could:

Figure 5.9.

The white circle can be edited in various ways to be nested inside the grey circle with 5 pixels all around instead of 10.

(1) edit the white circle with the mouse to make it bigger,

(2) specify the constraints explicitly using `ChangePropBySpec` to make the `DIAMETER`, `LEFT`, and `BOTTOM` be the appropriate offsets from the grey circle, or

(3) give the `ReCalcConstraint` command and use "Almost" to change the parameter of the rule from 10 to 5.

In any case, the picture and code will always be maintained correctly and the edited objects will have appropriate constraints with the other objects in the interface.

Chapter VI

Iterations

6.1. Introduction

A recognized problem with all Direct Manipulation systems is that repetitive actions are tedious. For example, if a procedure takes a list of strings to be displayed, the designer does not want to have to individually demonstrate where to display each one. Therefore, Peridot watches the designer's actions to try to infer when the previous objects might be part of a loop. If they appear to be, it queries the designer as to whether a loop is intended. If so, the statements are replaced with a loop statement, and the rest of the loop is executed. In addition, loops are important because they allow Peridot to support variable-length lists.

Research has shown that non-programmers have trouble with iterative constructs when presented in a conventional, programming-language way, but can handle them if they have a very simple structure [Musen 86]. Therefore, Peridot provides only two simple iterative constructs: loop for each element of a list, and loop for an integer number of times. This is sufficiently powerful to handle most interaction techniques, and the non-programmers who have used Peridot have found iterations easy to understand. In virtually all cases, Peridot automatically infers when an iteration is appropriate and asks the user if one should be used. If the designer says "yes," then the details of the control structure are handled automatically by the system. Editing of iterations is also supported in a straightforward manner.

Although the user interface to iterations is very simple, they present a fairly challenging implementation problem, because multiple items may participate in the iteration. In the menu of strings (Figure 6.1a), the loop simply draws one string from the list in each cycle. However, in Figure 6.1b, the iteration must repeat the rectangles as well as the string in each cycle. This chapter discusses the user interface for creating and editing iterations as well as how they are implemented.

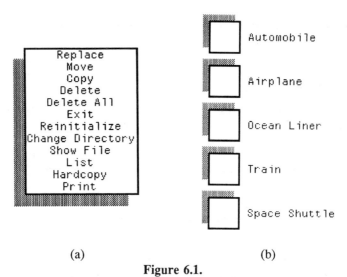

(a)   (b)

Figure 6.1.

Two interfaces that each use an iteration over a list of strings. (a) Menu of strings; each cycle of the iteration displays the single string object. (b) Property sheet; each cycle of the iteration displays three rectangles and a string.

6.2. User Interface for Iterations

Iterations in Peridot always require that the designer create the objects that will be displayed by the first two cycles of the iteration. As an example, in section 3.15, the designer placed the first two strings (Figures 3.15h and i). This allows Peridot to automatically calculate how the subsequent items of the iteration should change. Objects from the third cycle will be offset from the corresponding objects in the second cycle in the same way as the objects in the second cycle were offset from the objects in the first, and so on.

6.2.1. Loop Control

If the designer uses an element of a list in the first set of objects, and then uses an adjacent element of the same list in the second set of objects, Peridot will automatically infer that an iteration is possible. Currently, the list must be a parameter or active value of the interface. The list elements might be the names for strings (Figure 6.1a and b), the colors for rectangles (Figure 6.2), the height for rectangles (Figure 6.3), etc. In fact, any attribute of an object that can depend on a parameter can be the iteration control.

In addition, if the designer wants to iterate for an integer number of times (Figure 6.4), the explicit Iteration command can be used. The number can

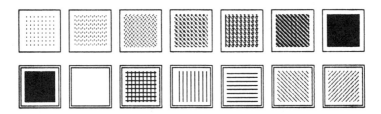

Figure 6.2.

Two different iterations over halftone shades for rectangles. The list contains the color values to be used for each interior rectangle.

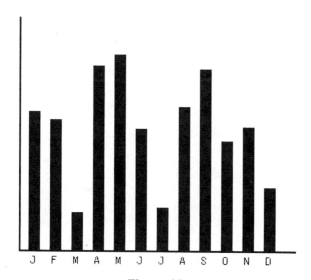

Figure 6.3.

Iteration over heights of rectangles, making a bar chart. The list contains the heights of each rectangle: (50 47 14 66 70 43 15 51 65 39 44 22).

Figure 6.4.

Iteration for an integer number of times.

either be a constant (e.g. 10) or it might depend on some parameter or active value (e.g. NumberOfBoxes).

Peridot allows the iteration to start at any element of the list and go in either direction (towards the front or back). However, more complex sequences clearly will not be supported (e.g., every other element of the list). These do not often occur in user interfaces, and if they are desired, the application program can simply pre-filter the items and provide a linear list. Extensions that would be useful, however, are nested and parallel iterations, as discussed in section 6.5.1.

6.2.2. Drawing Order

When multiple objects are displayed in each cycle of the loop, Peridot requires that the objects from the second cycle be drawn in the same order as the objects from the first cycle, and that all the objects be drawn consecutively. This makes it much easier to match the objects and determine what should change in each cycle. This restriction does not seem to be very severe, especially since the second group is usually created by using the copy command and then editing the parts that are different. Using the copy command insures that the objects in the second group are in the same order as those in the first group.

If the designer explicitly draws the objects in each group, however, care must be taken in the drawing order. For example, in Figure 6.5, the designer might draw BlackRect0001, WhiteRect0002, String0003 for the first cycle (where the string is the first element of a list), and then BlackRect0004, WhiteRect0005, String0006 for the second cycle (where this string is the second element of a list). If the designer had drawn the second group in a different order (e.g. BlackRect0004, String0006, WhiteRect0005), then Peridot would present a message that an iteration seems to be desired, but that the objects are not in the same order and so the iteration cannot be formed. Similarly, if some other, unrelated, object had been drawn between the two groups, Peridot would provide a similar message.

An interesting situation occurs if the object that is based on the list is not the last item drawn in the group. For example, in Figure 6.5, the drawing order for the first group might have been BlackRect0001, String0003, WhiteRect0002, which would result in the same picture. If the designer drew the second group from scratch (instead of using the copy command), then when the second string was drawn, the picture would be as in Figure 6.6. At this point, Peridot notices that an iteration might be desired, because the first two elements of a list have been used (BlackRect0001, String0003, WhiteRect0002, BlackRect0004, String0006), but the final object in the iteration

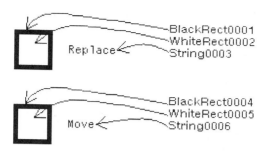

Figure 6.5.
Two groups of objects that will form the basis for an iteration.

(WhiteRect0005) has not yet been drawn. Peridot could wait to see if it is drawn next, but instead it simply presents a message telling the designer to use the explicit Iteration command when all of the objects have been drawn. The designer finishes the drawing, selects all six objects, and gives the Iteration command. This was simpler to implement, and is not a problem in practice since the copy command is usually used.

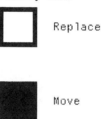

Figure 6.6.
The objects from Figure 6.5 drawn in a different order: the string is drawn after the black rectangle and before the white rectangle. This figure shows the picture after the second string is drawn.

6.2.3. Confirming Constants

Most of the attributes of objects in iterations are defined by relationships with other objects. For example, the position of the second string in the menu (Figure 6.1a) is centered below the first string, and the strings in Figure 6.1b are centered to the right of the rectangles. However, sometimes the position or size of an object is constant in the second group of objects. In this case, Peridot asks the designer to confirm the change in the constant number. For example, for Figure 6.7, Peridot might ask:

> For the LEFT property of the black rectangle [BlackRect0004]
> (marked with WRT), and the black rectangle [BlackRect0009]
> (marked with an N), the initial value is 10 and subsequent
> values will be offset by 3. Is this correct?
> (Yes, Almost (=Yes but change parameter), No):

The designer can confirm this (using y for "yes"), abort the iteration (n for "no") or type in new values for the parameters (a for "almost"). The most typical change is to make the offset be 0 so the objects will line up. Peridot might propose that the offset should be 0 if it is small, but there are a number of other ways to align objects, so if there is a non-zero offset, it is plausible that the designer did it on purpose.

Figure 6.7.

The two groups of objects with the second group at a constant position which is slightly offset from the first group.

6.3. Editing Iterations

When an iteration is created, the display is immediately updated with the rest of the objects. If the code window is visible, it is also updated, of course. If the designer does not like the way the iteration looks, it can be edited.

Another reason that an iteration might be edited is to specify an *exception* to the normal way that an iteration operates. For example, a special marker might be put in the list of strings for a menu that specifies that a line should be drawn, instead of providing a text string (Figure 6.8a), or an arrow might be used to signify when there is a sub-menu (Figure 6.8b).

Therefore, when the designer selects an object that is part of an iteration and gives an editing command, Peridot first asks if a modification to the iteration itself is desired, or whether there should be an exception. Exceptions are not yet implemented, but a preliminary design is discussed in section 6.5.2. Note that the designer does not have to be concerned about whether the objects to be edited are part of an iteration or not; any object can be selected directly and Peridot checks whether the object is part of an iteration before allowing the edit.

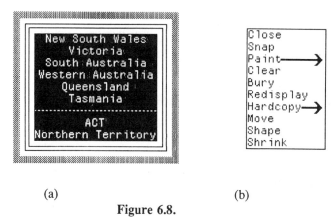

(a)   (b)

Figure 6.8.

Two types of exceptions in a menu. In (a), a dotted line is printed when a "_" appears in the list. In (b), an arrow appears for items that have submenus.

An important innovation in Peridot is the way that iterations themselves can be edited. If the editing operation is EraseSelection, then Peridot asks the designer if the entire iteration should be removed, or only the objects selected. If the entire iteration is chosen, then it is erased. However, if only the specific objects selected are desired, or if the editing operation is not erasure, then Peridot temporarily undoes the iteration and displays the original two groups of objects, which is called *suspending* the iteration. This is necessary for three reasons. First, it is much easier to insure that the designer's edits always make sense. If iterations were not suspended, and the designer changed the fourth item of the list, what would this mean? Second, the designer might make intermediate edits (such as deleting an object from one group) that would cause Peridot to be unable to show an iteration. Third, the value controlling the iteration might happen to have only 1 or 0 items in it when the designer decided to perform the edit, in which case there would not be two groups of objects to infer the loop relationships from. Returning to the original two groups of objects allows the designer to have full freedom to edit in any way desired, using all the conventional editing commands.

In fact, the exact original objects are not necessarily used. If, when asked about constants, the designer had specified that a different value should be used (Figure 6.7), then the original objects are modified to reflect those changes. This insures that the objects used for editing start off looking identical to the first two groups of objects in the iteration. As a convenience to the designer, constants in the second group of objects are modified to be offsets from the corresponding constants in the first group. For example, the size of the second black rectangle in Figure 6.7 will refer to the size of the first, so if the designer wants to change the size, only the first rectangle will need to be edited.

When the designer is finished editing, the iteration command is given, and Peridot will re-calculate the iteration from scratch. As a convenience, the designer does not have to select the objects that will be part of the iteration. Peridot automatically determines which objects to use based on information stored with the suspended iteration. The iteration is inferred just as if the objects were drawn the edited way originally. This gives the designer complete freedom in making edits.

6.4. Implementing Iterations

Iterations proved to be fairly complex to implement, primarily because multiple objects can participate in each cycle. The problems include: identifying which objects should participate in the iteration, matching up corresponding objects, calculating how they change, and then generating correct code. The code generation is complicated by the necessity to insure that the relationships between objects refer to the correct object.

6.4.1. Identifying and Matching Objects

When an iteration is inferred, Peridot counts the number of objects between the two objects that reference elements of a list.   For example, if the drawing order in Figure 6.5 was (BlackRect0001, WhiteRect0002, String0003, BlackRect0004, WhiteRect0005, String0006), and the objects whose values come from the list are String0003 and String0006, then there are 2 objects between them: BlackRect0004 and WhiteRect0005. Peridot looks for the same number of objects before the first one; here it finds the two objects BlackRect0001 and WhiteRect0002. These are the objects that will participate in the loop. If there are not enough objects before the first reference to the list then the user is notified that there seems to be an iteration, but the objects cannot be found. Next, the corresponding objects are checked to insure that they match, and if not, a similar message is displayed. In this example, the corresponding objects are:

```
BlackRect0001 <=> BlackRect0004
WhiteRect0002 <=> WhiteRect0005
String0003    <=> String0006
```

The matching checks the types (rectangle, string, circle, etc.) and the values (black, white, etc.).

When an iteration is explicitly specified using the Iteration command, the objects to iterate over have been selected (unless a suspended iteration is being re-instantiated). Here, the identifying step is obviously skipped, but the matching check is still performed. In addition, the objects are checked to see if they depend on any lists to determine if a numerical or list-dependent iteration is appropriate.

6.4.2. Calculating Changes

The next step is to check each attribute of the corresponding objects and see how they change[1]. If the attribute in both has the same value, then there is obviously no change. Otherwise, the value for the attribute in the first object is assumed to be the starting value, and the value in the second is assumed to be the offset for all subsequent cycles.

As an example, the first string of the menu in Figure 6.1a depends on the white rectangle for its position, and the second string depends on the position of the first string. In the iteration, therefore, all strings except the first will depend on the position of the string before it. Notice that this mechanism fits well with the inferencing rule ordering, where an object usually depends on the previously drawn object.

6.4.3. Generating Code

Once the expressions for the initial values and offsets for all attributes have been calculated, Peridot can generate the code for the loop. The primary problem here is insuring that the references refer to the correct object.

An object might refer to another object in its group, either forwards (e.g. BlackRect0001 referring to WhiteRect0002 in Figure 6.5) or backwards (e.g. WhiteRect0002 referring to BlackRect0001), or an object might refer to the corresponding object in the previous cycle of the iteration (e.g. BlackRect0004 referring to BlackRect0001). Clearly the constant names used for ordinary objects will not work, so a new scheme had to be invented to refer to objects.

Peridot therefore has the names for the objects in the iteration generated at run-time and uses these constructed names as the referents. Each object in the group is given a letter, and the name is generated by concatenating the name of the iteration (e.g. Iter0123), the letter for the object (e.g. C), and the count of the current cycle through the loop (which is in the variable I) using the

---

[1] Actually, the DRAWING FUNCTION and FONT attributes always use the value of the attribute from the object in the first group. If these attributes are different in the second group, then a warning message is printed.

function Name:

```
(Name `Iter0123 `C I)
```

Note that the I is not quoted; it will be evaluated each time to construct the name. In Figure 6.5, the object's names might be:

```
BlackRect0001 => Iter0123A1
WhiteRect0002 => Iter0123B1
String0003    => Iter0123C1

BlackRect0004 => Iter0123A2
WhiteRect0005 => Iter0123B2
String0006    => Iter0123C2
```

Therefore, every object receives a unique name at run time no matter how many times the loop iterates.

References to the objects are also changed to use the Name function with the appropriate arguments. For example, each white rectangle would use (Name `Iter0123 `A I) to refer to the black rectangle in the same group. In order to allow references to objects in the current as well the previous cycle, Peridot uses the following technique: for each attribute that changes in the loop, Peridot creates a temporary variable. This variable is initialized to the value for the attribute for the first object. The variable is set to the new value directly after the object is created.

For example if the drawing order for the objects in Figure 6.5 were (BlackRect0001, String0003, WhiteRect0002, BlackRect0004, String0006, WhiteRect0005), the code created for an iteration based on those objects might be something like:

```
(SETQ tmpY 456)
(FOR itervbl IN CommandStrings AS I FROM 1 DO
    (CreateRectangle
        (Name `Iter0123 `A I)    /* the name for this object
        -1                        /* the color (black)
        10                        /* LEFT
        tmpY                      /* BOTTOM
        20                        /* WIDTH
        20                        /* HEIGHT
        `(INPUT . REPLACE)        /* DRAWING FUNCTION
        (LIST itervbl I))         /* saved iteration values
    (SETQ tmpY `(PLUS -25 (Field ^(Name `Iter0123 `A I) BOTTOM)))

    (CreateString
        (Name `Iter0123 `B I)    /* name of object
        itervbl                   /* string value - from loop
        `(PLUS 24 (Field ^(Name `Iter0123 `C I) LEFT))    /* LEFT
        <centered with respect to ^(Name `Iter0123 `C I)> /* BOTTOM
        `(INPUT . REPLACE)        /* DRAWING FUNCTION
```

```
    (LIST itervbl I))          /* saved iteration values

(CreateRectangle
  (Name `Iter0123 `C I)       /* name of object
  0                           /* color (white)
  ´(PLUS 3 (Field ^(Name `Iter0123 `A I) LEFT))      /* LEFT
  ´(PLUS 3 (Field ^(Name `Iter0123 `A I) BOTTOM))    /* BOTTOM
  ´(PLUS -6 (Field ^(Name `Iter0123 `A I) WIDTH))    /* WIDTH
  ´(PLUS -6 (Field ^(Name `Iter0123 `A I) HEIGHT))   /* HEIGHT
  `(INPUT . REPLACE)          /* DRAWING FUNCTION
  (LIST itervbl I))           /* saved iteration values
```

A special form of quote is used (´) which evaluates only the arguments directly preceded by up-arrow (^) and puts a normal quote (`) before the expression[2]. Therefore, the value of tmpY after the first cycle (I = 1) will be:

```
` (PLUS -25 (Field Iter0123A1 BOTTOM))
```

This will be the value used for the BOTTOM of the black rectangle created in the second cycle. Therefore, the black rectangle from the second cycle will correctly refer to the black rectangle from the first cycle. The white rectangle refers backwards to the black rectangle in the same cycle, and the string refers forward to the white rectangle in the same cycle, all of which works correctly. The expressions are put into the attribute fields of the objects, and as discussed in Chapter 11, all the objects are created before any of the attributes are evaluated to get their numeric values, so the forward and backward references will work correctly.

As shown in the code, each object that is created in an iteration has associated with it the value of the two iteration variables: the name of the item from the list (itervbl) and the loop count (I). These are used by the mouse handler to return the iteration item that the mouse is over (section 9.9).

6.4.4. Saving the Objects

As mentioned in section 3.2.3, Peridot keeps a list of all the objects so that they can be redrawn in the correct order. Objects drawn in iterations are no exception to this; they can obscure objects drawn before the iteration and be obscured by objects drawn afterwards. Therefore, it is important to save the position in the overall drawing order list for the iteration objects. One consideration, however, is that the iteration may have no items displayed, but the position in the drawing order list must still be preserved in case it is redrawn later with more items. Therefore, each iteration inserts a dummy object into the

---

[2] This and other quoting problems have been a major source of difficulty in implementing Peridot.

drawing order list and the objects created during the iteration are stored as sub-objects of the iteration object. This makes the drawing order list hierarchical with two levels. This hierarchy is invisible to the designer. For example, the selection operation works the same for individual objects drawn by iterations as for other objects. It is not possible, therefore, to select the iteration object itself using the mouse, but this is never necessary.

6.5. Extensions

Iterations work very well and cover a large number of the repetitive tasks used in graphical interaction techniques. In addition to the extensions discussed above (providing constant lists to iterate over that are not parameters or active values, and making it easier to avoid dependencies that cause the iteration not to work correctly), this section discusses some others that would make iterations even more useful.

6.5.1. Other Forms of Iteration

Currently, iterations are only useful for things which are in a single line. It is often useful, however, to have multiple lines (Figure 6.9a) or even a rectangle of items (Figure 6.9b). While this can be simulated by having multiple one-dimensional iterations, as was done for Figure 6.9, it would be better for Peridot to support multi-dimensional iterations directly. This would probably require the designer to specify how to distinguish the dimensions. If the data was presented as a single list, the exception mechanism (next section) might be used to allow the designer to demonstrate where the break should be and where the next column or row should start. Otherwise, a list of lists might be used, where each sub-list would be a single row or column.

It is also sometimes useful to have a single iteration go through two or more different lists in parallel. For example, the height of bars in a bar chart (Figure 6.10) might depend on one list and the color of the bars on another list. To allow this would only require a small implementation extension to Peridot; the interface to the designer would not have to change.

6.5.2. Exceptions

Many graphical interaction techniques provide special markers or actions when the parameters have certain values. For example, a special marker might be put in the list of strings for a menu that specifies that a line should be drawn, instead of providing a text string (Figure 6.8a). This effect can be achieved in Peridot using Conditionals (Chapter 7), but then an extra parameter is required to determine when the graphic should appear. However, it would be

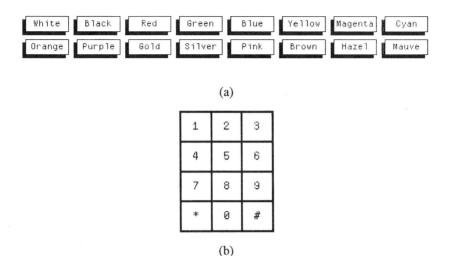

(a)

(b)

Figure 6.9.
Two useful extensions for iterations: (a) multiple lines and (b) two-dimensional.

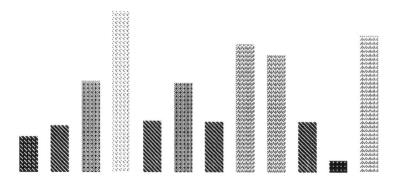

Figure 6.10.
Extending iterations to go through two lists in parallel: the height of the rectangles might depend on one parameter and the color on another parameter.

more convenient if Peridot supported exceptions for iterations that would be triggered by certain values of the list itself. For example, if a menu item has a sub-menu (Figure 6.8b), this might be signified by having that item be a list containing the sub-items, rather than a single atom. For Figure 6.8b the list might be:

```
(Close
 Snap
 (Paint (SetBrush SetSize SetColor))
 Clear
 Bury
 Redisplay
 (Hardcopy (ToAFile ToAPrinter))
 Move
 Shape
 Shrink)
```

Examples of the differences that might be detected are:

- the value is a particular constant which the designer would specify, e.g. NIL, "" (null string), or "_" (underline),

- the value is a different type (e.g. a list instead of an atom), or

- numerical properties such as equal to, greater than, or less than zero.

The designer would select the item that should be the exception and Peridot would automatically infer in what way it was different.

The graphics that result when the exception is noticed would be defined in the normal manner and could therefore be any combination of objects with dependencies to any other objects. This would make it easy to insure, for example, that the line in Figure 6.8a was the same width as the menu but a fixed height.

Exceptions might also be used to determine when an attribute in the iteration should have an abrupt change of value to provide multiple lines or two-dimensional displays. This might depend on a particular "break" value in the list, a fixed constant number of times through the loop, or a particular size being reached (e.g. the edge of the window).

6.5.3. Not Suspending the Iteration

Although suspending the iteration makes it much easier to implement editing, it is somewhat less convenient for the designer. Typically, an iteration is edited to adjust the spacing between elements so that the entire iteration will fit nicely with some other objects in the scene, so it would be useful if the entire iteration was visible during the edits. It might be possible to show the entire iteration during the edits, but still only allow the first two groups to be selected and edited. The other groups might be shown in grey to emphasize that they are "inactive." Of course, if some of them were already grey, it might be difficult to graphically depict that they are inactive.

Even more useful would be the ability to edit any of the groups and have the others adjust accordingly. For example, the designer might select the last group and move it, and the rest would adjust their spacing to insure that the last group ended up in the specified place.

6.5.4. More Clever Matching and Offset Calculations

Peridot could be more clever about finding objects that should participate in the iteration. This might alleviate the requirement that the objects be created consecutively and in the same order. This requirement is in contradiction with the principle of Peridot that inferencing only depends on the results of actions and not the trace (or order) that the actions were taken, so it would be appropriate to eliminate it. On the other hand, the restriction has not even been noticed by the designers who have used Peridot.

Another problem is that when the objects in the second group have attributes that are not constant, Peridot assumes that the third and subsequent groups should use the same value for the attribute as the second group. This works correctly when the attribute in the second group refers to attributes in the first group, which is usually the case. For example, in the menu, the second string is centered below the first, so each subsequent string is centered below the previous string. On the other hand, sometimes the second group has dependencies to objects that are outside of the iteration. In this case, all subsequent groups will have the same value for that attribute. This may cause all of the groups to appear in the identical place (directly on top of each other), which is usually an error. Peridot should try to detect this situation and propose an appropriate offset for the subsequent groups.

6.6. Chapter Summary

Iterations are very important because they save the designer tedious work and support variable length lists. Peridot provides iterations in a demonstrational manner that allows the designer to use them without programming. The designer draws two groups of objects, and Peridot automatically infers the need for an iteration if an object in each group has an attribute that depends on adjacent elements of a list. In other cases, such as when an integer number of cycles is desired, the designer can simply select the desired objects and give the iteration command. Peridot supports multiple objects in each cycle of the iteration and automatically calculates how the objects change from one cycle to the next. Currently, the objects must have been created consecutively and in the same order, but Peridot could be extended to relax this restriction. If the objects have numeric attributes that change, the designer is asked to confirm the numbers.

Iterations can be edited easily using any of the standard editing commands because Peridot returns the iteration to its original two groups of objects. This is called "suspending" the iteration. No previous system has allowed control structures to be edited in this manner.

The implementation of iterations is fairly complex due to the matching of the objects and the need to insure that name references among objects work correctly.

Iterations might be extended to support multi-dimensional and parallel loops, exceptions, editing without suspension, and more clever matching.

Chapter VII

Conditionals

7.1. Introduction

Many user interfaces involve choosing one or more from a set of objects. For example, the menu of Figure 7.1 allows the user to select a single item, and the property sheet of Figure 7.2 allows the user to select multiple items. It is also common for a marker of some sort to go on and off based on some criterion. Peridot uses a mechanism called *Conditionals* to handle these operations. These "Conditionals" are different from IF statements in conventional programming languages since they do not affect flow of control; they simply support choice items and blinking. They are called "Conditionals" because they are implemented using an IF statement in the generated code.

Figure 7.1.
The black rectangle is conditional.

Conditionals are a very important part of Peridot. They are used in all menus, property sheets, light buttons, etc. to show the current items, and to control any display that may optionally be displayed or invisible. They can also be used to display special marks on certain items (e.g. the illegal items in the example of Figure 3.15m). As shown in section 9.3.8.2, the value of a conditional is often set by the mouse, for example to change the selection in menus and property sheets.

As with iterations, Peridot uses a very simple form for conditionals so they will be understandable and easy to use for the designers. Conditionals are always controlled by the value of a parameter or an active value. The designers using Peridot have found this mechanism very intuitive. Conditionals can be specified by the designer, or they may be inferred automatically when some objects are declared to be dependent on the mouse. Conditionals are implemented using the same code as iterations, so the extra effort to implement them was minimal.

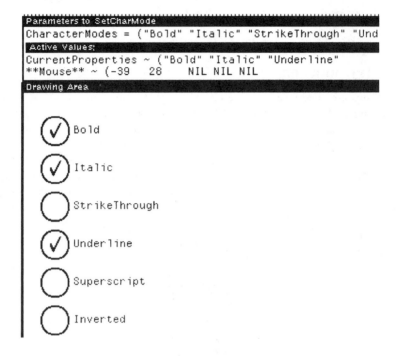

Figure 7.2.
The check marks are conditional on CurrentProperties.

7.2. User Interface for Conditionals

Conditionals are created in a postfix style. This means that the designer first draws the graphic objects that show when the conditional is true and then specifies what these objects should depend on. This allows the designer to use the standard drawing and editing commands to create the graphic objects. As with iterations, the objects that will be conditional must be created consecutively, just to make the implementation simpler. The conditional object in Figure 7.1 is the reverse video rectangle, in Figure 7.2, the conditional objects are the check marks, and in Figure 7.3, they are the four arrow icons. After creating the graphic objects that should be conditional, the designer can select them and explicitly give the Conditional command. Alternatively, as described in section 9.3.2 and shown in Figure 3.15o, the "simulated mouse" can be put on top of the object and the MOUSEDependent command given. In this case, Peridot will automatically infer when a conditional is desired.

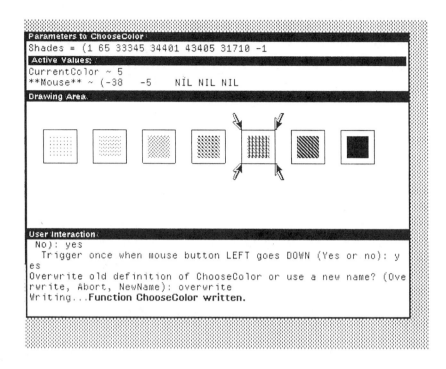

Figure 7.3.
The arrows are conditional on `CurrentColor`.

After a conditional has been specified or inferred, Peridot checks to see if the conditional objects have a relationship to any parts of an iteration. For example, when the black rectangle in Figure 7.1 was created, Peridot inferred that it was the same size and position as the string `Underline`, which was created as part of the iteration over `FontProperties`. If the objects selected to be conditional depend on different iterations, then Peridot issues an error message to the designer (this message has never been necessary in actual use of Peridot). When the objects depend on an iteration, Peridot guesses that the objects will be used to choose one or more items of the iteration. When the objects do *not* depend on an iteration, then the only option is for them to blink on and off.

Peridot then prompts the designer to select a parameter or active value that the conditional should depend on. For example, in Figure 7.2, the active value `CurrentProperties` determines which objects are marked, and in Figure

3.15m, the parameter IllegalValues determines which strings are shown in grey. As a convenience, if there is a single active value (not counting the input devices), then Peridot proposes that this be used.

The parameter or active value can control the conditional in various ways. Peridot automatically infers how it controls the conditional based on the type of its example value. The possible values types are:

(1) T or NIL

(2) the numerical index of element, e.g. 4 in Figure 7.1 and 5 in Figure 7.3,

(3) the name of an element, e.g. "Underline" in Figure 7.1,

(4) a list of T's and NIL's, where there is a T or NIL for each item of the iteration, e.g. (T T NIL T NIL NIL) for Figure 7.2,

(5) a list of indices, e.g. (1 2 4) for Figure 7.2, or

(6) a list of names, e.g. ("Bold" "Italic" "Underline") for Figure 7.2.

Option (1) allows for objects to go on and off, options (2) and (3) allows a choice of one element from an iteration, and options (4), (5) and (6) allow for multiple choices from an iteration.

The designer must confirm the guess of the control type, of course. This is because, as with other inferences, the particular example value for an active value or parameter might be ambiguous. For example, the "name" of elements for a list of colors is the integer representation of the color, so, in Figure 7.3, Peridot cannot tell whether the value for CurrentColor is the name of the element (option (3)) or its index (option (2)). Therefore Peridot always asks whether its inference is correct[1].

After the control is confirmed by the designer, Peridot immediately displays the conditional in all appropriate places. This may cause the conditional objects to disappear if the controlling value is NIL, or may cause the objects to appear in multiple places if allowed by the controlling value (e.g. Figure 7.2 and 3.15m).

---

[1] Currently, Peridot justs looks at the type of the value (e.g. integer). It could be slightly more intelligent and check whether the value is a legal example of the current iteration names. However, this would not eliminate all ambiguity. For example, in Figure 7.3, 1 is both a legal index and a legal name.

7.3. Editing Conditionals

When an edit command is given for an object that is part of a conditional, Peridot asks if the conditional itself should be modified (unlike iterations, there are no exceptions to conditionals). As with iterations, if the edit operation is erasure, the entire conditional can be removed, or only the selected objects. If the designer specifies that the conditional itself should be modified, Peridot suspends the conditional and displays only the original objects. These can then be edited normally. For the same reasons as for iterations, it is important to suspend the conditional during editing so that there will not be any ambiguity about the meaning of the edits. The conditional might be false, in which case the graphics would not be visible, or it might be displayed in multiple places, and the user might edit the different places differently, which would make it impossible for Peridot to calculate what to do. The designer gives the Conditional command when the editing is finished, and the conditional will be re-established.

7.4. Implementing Conditionals

Conditionals are implemented similarly to iterations. In fact, they share a great deal of the same code. The two steps for creating a conditional are to calculate the test (the "IF" part), and then to generate the code to perform the conditional. Since the designer is required to explicitly select all the objects that make up the conditional, the identifying and matching steps of iterations are not necessary.

7.4.1. Generating the Test

In order to determine how the active value or parameter controls the conditional, Peridot uses a very simple rule-based test. There are six rules, one for each possibility (section 7.2). The test part of the rule checks to see if the type of the parameter or active value is appropriate for this type of control:

(1) T or NIL

(2) number

(3) any non-list

(4) a list of T's and NIL's

(5) a list of numbers

(6) a list of anything

The rules are checked in that order, and, since more than one rule can pass, the designer is always asked for confirmation, using a message associated with the rule. If the designer answers yes, then the action part of the rule returns code to use at run-time to test the value to see if the conditional should be on. If the designer answers no, then the system continues though the rules. If none are confirmed, then the conditional is aborted.

7.4.2. Code Generation

The most common case is for conditionals to be displayed over one or more items from an iteration, as shown in Figures 7.1, 7.2 and 7.3. In order to implement this case in a simple way, Peridot copies the loop control from the associated iteration, inserts the generated test, and wraps these around the creation routines for the objects that will be part of the conditional. Of course, the objects must be modified to use the (Name `CondVbl0143 `A I) form discussed in section 6.4.3 to refer to other objects that are part of the conditional. In addition, references to objects that are part of the iteration must also be modified to use that form so that the conditional will appear with the appropriate iteration item (rather than the particular example object that was demonstrated).

For conditionals that are not part of an iteration (choice (1)), Peridot creates a dummy iteration to maintain consistency:

        (FOR I FROM 1 TO 1 AS itervbl DO ....)
In order to use a single procedure to handle both iterations and conditionals at run time, the only other change is to make normal iterations use T for the "IF" test. Then all iterations and conditionals have the same structure and can be executed identically.

7.5. Extensions

Conditionals work very well and provide the needed functionality. The main extensions that seem appropriate would be to allow the conditional objects to be displayed when the active value or parameter is NOT true, and to have Peridot automatically identify which objects should be put into the conditional. This latter extension would make conditionals more like iterations, since with iterations Peridot infers which objects should be included in the loop. Since there is only a single set of objects for a conditional, however, it is harder to identify the related objects, but the object-object relationships will almost always suffice to identify which objects should be included.

An interesting idea is to try to extend conditionals to handle many other kinds of optional or changing behavior. For example, conditionals might support parameters that control the way that the interface works and looks. A parameter might determine whether the items in a menu are left-justified or centered, and another parameter might determine whether the left or middle mouse button is used in the interaction. In these cases, both possibilities would be demonstrated and Peridot would prompt for the parameter or active value that would determine which one to use. The Tinker system [Lieberman 82] has a similar facility, although the code for each branch of the conditional must by entered textually rather than demonstrated.

Other extensions would be to use conditionals to handle iteration exceptions, discussed in section 6.5.2, and mouse exceptions, discussed in section 9.10.3.

7.6. Chapter Summary

Conditionals provide the mechanism to handle objects that appear and disappear, and the choice of one or more items from an iteration. By combining all these behaviors into one simple mechanism, the user interface for Peridot is greatly simplified. All conditionals depend on a parameter or active value which controls where the conditional objects will be displayed. The designer creates one or more graphical objects that will depend on the parameter or active value, and then selects them and gives the `Conditional` command. Alternatively, a conditional will be automatically inferred when the objects are specified to depend on the mouse, as explained in section 9.3.2. The controlling parameter or active value can be `T` or `NIL` if the objects will go on and off, and can control the choice in one of five ways if the conditional chooses one or more items from an iteration. Of course, as soon as the conditional is confirmed by the designer, Peridot immediately updates the display to show the conditional in the appropriate places based on the current value of the controlling parameter or active value.

As with iterations, conditionals must be suspended to be edited. This insures that the designer can use any of the normal editing features and Peridot will not get confused about what the edits mean.

The implementation of conditionals is very much like that of iterations. In fact, iterations are modified to have a test that is always true, and all conditionals are forced to have a loop, so that the same code can be used to execute conditionals and iterations.

Chapter VIII

Active Values

8.1. Introduction

The key to providing an easy-to-use mechanism for handling pictures that can change at run-time is to have a simple technique for controlling the dynamic state. Peridot uses *active values* for this control, and they have proven to be powerful, efficient to implement, and easy for the designer to use. As described in section 1.1, active values are like parameters to the procedure except that they can change at run time. When a graphical object depends on an active value, a *data constraint* is automatically created, so the object will change immediately when the value is updated. The designer can create references to active values in the same way as references to parameters to the procedure, so creating these data constraints requires no extra knowledge for the designer.

The only previous UIMS that uses active values is GRINS [Olsen 85a] although similar ideas have been used in many process monitoring and control systems (see section 2.4.2).

Active values can control objects in many ways. The value can be a number that varies in a range and controls a linear interpolation (such as the scroll bars of Figures 5.4 and 5.6), it can contain the control value for a conditional and determine where the conditional is true, as in Figure 7.2, or it can contain the position of an object being dragged with the mouse. In fact, anywhere a reference to a parameter is allowed, Peridot will support a reference to an active value instead to allow for run-time updates. This includes any combination of the position, size, and value (color, string, or bitmap picture) attributes of an object.

Active values can be set by the application program at any time to update the graphics. In addition, application routines can be attached to active values and these will be called when the active value changes, and thus are used to pass information back to the application programs. This provides an appropriately abstract interface to the applications. The implementation of the connection between the active values and the graphics is hidden from both application programs and the designer (it might use message passing, procedure calls, etc.). In addition, the application can deal in its own abstract units (e.g. 0 to 100 for the progress indicator in Figure 5.3b, and the string names of the font properties in Figure 7.2), and be totally independent of how these values are represented graphically or set by input devices. Therefore, the graphics can be changed arbitrarily and the application code is not affected.

When deciding which values should be active values and which should be parameters, the designer needs to determine whether the value needs to change while the procedure is running. For example, for a pop-up menu, the names of the choice items probably will not change while the menu is displayed, but for a fixed menu that is displayed continuously on the screen, the items in the menu might need to change based on context. Alternatively, all of the possible choices might appear all of the time, so they would be passed as a parameter, but some items might be marked as illegal. These would not be selectable using the mouse, as shown in the example of section 3.4 and discussed in section 9.5. In this case, an active value might be used to communicate which values are illegal so they could change.

Active values are also used to handle input devices, as described in Chapters 9 and 10. There is a special active value for each input device (e.g. **Mouse** for the mouse), and interactions are attached to these active values. These interactions generally change the values of other active values to modify the picture at run-time. For the mouse, the interactions are generated automatically, as described in Chapter 9.

Application-supplied procedures can be attached to active values and will be called when the active value is set, when it changes value, or when it changes by more than a specified threshold. If a procedure is attached to the active values for input devices, *semantic feedback* (defined in section 1.1) can be easily provided. A special mechanism attached to active values also allows the Peridot-created procedure to exit and return a value to the program that calls it.

The active values are displayed on the screen in the top Peridot window (Figure 8.1) and the displayed value is updated when the value changes. This makes the system more understandable since the state of the system is always visible; the designer does not have to try to remember the values of the variables. Another factor which makes them easy to use is that after objects have been made to depend on active values, the value of the active value can be easily changed by the designer to view the effects on the objects and verify the behavior.

8.2. Examples of Using Active Values

The example of Figure 3.15 used an active value to control which menu item the black rectangle was displayed over. In Figure 3.15o, the rectangle is defined to depend on the active value ReturnValue which contains the name of the item to use and is set by a mouse interaction. A conditional is created automatically which uses ReturnValue as the control, and this conditional is reevaluated whenever the active value changes.

Similarly, in Figures 5.4, 5.6 and 5.7, linear interpolations use active values as the control values. The position of the indicators will therefore be updated whenever the active value changes.

Figure 8.1 shows a more complex interface created using Peridot. This interface is controlled by 7 different active values. One contains the position of the entire window, and this is updated by the mouse as the window is dragged around, which is triggered by pressing in the icon in the lower right corner. Another contains the size of the window, and this is updated by the mouse as the window changes size after pressing in the icon at the upper right. Controlling the view of the picture inside the window are two pairs of active values: one pair for x and one for y. For each, there is one active value for the position of the origin of the picture and one for the percent of the picture visible. The position active values are updated by the mouse when the user manipulates the scroll bars or presses over the arrows, and an application procedure updates the percent-visible active values whenever the size of the window changes. Finally, an active value controls when the procedure should exit, and is set when the user presses the mouse over the STOP icon.

8.3. Creating Active Values

When the designer starts to create an interface using Peridot, the names of the parameters and active values must be typed, along with an example value for each. As described in section 3.2.5, the example values allow the system to show how the interface will look to the end user, and they are also used to infer how the active value should control conditionals and mouse dependencies.

The user interface designer can create as many active values as needed and give them arbitrary names. There will typically be one active value for each part of the interface that can change at run-time, as shown above.

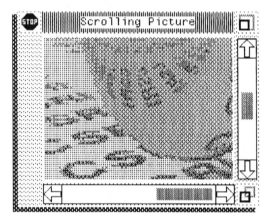

Figure 8.1.

A complex interface created entirely by Peridot. The window can be moved or changed size, and the picture can be scrolled in either x or y. This is controlled by 7 active values. An application procedure is called to display the picture and calculate what percent of it is displayed in the window, but all other manipulations are handled by Peridot.

8.4. Setting Active Values

In Lisp, all variable assignment is performed using functions (such as SETQ). Similarly, to set an active value, an application program simply calls the Peridot function SETActive. In its simplest form, it is like the Lisp function SET, and a typical call might be:

        (SETActive `ScrollPercent 64)

which will set the value of the active value ScrollPercent to 64 and cause any graphics that depend on it to be updated.

In addition, SETActive has a number of special forms that have proven useful for various Peridot actions. These are primarily used internally by Peridot, but they are also available for use by applications, if desired. The general definition of SETActive is[1]:

  (SETActive <name> <new value> <index> <how change>)

The <new value> can just be a new value for the object, but it can also be one of three special forms. These are for incrementing numbers, toggling booleans, and a special value to signal that interactions are complete. To increment or decrement an active value, the form can be (+ <inc>), as in:

  (SETActive `ScrollPercent `(+ 3))

which will increment the value of ScrollPercent by 3. The amount to increment by can be a positive or negative integer or any floating point number. If the active value does not contain a numeric quantity, an error is raised. Similarly, the special form TOGGLE can be used to toggle an active value which acts as a flag:

  (SETActive `BlinkControl `TOGGLE)

If the old value for the active value was T, it is changed to NIL, if NIL, it is changed to T, and otherwise an error is raised. A final special form is only used when SETActive is called by the mouse device handler. Here, the value is **DONE** which does not change the value at all, but simply causes any application procedures that have interaction-complete notification to be called (see section 8.5). If the actual strings (+ <inc>), TOGGLE, or **DONE** are desired as the value, the caller can always make them into Interlisp strings (e.g. "(+ 4)"), since Peridot displays strings and non-strings the same way.

The <index if list> parameter to SETActive can be used to set a particular value in a list. If the active value is a list, and <index if list> is an integer, then the element of the list with that index is set and the rest of the list is unchanged. For example:

  (SETActive `CurrentStates T 4)

will turn the fourth element of CurrentStates on and leave the other elements unchanged.

---

[1] Remember that functions in Interlisp-D can be called with fewer than the defined number of arguments, and the arguments that are not provided use NIL.

Finally, the `<how change>` parameter allows a number of special operations to be performed on the value. `<how change>` can be:

- `NIL`: set the value normally,

- `APPEND`: assuming the active value is a list, add the `<new value>` to the end (if not a list, then raise an error),

- `SETAPPEND`: similar to `APPEND`, but only adds `<new value>` if the item is not in the list already,

- `REMOVE`: assuming the active value is a list, removes the `<new value>` from the list if it is there (no action if not there),

- `SETREMOVE`: identical to `REMOVE`, or

- `SETTOGGLE`: assuming the active value is a list, if `<new value>` is a member of that list, then remove it, otherwise append it.

Although the application program is free to use these forms when setting active values, they are typically used when the mouse handler wants to set a conditional (section 9.9) in which case the `SETActive` call is generated automatically by Peridot. The `<how change>` options make supporting the various ways an active value can control a conditional much simpler.

In addition to being set by applications programs using the `SETActive` procedure, Peridot also allows active values to be set by the designer. This allows the designer to test out how the graphics will change as the active value changes and therefore to check the current interface. The designer simply selects the active value, gives the `SetActiveValue` command (which is in the submenu of `FixActive`), and types in a new value[2].

8.5. Out of Range Handling

An important consideration is what to do when an active value is set outside of its expected limits. This is obviously most important when the active value is set by an input device, but it can also be useful for preventing application programs from setting values incorrectly. An application-defined procedure can be supplied which takes the proposed value as a parameter and returns the value to use. Alternatively, one of Peridot's built-in range checking routines can be used if the value is numeric. The built-in routines take a minimum and

---

[2] Peridot might be extended to allow the designer to test the interface by setting the active value to be different values using a slider, as is done in PVS [Foley 86]. Of course, the slider would be created using Peridot.

maximum value and an action to perform when the value is out of range. The actions supported by Peridot are:

(1) raising an error exception,

(2) pegging the value to the nearest legal value (MIN or MAX),

(3) wrapping the value around to the other extreme (MOD), and

(4) allowing the value to go outside the range. This choice is obviously the same as having no range checking at all.

Normally, the designer explicitly selects which option is desired from a menu, and then types in the minimum and maximum values for the range or the name of the application procedure to be called. In one case, however, Peridot automatically sets up an out-of-range check, which the designer can override if necessary. This happens when the designer specifies that a linear-interpolation (section 5.6), such as a scroll bar, depends on an active value. Here, Peridot asserts a clipping operation (option (2)) to keep the active value from going outside the range allowed for the interpolation. This will therefore keep the associated graphics from going out of bounds.

The option to use an application-supplied procedure is very useful for providing semantic feedback. The procedure is invoked whenever SETActive is called to set the associated active value. This procedure is called with two parameters: the proposed new value for the active value, and an extra parameter which the designer specifies. The active value is set with the value that the routine returns. For example, to enforce simple gridding, where a value is only set with multiples of GridAmt, the following simple application-supplied procedure could be attached to the active value:

```
(DEFUN SimpleGridding (proposedVal GridAmt)
    ((INTEGER_DIVIDE proposedVal GridAmt) * GridAmt))
```

GridAmt is the extra parameter used for this procedure. Much more complicated procedures can be used to filter the data, of course. This can be used to provide non-linear gridding, gravity (where the value jumps to some semantically meaningful value when it is within some threshold), and other data manipulation that require application-specific knowledge.

8.6. Application Notification

In order to provide semantic feedback, it must be possible for application procedures to also be called when "interesting events" occur. Peridot therefore provides a second way for application procedures to be attached to active values, and the designer can control how often these are called. As an example,

Figure 8.2 shows a graphical potentiometer for setting grey shades (the end user can move the diamond with the mouse). The position of the diamond and the number in the left box are directly tied to the active value SliderValue using linear interpolation, but the halftone representation of the corresponding grey shade is calculated using an application-provided procedure and set into the active value CorrespondingColor. The rectangle on the right uses the value of CorrespondingColor as its color. The conversion function is called whenever the SliderValue value changes, which causes the value in CorrespondingColor to change, which causes the color in the box on the right to change, so the picture will always be correct.

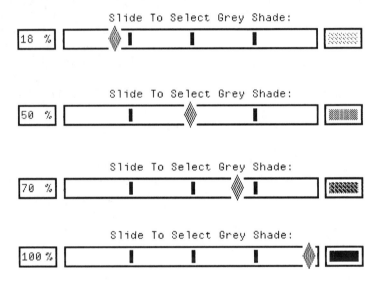

Figure 8.2.
Multiple views of a graphical slider. The diamond and the numerical percent (on the left) depend directly on the active value SliderValue and show its current value. An application procedure called CalculateHalftone is attached to the active value. The designer specifies that CalculateHalftone should be invoked whenever the value in SliderValue changes. The output of CalculateHalftone is set into a different active value, which controls the color of the rectangle on the right.

It is important to emphasize that this allows the application program to have *fine-grain control* over the interface. Most other UIMSs only provide coarse-grain control so they cannot handle this kind of semantic feedback. The application can control feedback, default values, and error detection and recovery at a low level and this operates fast enough to be in the inner loops of mouse tracking and other input device handling.

The application procedure is called with the value of the active value as a parameter. As with application-supplied range checking, the procedure might also take another parameter, and the designer can type a value to be used. If the procedure returns a value, the designer can select a different active value to be set with the return value[3]. This was used in Figure 8.2 to set `Correspondingcolor`.

The designer can choose from a menu how often the application program is called. The choices are:

(1) whenever the active value is set (including when it is set to the same value that it already is)—this is useful as a trigger,

(2) whenever the value changes,

(3) whenever the value changes by more than some threshold,

(4) when an interaction is complete (e.g. when the mouse button is released after moving the diamond in Figure 8.2), and

(5) never.

In the example above, the application procedure (`CalculateHalftone`) is called whenever the value changes (option (2)), and this is the most common choice. Sometimes the others are useful, however. The one-dimensional slider I/O device (section 10.2) sets its active value to UP each time the slider is moved one increment up, and DOWN for each increment down. The first choice (whenever the value is set) should be used here since the active value will be set to UP repeatedly while the user is moving the device up in a continuous fashion.

The threshold choice (number (3)) is useful for increasing efficiency (so the application is not notified too often), and it is also useful for controlling animations. A special system-provided active value is the clock (section 10.3), and animations (e.g. blinking or moving at a specific speed) can be tied to the clock using the threshold notification.

---

[3] If the application procedure wants to set the *same* active value that it is attached to, the out-of-range application calling mechanism should be used instead, in order to avoid infinite recursion. In both, the application procedures are called with the same arguments, so the same procedures can be used in both places.

An example of when the interaction-complete (4) choice would be used is the half-tone shade editor of Figure 3.7. Here, the graphical slider can be moved up and down, and the textual number and rectangle are updated continuously, but the four-by-four pixel representation is not updated until the mouse button is released (for efficiency reasons). Therefore, the procedure which calculates the pixel representation and sets the associated active values is attached to the slider using interaction-complete notification.

8.7. Returning from the Created Procedure

The designer needs a way to cause the procedure being created with Peridot to exit and return to its caller. For example, a pop-up menu procedure might exit when the mouse button is released and return the item that the mouse was last over. Peridot provides a special command (Add-Return-Stmt) to specify this, but it is implemented using the same mechanism as application notification. The designer selects an active value, gives the Add-Return-Stmt command, and then selects from a menu when the procedure should return. In addition to the choices listed in the previous section, an additional choice is available:

(6) whenever the active value is set to a particular value.

For this choice, the designer is prompted to type a value to compare with the active value. Peridot automatically attaches a special procedure to the active value which causes the interface procedure to exit if appropriate. A pop-up menu might use interaction-complete to define when it should return, as shown in the example of section 3.4.

8.8. Implementation of Active Values

Active values are not very difficult to implement, and can be provided efficiently with many different kinds of operating systems. In order to determine what graphic objects to update when the value changes, Peridot saves a list of those that depend on each active value. Whenever a conditional, iteration, or attribute of an object is made to depend on an active value, Peridot saves a reference to the object with that active value. In addition, if the active value is a list and the reference is to a particular element of the list, then the active value saves the index of the element referred to, so the objects will not be redrawn if a different element of the active value changes.

When the SETActive procedure is called, Peridot first executes any out-of-range checking on the value (section 8.5). Next, the screen display (in the top Peridot window) for the active value itself is updated[4]. Next, SETActive checks to see if there are any objects that depend on the active value. If so, the objects and all the objects that depend on those objects are erased and redrawn. This must be done in the correct order, of course, to maintain the relative drawing order for the graphical objects. Finally, any application notification procedures attached to this active value are called (section 8.6). Some of these procedures might cause SETActive to be called recursively to set other active values, as in Figure 8.2.

Before calling any application procedures for out-of-range handling or application notification, Peridot first checks to see if the procedures have been defined by the application. If they are defined, then they are called. This allows the interface to operate as it will be used by the end user. If the procedures are not defined, however, Peridot simply prints a message in the prompt window telling what procedure would have been called and what its arguments would have been. This allows the designer to execute an interface before the application code has been written (not even "stubs" need to be provided). If the application procedure would have set another active value, the designer can explicitly set it to continue with the simulation of the interface.

Currently, the application procedures for range checking and application notification are simply saved in a list and are called directly from the SETActive routine. This has the severe disadvantage that if the application procedure has a long processing delay or breaks with an error, the user interface will stop. On the other hand, if the application can be trusted to be quick, it is a very efficient and simple mechanism. If the application is not trusted, and the underlying operating system has an efficient inter-process communication (IPC) mechanism, then the application notification can use IPC calls to protect the user interface. Fast message passing seems particularly appropriate; a message could be sent to a process for the application when the active value changes, and a return message might cause the same or other active values to be set. Adagio [Tanner 86] or Sassafras [Hill 87b](Appendix B) might provide an underlying structure on which to build this message passing. In addition, active values might be implemented using database trigger techniques [Buneman 79] or entirely new mechanisms such as the "logical tuples" in Linda [Ahuja 86]. Some artificial intelligence development systems, such as LOOPS [Stefik 86]

---

[4] Of course, if the procedure is running outside of Peridot as part of an application, there is no display to update; see section 11.3.

and KEE [Ramamoorthy 87] support a form of active values directly, and these could be used. In any case, no complex constraint-satisfaction techniques or other non-linear-time algorithms are ever needed. The important point is that active values are efficient and provide an appropriate abstract interface to the functionality and will hide the various implementation techniques from the non-programmer designer and even the application program.

8.9. Benefits of Active Values with Data Constraints

Active values with data constraints seem to be a very good idea and one of the important contributions to Peridot's success. They are a fairly intuitive way to connect together various parts of the interface that can change at run time and can be implemented efficiently. A single active value can have multiple displays and interactions associated with it, so the value can be displayed and set in different ways, depending on the needs of the end user. For example, the active value for SliderValue is used in two displays in Figure 8.2. An example of multiple interactions setting the same active value is the half-tone editor in Figure 3.7 which allows the grey shade to be set by moving a slider or explicitly turning on and off pixels.

In addition, active values can be used to extend whatever Peridot supports. If some kind of interaction or special effect is not provided directly, then a very short procedure can usually be written to perform the action by querying and setting active values. For example, if Peridot did not support exceptions to mouse interactions as used in the example of section 3.4 (where the mouse is not allowed to go over certain items controlled by whether a conditional is true), this effect could be easily achieved by having the following trivial Interlisp-D function as the application-defined out-of-range checking procedure:

```
(DEFUN CheckIllegal (activeVal exceptionList)
    (IF (MEMBER activeVal exceptionList) THEN NIL
    ELSE activeVal))
```

Active values also allow the end user to provide arguments for commands in any order. The designer simply provides an active value for each piece of data that will be input, along with some appropriate technique for specifying the value, and then the end user can set or adjust the values of each independently, in any order or even in parallel. In addition, it is easy for the application program to provide appropriate defaults for any values simply by setting the appropriate active value, and these may be calculated based on the values of other active values to provide semantic defaults. Most previous UIMSs have not allowed the end user to specify arguments for commands in different orders or supported semantic defaults.

Active values allow Peridot to also support semantic feedback, since application-supplied procedures can be called in inner loops to filter data from input devices.

Another important advantage of active values is that they support multiple processing easily. If the application program is implemented as multiple processes, then they can each call and be notified by SETActive independently. In addition, multiple input devices can be operating concurrently by setting their associated active values whenever they change. Whatever graphical objects and application procedures that depend on these devices will be notified appropriately. Chapter 10 discusses the use of multiple input devices concurrently.

A related advantage is that active values allow Peridot to provide application (internal) control, UIMS (external) control, and parallel (mixed) control [Tanner 85]. If the procedure is set up to return the desired value (as with the pop-up menu of Figure 3.15), then the application can simply call the procedure and use the result (application control). In this way, Peridot can be used to create a conventional library or "tool box" of interaction techniques. On the other hand, the interface can be set up as a set of interactions with application procedures called when values change (UIMS control). An example of this is the application procedure attached to the scroll bar of Figure 8.1 which is called whenever the user moves the scroll bar indicator with the mouse or presses on an arrow. Of course these can be combined to achieve parallel or mixed control.

8.10. Extensions

One interesting user interface extension of active values would be to allow the designer to *demonstrate* how out-of-range values should be handled and when an application procedure should be called. For example, to demonstrate which out-of-range action is desired, the designer might type an out-of-range value for the active value and then either type the desired value that should be used or graphically move the object associated with the active value to the desired place. However, since there are only a small number of choices and they are easy to understand, the specification technique seems sufficient here.

It is often the case that the application procedure attached to an active value performs some simple arithmetic or test on the value to calculate the return value. Allowing the designer to simply type these expressions would make the designer less dependent on a programmer to provide small procedures to handle these cases.

There are a number of implementation problems that should be removed to improve the handling of active values. The most important is that Peridot should be smarter about what needs to be redrawn when an active value changes. As discussed in section 5.9, when a object changes, it is non-trivial to calculate which other objects need to be updated. For active values, Peridot currently erases and redraws only the objects that directly depend on the active value and the objects that depend on those objects. Objects that happen to be in the same place on the screen as the updated objects are not redrawn. This means that the updated objects may leave white holes in other objects (since objects are erased to white). As a partial fix, Peridot currently checks to see if an object was drawn using XOR, and if so, erases it using XOR rather than drawing with white, which usually restores the original picture. Techniques from [Olsen 85b] might be used, or Peridot could support saved bitmap pictures (for the picture underneath the object that is moving) so objects could move smoothly over arbitrary backgrounds, as is done in many systems. The algorithms for handling this are well-known and inexpensive and could be easily integrated with Peridot.

Another useful feature would be some kind of modularization of active value names. Currently, all active values are globals. This makes it difficult to have two instantiations of the same user interface, and makes it important that different interfaces use different active value names. This problem is inherent in Interlisp-D since there is no modularization mechanism provided in the language. If Peridot was ported to some other language, possibly that language's modularization mechanism could be used. For example, Common Lisp (another popular Lisp dialect) does support modules. Otherwise, Peridot would have to invent some modularization technique internally, such as creating unique names for each instantiation and associating active values with these names.

A trivial implementation problem is that currently only one application-defined procedure and one range checking procedure is allowed on an active value or any of its elements if it is a list. There are occasions where this is not sufficient and multiple procedures are needed. It would be important with multiple procedures to be able to specify what order they should be applied, especially for the out-of-range handling.

Finally, it is possible to set up application procedures so that they form an infinitely recursive loop. For example, if active value A has an application procedure that calculates and sets active value B, and another application procedure is attached to B and sets A, this can cause an infinite loop. Peridot could easily detect this case, which would allow two active values to be tightly coupled in this way while freeing the application programmer from having to deal with this problem.

8.11. Chapter Summary

Active values are like parameters to the procedure except that the value can change while the procedure is running. They can be set by input devices or application procedures and the graphic objects that depend on them will be updated immediately. Although the normal form for the SETActive procedure, which sets active values, is similar to the standard Lisp variable assignment, extra parameters are available chiefly to make handling the mouse simpler.

Various forms of out-of-range handling for active values can be specified by the designer, and one kind is automatically supplied when a linear interpolation is created. Application-defined out-of-range checking, along with application procedures called when the active value changes, allow semantic feedback and UIMS (external) control since the application can be called in inner loops of tracking. For application-notification, the designer can specify how often the procedure is called. Active values are also used to control when the Peridot-created procedure exits (returns to its caller).

Active values are implemented efficiently in Peridot, and can also be implemented efficiently in various forms of operating systems and database systems.

Active values are an important part of Peridot's success and provide the "hook" to allow additional features to be added when necessary.

Chapter IX

Handling the Mouse

9.1. Introduction

When creating highly-interactive, direct manipulation interfaces, one of the most difficult design and implementation tasks is handling the mouse and other input devices. One of Peridot's primary innovations is allowing the input devices to be programmed by demonstration. This operates in a manner consistent with the rest of the Peridot user interface.

The design of the mouse interaction portion of Peridot may seem "rougher" than other parts of the system. This is due to the fact that there are no other systems that allow mouse interactions to be programmed by demonstration and so everything that Peridot provides is an innovation. Previous systems have handled some aspects of graphical constraints and control structures (iterations and conditionals) by demonstration, so there was more background research for those parts of Peridot.

Each input device is attached to its own active value. For example, the mouse has an active value, called **Mouse**, which is a list of five items: the *x* position of the mouse, the *y* position, and a boolean for each of the three buttons[1]. An example of the value for **Mouse** is (49 102 NIL T NIL).

Clearly, the mechanisms described in the previous chapter can be used to attach the input devices' active values to active values controlling the graphics. The techniques of section 8.5 could be used to restrict the values to certain limits and the application would be notified when appropriate (section 8.6).

If this was all that was provided, however, then code would have to be written for each mouse dependency to cover all of the requirements. The main problem is that interaction techniques need to be activated only under certain conditions. For example, a typical pop-up menu has an inverting black rectangle that follows the mouse (Figure 3.15), but only while the mouse button is held down over the menu. When the mouse button is released, the current value is returned.

---

[1] Of course, some systems may provide more or fewer items for the mouse. For example, the Peridot definition should probably be extended to include a bitmap (icon) to use as the tracking symbol.

This chapter discusses the extensions that make it possible to define mouse-based interactions by demonstration. The next chapter discusses some other input devices (one-dimensional sliders, toggle buttons, and a clock) that Peridot supports.

A particular interface may be composed of multiple mouse interactions, where an "interaction" is the setting of one active value based on one positioning of the mouse with one particular button configuration.

9.2. The "Simulated Mouse"

Ideally, the designer would simply use the various input devices in the same manner as the end user, but this has three main problems:

(1) All of the end user's devices may not be available to the designer (for example, in designing the user interface for a flight simulator).

(2) The mouse input device is also used for giving commands to Peridot, so disambiguating actions meant for Peridot from those that the end user will perform is difficult.

(3) It may be difficult to keep the input device in the correct state (e.g. with a button held down or at a certain location) for the entire time it takes to specify the actions.

Therefore, Peridot uses simulated devices for the devices that have these problems. The *simulated mouse* is a small icon which represents the real mouse (see Figure 9.1). It has three buttons (the three white areas in Figure 9.1a) even though the real mouse only has two buttons (an example of problem (1)). To move the simulated mouse, the designer points with the real mouse at its "nose" and holds down a real mouse button. The icon will follow the mouse while the button is pressed. If a real mouse button is pressed over one of the simulated mouse's buttons, then the state of the simulated button toggles. Black represents the button depressed, and white represents the button released.

Some people have suggested that two physical mice might be used rather than a simulated mouse. One mouse would represent the user and the other would be used to give Peridot commands. With most computers today, however, it would be difficult to attach another mouse. Furthermore, this approach does not solve the third problem mentioned, since the designer would have to hold the mouse buttons down while giving commands, which would be inconvenient.

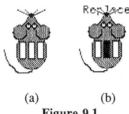

(a)   (b)

Figure 9.1

A simulated "mouse" pointing device with three buttons. The device can be moved by pointing at the "nose" (using a real pointing device), and the buttons can be toggled by pressing over them. In (b), the center button is pressed over the word Replace.

9.3. Making Actions Mouse Dependent

9.3.1. Example

In the example of Figure 3.15 (section 3.4), the black rectangle that shows which menu item is selected was made mouse dependent. To do this, the designer only had to position the simulated mouse over the box, toggle the simulated mouse's left button, and give the MOUSEDependent command. Peridot then asks a number of questions: if the black box should be a conditional (yes), what active value should be set with the current value (ReturnValue), if that active value contains the name of the menu item to use (yes), if the operation should happen for any of the menu items (yes), whether the operation should be continuous while the mouse left button is down (yes), whether the operation should stop being continuous if the mouse moves off of the menu items (yes), and what value should be used when the mouse moves off the menu items (NIL). These questions are explained in the following sections.

As another example, suppose the designer wants the indicator in the scroll bar of Figure 9.2a to move with the mouse when the middle button is down. The indicator is first defined as a linear interpolation (section 5.6), and then the simulated mouse with its middle button down is moved over the bar (Figure 9.2b). When the MOUSEDependent command is given, Peridot asks if the grey box should move in a range with the mouse (yes), whether the interaction should start only when the mouse is pressed over the grey box (yes), whether the interaction should be continuous while the middle button is down (yes), whether the middle of the indicator box should be attached to the mouse (yes), and whether the operation should stop working if the mouse moves off of the grey box (no).

(a)   (b)

Figure 9.2.

To make the indicator box in the scroll bar (a) move with the mouse, the designer moves the simulated mouse over the box (b), gives the MOUSEDependent command, and answers some questions.

9.3.2. Selecting the Objects

As shown in the above examples, it is very simple to make an action depend on the mouse. Using the postfix style, the designer first defines the graphics, then moves and presses buttons on the simulated mouse to show where and when the action should take place, and then gives the MOUSEDependent command. The position of the simulated mouse shows where the mouse should be for this interaction to happen. It turns out that in many cases, the object under the mouse happens to be the graphic object that should depend on the mouse. For example, in Figure 9.2, the grey rectangle should follow the mouse when the mouse is over it. The position of the simulated mouse therefore tells Peridot both the affected object and the position. In other cases, the designer must explicitly select the objects that should be affected by the mouse. In Figure 9.3, four arrow icons are used to show the current selection, and the designer wants them to be set by the mouse. In this case, the arrows must be explicitly selected before the MOUSEDependent command is given because there is more than one object that should depend on the mouse, and because the mouse position when the operation should occur (over the rectangles) is not over any of the arrows.

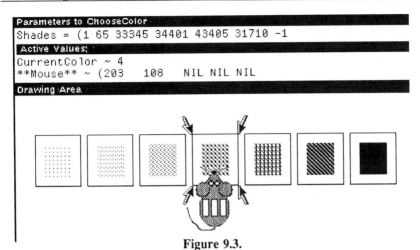

Figure 9.3.
The four arrows must be explicitly selected before giving the MOUSEDependent command to make them depend on the mouse.

9.3.3. Inferring the Dependency

Peridot uses the type of the graphic objects to guess how the objects should depend on the mouse. The possibilities that Peridot checks are:

(1) If the object selected is an active value, then it can be set to a special value when the mouse interaction occurs.

(2) If all of the objects are part of a conditional already, then a conditional is inferred. The conditional must depend on an active value so it can change at run-time.

(3) If one of the graphic objects depends on a linear interpolation, then Peridot infers that the mouse should move the object in that range. Again, the linear interpolation must depend on an active value.

(4) If the objects are all copies, then Peridot infers that a copy is desired at run time (the mouse will cause new copies of the objects to be created). This would be useful for creating a menu of selectable items, as in Figure 9.4. This option has not been implemented yet.

(5) Peridot infers that the objects should be made into a conditional and that the conditional should be set by the mouse.

(6) Peridot infers that the objects should move or change size with the mouse.

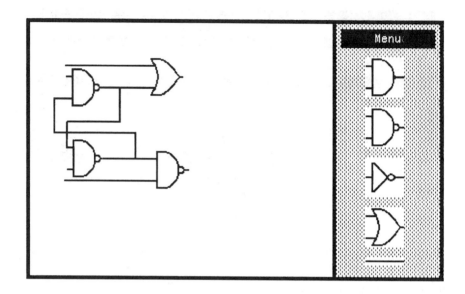

Figure 9.4.
A circuit design program that might be created using Peridot if it were extended to handle copies at run time. A new logic gate is needed each time the mouse is pressed over one of the items in the menu on the right. The application would have to provide procedures to insure that the lines connecting the copies were only in the correct places (e.g., attached to the circuit elements and not having two outputs connected together).

As with other parts of Peridot, these options are tried in order until one of the tests succeed and the designer confirms that this is what is desired. The last two options can be valid for any objects, so they will always be asked if the first four tests fail. The order of the last two is changed, however, depending on whether the objects depend on an iteration or not. If the objects have an attribute that depends on part of an iteration, then the conditional option (5) is more likely, so it is asked before (6). Otherwise, option (6) is asked before option (5). Note that option (5) is just an optimization to help the user, since an explicit conditional could have been made first (using the Peridot Conditional command) and then option (2) would apply. To perform option (5), Peridot effectively calls the Conditional command, so the designer has to answer all of those questions (see Chapter 7), and then option (2) is used.

9.3.4. Inferring Where the Action Should Happen

After the form of the dependency is established, Peridot tries to guess where the mouse should be for this action to take place. Typically, mouse interactions should only happen when the mouse is in a certain area. For example, pressing a mouse button on the up-arrow in the scroll bar of Figure 9.5 might perform a particular interaction, and this interaction should not happen if the button is pressed anywhere else.

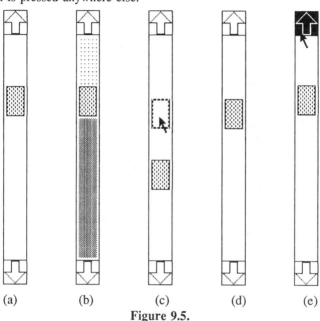

(a)	(b)	(c)	(d)	(e)

Figure 9.5.

A complete Macintosh-style scroll bar programmed by demonstration (a). This uses two invisible rectangles, which have been made visible in (b) by changing their color. When the button is pressed over one of these boxes, the scroll value changes by a specified amount (one page). The dotted-line box (c) appears when the button is pressed directly over the indicator box and follows the mouse while the button is held down. The indicator box jumps to the position of the dotted-line box when the button is released (d) and the dotted-line box disappears. Pressing on the arrows causes them to reverse video (e) and increments or decrements the scroll amount. Holding down on the arrows causes the value to be changed continuously, after a short delay. This interface was defined entirely by demonstration. It is composed of 8 interactions and took 30 minutes to create.

To find the object that the mouse should be over for the interaction to work, Peridot looks at the position of the simulated mouse. Peridot checks each of the objects at that position in order from top to bottom (most recently created to oldest). For each object in turn, Peridot checks to see if the object is part of an iteration. If so, Peridot asks the user if the action should happen when the mouse is over *any* of the items of the iteration. In order to make it more obvious which iteration is referred to, Peridot selects all the items of the iteration. The animated border which shows the selection makes it very clear which iteration is in question[2]. If the designer types "no" or the object is not part of an iteration, then Peridot asks about the object itself. If the designer types "no" to the object itself, the next lower object is queried (as part of an iteration and then by itself), and so on. Finally, if all the objects have been exhausted, or if the simulated mouse was not over any objects, Peridot asks if the action should happen no matter where the mouse is. If the designer says "no" to this, the MOUSEDependent command is aborted.

As an example, in the menu of Figure 3.15, the system notices that the simulated mouse is over the string Copy and guesses that the designer wants the operation to happen if the mouse is over any of the items in the iteration. This is correct, but if the designer had said "no," then Peridot would have asked if the operation should happen when the mouse is only over the single string Copy. If the designer had said "no" again, Peridot would have asked about the white rectangle, then the black rectangle and finally the grey rectangle, since they are all under the simulated mouse. In this case, none of the other choices are appropriate, but in the scroll bar example of Figure 9.2, the designer might want the indicator bar to follow the mouse when the designer presses anywhere inside the black rectangle. In this case, the designer would answer "no" when asked whether to trigger over the grey rectangle, and "yes" when Peridot then asked whether to trigger over the black rectangle.

9.3.5. Inferring the Mouse Buttons that Cause the Action

The next step is to infer the state of the mouse buttons that should cause the action. Peridot currently does not support chording—when two buttons are held down together (because the Interlisp-D mouse does not report it; see section 3.3.1), so the choices are a particular button down or a particular button up after single or multiple clicks. In addition, for each, the action might happen *continuously* while the button is in that state or *once* when it goes into that state.

---

[2] Peridot uses selection as a user interface *output* technique, as well as an input technique since it is a convenient way to draw the designer's attention to objects on the screen.

As an example of the difference, the inverting rectangle in the menu of strings (Figure 7.1) will follow the mouse while the button is pressed (this is "continuous"), but the property sheet items (Figure 7.2) toggle when the mouse button goes down ("once"), and nothing happens if the mouse is moved while the button is held down.

Peridot has used three different schemes for allowing the designer to specify which of these choices is desired. While none of these is clearly superior, the last one, which Peridot is now using, seems best.

The first attempt used the simulated mouse buttons to demonstrate whether the button should be up or down, and then explicitly asked the user whether the action should be continuous or discrete.

Figure 9.6.
A different form for the simulated mouse that allowed the designer to open and close the eyes by pressing on them with the real mouse.

The second method tried to eliminate the question and provide a demonstrational interface for specifying whether the action should be continuous or discrete using an elaborate mechanism. The simulated mouse was changed to have eyes that could open and close (Figure 9.6). Pressing on the eyes caused them to toggle state. A history of the button transitions was kept when the eyes were open. When the eyes were closed, the history was reset and nothing was saved. Demonstrating the various conditions required the following actions:

- For "once" when a button goes down, the designer would have the button up (white) when the eyes became open, and then press it down (the mouse would "see" the button going down).

- For "continuously" while down, the designer would have the button down when the eyes became open and do nothing afterwards (no transitions) (the mouse would not "see" the button go down).

- For "once" when a button goes up, the designer would have the button down (black) when the eyes became open, and then have it come up (the mouse would "see" the button going up).

• For "continuously" while up, the designer would have the button up
   when the eyes became open and do nothing afterwards (no transitions).

This scheme appeared to be too complex and hard to remember. The mouse
buttons were often left in the wrong state and it was hard to remember to toggle
the eyes. In addition, it did not scale up to handle multiple clicks (see the next
section). Therefore this method was abandoned.

The technique that is now in use is more like the first and uses the normal
simulated mouse shown in Figure 9.1 (the eyes stay open). Here, the two most
common situations, which are "once" when a button goes down and "continuously" while a button is down, are the easiest to specify, and the two least
common are harder. The simulated mouse always keeps a history of button
transitions. If the final state is button down, then this means "continuously"
while down. If a button has been toggled down and then up, then this means
one of the other three, and the designer is asked in order if it means (1) "once"
on the down transition, (2) "once" on the up transition, or (3) "continuously"
while up. Since the "up" cases are rarely used, this seems to be an appropriate
compromise. The problem is that the designer sometimes forgets which button
state means what. Fortunately, the questions confirming the state are very clear,
and the designer is allowed to abort and reset the buttons if they are set
incorrectly.

Other techniques that were considered but not implemented included having
a special button on the simulated mouse that means continuous, and having the
buttons be four-state instead of two. Neither of these seemed especially obvious or compelling, but more work could be done in this area.

9.3.6. Inferring Multiple Clicking

Peridot supports multiple-clicking (pressing and releasing the same button
multiple times within a specific time interval). Multiple clicking must be handled specially for two reasons: the second and subsequent clicks must happen
within a certain time period, and if they do happen, then operations on fewer
clicks should not happen. For example, if there is a single click action and a
double click action in the same area, the single click action should not happen
if the user double-clicks. Therefore, the single click action must wait to see if a
double click happens before executing its action. Peridot supports an arbitrary
number of clicks leading up to the command, and different interactions can be
defined for each number of clicks. For example, one interaction might happen
on double-click and another on 5-clicks, with no interactions for 1, 3, or 4
clicks.

The user interface for multiple clicking is very simple. The designer toggles the simulated mouse buttons the desired number of times and this is remembered in the mouse history. The ResetMOUSE command will normally be used before doing this to delete the history. The amount of time that the designer takes in pressing the simulated mouse's buttons is not recorded; the designer is explicitly prompted later for the multi-click wait time. After toggling the buttons the appropriate number of times, the designer will leave the button in the appropriate state (up or down) to signal whether continuous behavior was desired. When the MOUSEDependent command is given, Peridot counts the number of button down transitions in the history and asks if this is the number that should be used. If not, the designer can answer ''no'' and the click count will decrement, or ''quit'' and the regular, not-multiple-click questions will be asked.

Once a multiple click action has been confirmed, Peridot looks for other mouse actions using the same button in the same place (therefore the location (section 9.3.4) must be asked before the buttons). If any are found, Peridot asks the designer if the other interaction should wait for the new one. If so, the interactions are linked together so they will be mutually exclusive. This question is asked because it is possible that the designer would want the single click and multiple click actions to both operate independently in the same place. For example, in the Macintosh, a single click causes an icon to be selected and a double click causes the icon to open. The selection action happens whether or not the double-click operation happens. Alternatively, the Symbolics Lisp machine [Weinreb 81] uses single, double and triple clicks to bring up different menus, so these would be mutually exclusive.

Peridot must search for multi-click interactions every time a new mouse interaction is defined, even if the new one is a normal single-click interaction. This is because a previous multi-click interaction may be in the same place as the new single click interaction and Peridot does not restrict the designer to demonstrate the interactions in any particular order. Of course, this search is done at design time and the run time operation does not have any time penalty for non-multi-click operations.

Currently, Peridot assumes that all multi-clicks at the same place will use the same timeout (the wait before the button presses are considered two separate single clicks instead of one double click). The time is therefore stored with each group of mutually exclusive interactions. If the designer is defining a new multi-click interaction, Peridot queries how long the wait should be (with a default of 1/2 second). The designer can type a number or demonstrate the interval by pressing on the real mouse buttons.

9.3.7. Parameters for Continuous Interactions

In order to handle the wide range of interactions desired, Peridot provides various conditions under which a continuous operation will work. When an action is specified to be continuous, Peridot asks a series of questions. The first is whether the operation should only be continuous when the mouse is over certain objects. For example, pop-up menus usually remove the selection when the mouse goes outside the menu. On the other hand, the Macintosh scroll bar goes up and down while the mouse button is held down even if the mouse is moved outside the scroll bar (the y value for the mouse is used and the x is ignored). Peridot therefore asks if the operation should continue when the mouse goes out of the bounds. The designer can specify that the operation should be continuous everywhere, only when over the objects that the interaction is defined for (e.g. the string names in the menu), or over any other single object that the designer selects.

If the designer specifies that the operation should not be continuous everywhere, then Peridot inquires what value should be used when the mouse goes outside. The designer can type a value or * to use the last value of the interaction before the mouse went outside (which would be used, for example, by a scroll bar that only operated while the mouse was inside). For the menu, the designer might type NIL, 0, or " " (null string) to show that nothing should be highlighted when outside.

9.3.8. Parameters to the Action

The final set of questions deal with specifying any necessary parameters to the particular action. Each type of operation (setting an active value explicitly, a conditional, a linear interpolation, dragging and changing size, or copying) has its own parameters.

9.3.8.1. Parameters for Setting an Active Value

Since active values are used to control anything that can change at run time, all of the mouse actions affect active values. The other actions (conditional, linear interpolation, etc.) affect an active value indirectly through changes to graphics. With the action described here, however, the designer can select an active value and have it set directly when a mouse interaction occurs. For example, when the end user presses on the STOP icon in Figure 9.7, the active value controlling the stop action is set to T so the window will be removed. Graphics might explicitly depend on this active value or an application procedure might be called when it is changed.

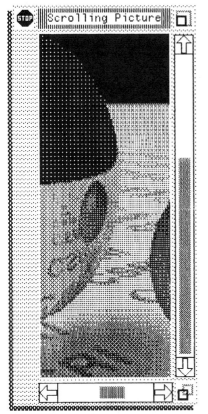
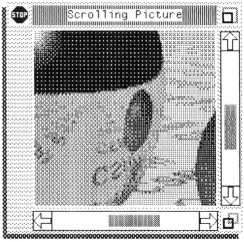

Figure 9.7.

Two views of a window created by Peridot. (Note: this is the same interface that was shown being created in Figure 8.1.) The picture can be scrolled horizontally or vertically either by pressing and moving the indicator boxes or by pressing on the arrows. The window's size can be changed by pressing on the icon at the upper right, and the position can be changed by pressing on the icon at the lower right. An application program is called to display the picture inside the window, but all of the interactions are handled entirely by Peridot, and were created by demonstration without programming.

Peridot supports a number of different ways to set an active value based on the mouse. In order to guess which way is appropriate, the type of the example value of the active value and the type of the object that the action depends on (the "where" from section 9.3.4) is used. The possibilities are:

(1) If the active value is a boolean (T or NIL), Peridot asks whether the active value should be toggled, set or cleared.

(2) If the active value is a number and if the object that the mouse is over is part of an iteration, then Peridot will ask if the active value should be set with the iteration loop count.

(3) If the active value is not a list and the simulated mouse is over part of an iteration, then Peridot asks if it should be set with the value of the iteration variable for this loop.

(4) If the active value is numeric, Peridot asks if it should be incremented by some amount, which can either be positive or negative. This is the option used for the arrow icons in the Macintosh-style scroll bar (Figure 9.5).

(5) If the active value is a LITATOM (any atom other than a number), then Peridot asks if it should be set with the name of the object that the mouse is over.

(6) If the active value is a pair of numbers, then Peridot asks if it should be set with the location of the mouse.

(7) Independent of the type, Peridot asks if the active value should be set with some constant value. (This actually covers choices (1) and (4), but they are provided so the designer does not have to know the special SETActive forms to achieve those effects.)

9.3.8.2. Parameters for Conditional

If the conditional allows multiple items to be selected (such as the property sheet in Figure 7.2), then Peridot asks whether the mouse action should cause the new value to be added to the list, removed from the list, or toggled (removed if there, added if not).

9.3.8.3. Parameters for Linear Interpolation

An interesting advantage of the demonstrational technique is that Peridot can infer what part of the object should be attached to the mouse during dragging based on where the mouse was placed (see Figure 9.8). Peridot checks to see if the designer placed the mouse in the center, at a corner, or in the middle of one side, and asks the designer for confirmation of the inferred position[3]. Of

---

[3] Another useful option would allow the object to be moved from the exact position where the mouse presses. This requires that the offsets from the original mouse position be saved for use while the mouse is moving, and so has not been implemented.

course, if the linear interpolation is only in one dimension (e.g. up and down), then Peridot need only ask about that direction. If the designer specifies that the guess is incorrect, then other parts of the object are guessed until the correct place is found or the designer aborts the process.

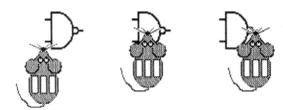

Figure 9.8.
Demonstrating that an object might be attached to the mouse in various places for dragging: bottom-left, center, and center of right side.

9.3.8.4. Parameters for Dragging or Changing Size

This type of action is useful when the active value should be set with the absolute (screen specific) pixel size or position of an object. If a transformation to abstract coordinates is desired, then linear interpolation (previous section) would usually be preferred.

When the designer specifies this choice, Peridot asks which properties of the object should change with the mouse. The options are: x, y, position (x and y together), width, height, or size (width and height together). The position of the simulated mouse is used to guess what part of the object should be attached to the mouse during the changes, as described in the previous section. Due to an implementation problem, changing size will only work from the right and top[4], but moving can be from any side, corner or middle. For this action, Peridot prompts for an active value to set with the properties of the object that change.

Examples of using this action are the bar chart of Figure 6.3, where the heights of the bars can be adjusted with the mouse, and the window of Figure 9.7. For the window, the icon at the top-right causes the window to start changing size with the mouse, and the icon at the bottom-right causes the

---

[4] Changing size from the left, bottom or middle requires that both the size and position of the object be adjusted, since regions are defined using LEFT, BOTTOM, WIDTH, and HEIGHT. It would be fairly easy to construct the expressions that would handle this, however.

window to move with the mouse. These interactions (as well as the scrolling, of course) are handled entirely internal to Peridot; the application procedure that handles the picture in the window is simply notified of the new size and position.

9.3.8.5. Parameters for Copying

Copying objects at run time is not implemented yet, but it may be useful for some interfaces such as Figure 9.4. Peridot would prompt for an active value to set with the name and type of the new object. Typically, the application program will attach a notification procedure to this active value so that it can keep track of what the user has created. The copy interaction would typically be followed by a dragging or linear interpolation operation, so the new objects would be in a different place from the originals.

9.4. Running the Interaction

As soon as all of the parameters to the interaction have been typed or confirmed, the designer can move the simulated mouse around and toggle the buttons to see if the interaction works as expected. The real mouse can also be used by going into "Run Mode" using the Run-Procedure Peridot command. In run mode, the real mouse works as it will for the end user. This is very useful since the simulated mouse is somewhat clumsy for running the interface. While in run mode, the mouse cannot be used to give Peridot commands. To leave run mode, the designer hits the keyboard key labeled "Stop." In addition, if the procedure being created exits because an active value is set to the appropriate value (section 8.7), run mode will be exited and the return value will be printed in the prompt window[5].

9.5. Exceptions to Mouse Dependent Actions

Sometimes it is desirable for a mouse action *not* to happen under certain circumstances. For example, the mouse interaction for the menu of Figure 3.15 should not happen when the mouse is over one of the illegal items. Currently, Peridot allows any conditional to define when an mouse exception should happen. If exceptions to iterations (section 6.5.2) were implemented, then mouse exceptions could be based on them also.

---

[5] If Peridot is not in run mode and the active value is set to a value that causes an exit, for example by using the simulated mouse, the return value is simply printed in the prompt window.

To define a mouse exception, the designer only has to select an object that is part of the conditional (as in Figure 3.15o), and give the MOUSE-Exception command. Peridot guesses which interaction this should refer to based on which interactions use the same active value or iteration, and confirms this with the user. The value to use when the exception occurs is the same as the value used when the mouse goes outside the object (section 9.3.7), and the designer is queried if this value has not been specified.

Now the interaction can immediately be exercised to see if the exception works correctly.

9.6. Editing Interactions

It is very easy to edit static pictures in Peridot since they can be easily selected and redrawn. It is harder to select dynamic and ephemeral things such as interactions, however, since they often do not have visual representations on the screen. Some systems have required the user to learn a textual representation for the actions in order to allow editing (e.g. [Halbert 84]), but this is undesirable. Therefore Peridot allows interactions to be edited in a number of ways. First, an interaction can be re-demonstrated, and Peridot will inquire if the new interaction should replace the old one or run in parallel. Running in parallel is often used since multiple interactions may affect the same active value. For example, pressing on the arrows for the scroll bar in Figure 9.5 and moving the indicator up and down will affect the same active value (ScrollPercent). The second way to edit interactions is to select an active value and give the DeleteInteractions command. Peridot then prints a description of each interaction in the prompt window and asks if it should be deleted.

Any system that allows editing will have a certain "grain" finer than which items must be re-entered from scratch. For example, drawing packages rarely allow a rectangle to be edited into a circle (keeping some of its properties); instead, the rectangle must be erased and a circle drawn instead. Similarly, the grain chosen in Peridot for mouse interactions is one entire interaction. Since individual interactions are small (e.g. setting an active value when the left mouse button goes down over a menu item), this should not be a large burden. A complex interface, such as the scrollbar of Figure 9.5, is typically constructed from a number of small interactions, each of which takes only a few seconds to define. The added complexity for the designer of learning extra editing commands does not seem appropriate given the ease of re-specification. If this turns out to be obnoxious to designers in the future, however, then it would not be too difficult to allow the various parts of the interaction (the active area, the buttons, the action, the exceptions, etc.) to be edited separately.

9.7. Some Techniques for Creating Desired Effects

Occasionally, designers may want to provide an interaction which is not directly supported by the capabilities described above. Often, the effect can be achieved by using some "tricks" or techniques that still do not involve programming, but other times, a small "helper" procedure is needed.

One of the most useful techniques is to create an invisible rectangle and have the operations occur when the mouse is over it. An invisible rectangle can be drawn by making its color be white and its drawing function OR or XOR. It will then never be visible. While defining the interaction, it might be convenient to use some other color for the rectangle so the designer can see it, and then edit the color to be white when the interaction has been defined.

An example of the use of this technique is in demonstrating the unusual behavior of the Macintosh scroll bar (Figure 9.5). When the user presses above the indicator box, the document is scrolled one page up, and below the box, the document is scrolled one page down. To scroll to a particular part of the document, the user points to the indicator box itself and drags it while holding the button down. The designer can program this entire interface in Peridot using eight interactions (including two for each arrow) and two invisible rectangles. The rectangles are placed above and below the indicator box and attached to it, so they change size with the movement of the indicator box.

Another use of invisible rectangles is to make the mouse active area be larger than the objects displayed. For example, the menu of Figure 3.15 has the feature that the names are only selected when the mouse is directly over the name; to the side of the name but still inside the menu box is considered outside. If this is not the desired behavior, then invisible rectangles can be placed over each name that are the full width of the menu box and the interaction can be defined using these. This would add only two extra steps to the example (drawing the boxes over the first two elements of the iteration in Figures 3.15h and i); all other changes would be handled automatically.

When an operation is not directly available in Peridot, usually a small application procedure can be created which sets an extra active value to provide the effect. For example, to change the color of the menu bar as it moves over illegal items (rather than having it not show up at all), the following procedure could be attached to the active value for the position of the bar:

```
(DEFUN ChangeColorIfIllegal (activeVal illegalItems)
    (IF (MEMBER activeVal illegalItems) THEN Grey
    ELSE Black))
```

The output from this procedure would be used to set the active value controlling the color of the bar.

9.8. Other Designs for Handling the Mouse

Originally, the design for how mouse-based interactions would be performed was entirely different [Myers 86b]. There were to be two different modes: one for designing the static, background picture and one for defining the interaction. In interaction mode, the designer was going to move the simulated mouse or change its buttons first, and then perform some operation, such as moving an object or drawing a new object. Peridot would then create a conditional statement that would be triggered by the input device state and position. Iterations (e.g. perform this operating until a button is hit), exceptions, and special cases would be specified using the iteration and conditional commands.

As a specific example, to specify the menu of Figure 3.15, the simulated mouse would first be moved over one of the menu items, and then the designer would draw a black inverted rectangle over that item. The designer then would move the simulated mouse off to the side and explicitly erase the black rectangle. Peridot would infer that the box should be erased when the mouse is no longer over an object. The designer would then perform this action on another string, or explicitly specify an iteration, and the code that handles highlighting would be completed. Next the designer would press one of the simulated mouse's buttons and specify that the object under the mouse should be returned. From this, the system would infer that the procedure should be exited upon button press.

This design seems somewhat more demonstrational than Peridot's current design, but it proved unsatisfactory for a number of reasons. First, it was extremely difficult to generate correct code, and the code that was produced seemed very special purpose. Each operation had a test wrapped around it to determine when it should occur (e.g. when the mouse is over an iteration item). Synchronizing all of the drawing and erasing operations and insuring that they affected the correct objects was a major problem. It was also not clear that this mechanism would extend to types of interactions other than menus. In addition, having a separate interaction mode was very annoying. Finally, the code structures did not integrate well with active values and conditionals.

9.9. Implementation

Using active values made the implementation of mouse-based interactions fairly easy. Each input device has an associated active value which is updated by the real devices. The association between the physical devices and their active values is implemented in Lisp code. For the mouse, the simulated mouse updates the **Mouse** active value, and the real mouse updates it when in "Run Mode." Of course, when a Peridot-created interface is used as part of a real application (see Chapter 11), the mouse active value is always updated by the real mouse.

To make operations depend on the mouse, special objects, called MouseWatchers are created which appear to the implementation to be normal graphical objects. These objects are never seen by the designer. MouseWatchers are made to depend on the mouse active value. If the interaction depends on a particular button, then the dependency is on the part of **Mouse** that represents that button. For example, since the mouse active value has the form (x y left middle right), for the middle button, the dependency would be on element 4 of **Mouse**. When the mouse active value changes appropriately, the interaction objects are "redrawn" using their drawing routine (the function in the DRAWFN field of the object). The routine in this field for MouseWatchers is special, and it checks the state of the buttons and the position of the mouse to see if the interaction should really be run. If so, then some other active value is set appropriately, which automatically causes any associated graphics to change and application procedures to be called as appropriate. The calculation of how to set the other active value is made based on the type of the update, and often uses the special forms of SETActive described in section 8.4.

The main complications to this algorithm are for supporting continuous interactions, special values to be used when the mouse goes outside the objects or over exception values, and handling multiple clicking.

For continuous mode, the SETActive routine had to be modified to enable MouseWatchers to arrange for the drawing function to be called when the mouse moves (rather than just when the button changes) while in continuous mode. For efficiency, however, the MouseWatcher procedures should not be called until the appropriate button is pressed when not in continuous mode. To implement this, the drawing function adds the MouseWatcher object to a special list for the mouse active value when continuous mode is entered and removes the object from the list when continuous mode is finished. While in continuous mode, if the mouse moves outside the object, the special outside value is used instead of the normal value for the active value being set.

Similarly, if there are exception areas, then these are checked before the normal processing.

Often, it appears that the constraints between graphical objects and the active values they depend on are bi-directional when the mouse can move the graphical objects. For example, the indicator box in the scroll bar of Figure 9.5 can be moved up and down with the mouse and this will cause the associated active value to be set, or the active value can be set by an application and this will cause the box to move. In fact, however, this is implemented with two separate uni-directional constraints: the original constraint that ties the position of the box to the value of its active value, and a new constraint that ties the active value to the position of the mouse. This scheme provides the effect of bi-directional constraints (either the active value or the object can be changed and the other will be adjusted), without the inefficiency and complexity of constraint-satisfaction algorithms.

The multi-clicking mechanism was rather difficult to implement. Here, it was necessary to delay the processing of smaller-numbered clicking operations until after a timeout had elapsed in order to check whether the mouse button would be pressed again. Unfortunately, it is not possible to simply have the DRAWFN procedure wait, since this would prevent other processing. Therefore, it was necessary to fork off a process and have that process wait while allowing the main process to continue. Interlisp-D's multi-processing system (section 3.3.1) was very helpful for this.

When there are multiple interactions that are mutually exclusive for multi-clicking, they are linked together as described in section 9.3.6. The first interaction in the list is marked and the maximum number of clicks in the group is saved. The first interaction is responsible for updating the button press counter. At each press, it compares the current time with the time of the last press to check whether to start the count over or increment the counter.

Each interaction, including the first, checks the counter against the number of clicks that it is expecting (for example, a double click interaction checks to see if the counter is 2). If so, and if this interaction is the maximal one, then it can run. For example, if there is a single, double and triple click, then the triple click is the maximal one. If it is not the maximum, then it forks off a process to wait the appropriate amount of time. When the process times out, it checks to see if the click count is still the same as it was expecting, and if so it runs. If not, it just aborts because there were more clicks. As an optimization, this process is explicitly killed if the count is incremented after the process is created.

Although somewhat complex, this multi-click mechanism is, of course, implemented internal to Peridot and the complexity is invisible to the designer. The appropriate effect is achieved, however, and it could be easily extended to handle some other effects, such as having the double click timeout be different from the triple click timeout, etc.

9.10. Extensions

9.10.1. General

The method for defining the mouse-based interactions described above fits in very well with the other structures in Peridot (conditionals, active values, linear interpolations, etc.) and has a similar style (postfix specification, demonstrational, etc.). In addition, it covers a large variety of interaction techniques, styles and mechanisms, and is implemented efficiently.

Unfortunately, there are a number of interactions that cannot be created without writing application code, and it is hard to argue that the mechanism is truly general. The proposed extensions will help, but the basic problem is that no-one has invented an underlying theory or model of the basic units out of which all interaction techniques can be constructed. It was not a goal of this research to invent such a model, but if future research provides one, then Peridot can be profitably modified to incorporate it.

It would also be interesting to investigate radically different ways to demonstrate how the mouse should control the interaction. The original method proposed (section 9.8) could be reexamined based on the knowledge from the current implementation to see if it can be made to work effectively. Another approach is to hard-code the *behaviors* of the interactions (e.g., the menu behavior, the dragging behavior, etc.) and allow the pictures to be defined arbitrarily. This is similar to the mechanism in Trillium [Henderson 86]. Peridot did not use this approach because one of its goals is to support the investigation of new interaction behaviors.

9.10.2. Support For Sequencing

One common situation is that the result of one interaction will be to start another interaction. For example, when the mouse moves down out of the top bar in the Macintosh, a pop-up menu appears. Peridot does not support this type of sequencing directly; it is up to the application program to specify it. Sequencing (which is basically the syntax of the interaction) has been the chief emphasis of many UIMSs, so there are a variety of existing techniques to choose from here. Good candidates would be transition networks [Jacob 85], grammars [Olsen 83], Event Response Systems [Hill 87b], or direct links [Granor 86]. Alternatively, the ideas in Peridot might be extended to handle sequencing by demonstration, as described in section 13.7.5.

Sequencing support would also be useful internally in Peridot. Currently, the implementation of continuous interactions is fairly special-purpose. It would be better if the designer could specify (1) an action to start the interaction, (2) operations to perform when the interaction begins, (3) operations to perform while the interaction is in progress, (4) actions that specify the end of an interaction, and (5) operations to perform at the end of an interaction. A powerful sequencing system would allow multiple paths through an interaction. This would allow, for example, an object to be moved about while the left button is down, but if the right button is hit while dragging, then the object would be deleted [Hill 87b].

9.10.3. Extensions to Mouse Exceptions

Without modifying the current structure radically, it would still be possible to significantly improve how mouse exceptions are handled to make them easier to specify and more powerful.

For example, exceptions might be specified by demonstrating the graphics (or lack of graphics) that should appear and the conditions under which this should happen. A similar procedure to that used by the `MOUSEDependent` command would be used to generalize the demonstration.

The simplest extension would be to allow the exception to cause arbitrary active values to be set with specified values, rather than just providing a fixed value. Another general mechanism would be to allow mouse interactions to act whenever the mouse was over a conditional object (rather than just over an iteration or a simple object as now), and possibly over the negation of the conditional (everywhere it is false). This should not be difficult to add. Exceptional behavior for one interaction would then simply be defined as another interaction which operated over a conditional. The system would notice that two interactions operated at the same place with the same buttons and would ask if they should be mutually exclusive or not. Exceptions would then not need a special command, they could have arbitrary graphical presentations and values for active values, and they could be created by demonstration.

9.10.4. Eliminating the Need for Invisible Rectangles

Most designers who have used Peridot seem to assume that if a conditional is defined on an iteration, then the mouse will operate anywhere that the conditional is displayed, rather than where the iteration itself is displayed. For example, for the menu of Figure 9.9, the bar which shows which item is selected is much larger than the strings from the iteration. The mouse interaction is defined by default only when the mouse is directly over the strings, however. Peridot could probably notice when the conditional has a larger area than the iteration item and propose that a bigger area be used, so an invisible rectangle would not have to be created.

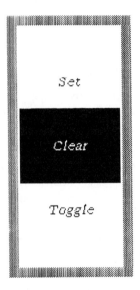

Figure 9.9.
Menu with large marker.

For the cases when invisible rectangles are created, there is clearly no reason why they should be drawn. Peridot should detect when an object is going to be invisible and save some expense at run time by not drawing it. The region of the object will still have to be calculated, of course, since interactions are likely to depend on it.

9.10.5. Other Extensions

There are many ways that the user interface of Peridot for mouse interactions could be improved. One area is the specification of "once" versus "continuous" as described in section 9.3.5. Another area that could be improved is the way that Peridot describes interactions to the designer. Peridot lists interactions for three reasons: on designer request, when an interaction is being deleted, and when a multi-click interaction may be mutually exclusive with another. Currently, Peridot prints in the prompt window some properties of the interaction such as the buttons required and the object it is defined over. It would be cute if instead Peridot ran a small animation of the interaction in operation using the simulated mouse.

It would also be interesting to see if some of the questions that Peridot asks about interactions could be replaced with a demonstrational action, and whether this would be easier for the designer to use. For example, the designer might demonstrate that an action should be continuous by demonstrating it happening twice without changing the button state. This was not done because it would typically take much longer to demonstrate the action a second time than to answer a question as to whether it was continuous or not. Section 3.2.2 discusses how the choices for setting a boolean might be demonstrated.

9.11. Chapter Summary

Peridot is the first system to allow the interaction part of user interfaces to be created by demonstration. A "simulated mouse" is used to represent the real mouse, and its position and button status are used to demonstrate what the interaction should depend on. The type of the object that the mouse is over and the type of the example value for the associated active value are used to guess how the mouse should affect the graphics and the active value. The choices supported by Peridot are to set an active value directly, set a conditional, move an object within a linear interpolation, or move or change the size of an object unconstrained. Associated with each operation are a position (which may be anywhere, over a particular object, or over any object of an iteration), and a button status (down or up, single or multi-click, once or continuous). The designer is then prompted for any further parameters to the operation. After an interaction is defined, it can be run immediately with the real or simulated mouse, edited, and exceptions can be defined for it.

The current user interface of Peridot is well integrated with the rest of the system and has the same style. Other user interfaces have been investigated, however, and it is clear that Peridot's can still be improved.

The implementation of mouse interactions was made fairly straightforward by the use of the powerful active value mechanism. The chief difficulty was to provide multiple clicks since they require waiting for a period of time, whereas active values assume all updates will be virtually instantaneous.

There are many extensions possible for demonstrating mouse-based interactions and much future research in this area would be appropriate. Peridot has demonstrated that this research can result in a powerful system that can make defining of highly-interactive mouse-based interfaces possible for non-programmers.

Chapter X
Other Input Devices

10.1. Introduction

One of Peridot's important goals is to allow investigation of new types of interactions. One promising area is the use of alternative input devices. Human factors experiments have demonstrated that novices can perform some tasks easily and more quickly using special input devices in the left hand while the mouse is used in the right hand [Buxton 86]. For example, the left hand might be controlling a one-dimensional slider or a knob which adjusts the size of a square, while the other hand is positioning it using a mouse (Figure 10.1). An important feature of these interfaces is that multiple devices are in operation at the same time. This concurrency makes it fairly difficult to implement these interfaces in conventional programming systems.

The use of active values in Peridot, however, makes handling multiple concurrent input devices very easy. Since multiple active values can be updated in parallel and the effect of different active values is independent, multiple input devices can be active at the same time. The application program can be totally ignorant of this parallelism by supplying independent procedures to filter or handle the separate input devices. Alternatively, the application can synchronize and control the devices in any desired manner while still allowing the user interface designer to specify the graphical relationships. This assumes, of course, that the underlying programming language or operating system has adequate support for fine-grain multi-processing, as discussed in section 8.8.

A common input device that is often used in user interfaces, at least indirectly, is the clock. For example, a window might start scrolling continuously after the mouse is held down over a certain area for a certain length of time.

Peridot uses active values and demonstrational techniques to make the use of multiple devices easier. Currently, Peridot supports the clock and a custom-built slider and button box which contains four buttons and two one-dimensional sliders (Figure 10.2). These have features in common with a wide variety of other input devices that are often attached to computers. Therefore, they show how easily the techniques in Peridot can be used to support multiple input devices operating in parallel. This chapter discusses these devices and how further devices could be added to Peridot.

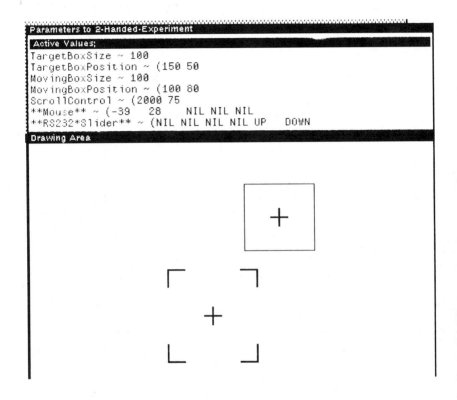

Figure 10.1.
The size of the box is controlled with the left hand at the same time that the position is controlled with the right hand.

10.2. The Slider and Button Box

The one-dimensional slider box shown in Figure 10.2 is representative of a class of devices that are often attached to computers. The buttons represent any set of switches, and the sliders represent any unconstrained (continuously varying) one-dimensional quantity, such as rotary knobs that can be turned continuously.

As explained in the previous chapter, every input device is associated with an active value. The active value for the slider box is called **RS232*Slider** and has the form (NIL T NIL NIL UP DOWN) where each button is represented by a boolean (T or NIL) and each slider is represented by a value which is set to UP or DOWN each time the device moves one increment

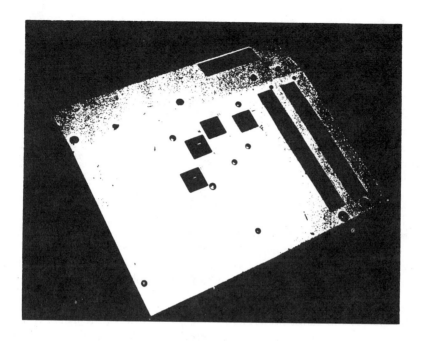

Figure 10.2.
Photograph of the custom-built slider and button box.

in that direction. Clearly, any button box can be represented by a set of booleans (or a set of enumerated types if the buttons have more than two states). If the sliders had been knobs instead, the value might be set to COUNTER-CLOCKWISE or CLOCKWISE rather than UP and DOWN, but the effect would be the same.

In order to have the display of a set of objects dependent on the state of a button and therefore blink on and off, it is only necessary to have the objects be conditional on the associated boolean active value.

To have the slider increment or decrement a number, a special application procedure is needed[1]. UpDownAdd was written as follows:

---

[1] If active values were extended to allow the designer to type in expressions as suggested in section 8.10, this operation could be performed without writing any code. The other active value would be set to the specific values (+ <inc>) or (+ -<inc>) when the slider was set to UP and DOWN respectively.

```
(DEFUN UpDownAdd (val inc)
    (IF (EQ val 'UP) THEN (LIST '+ inc)
    ELSE (LIST '+ (MINUS inc)))))
```
This simple procedure generates the appropriate form for SETActive to incre-
ment or decrement an active value based on whether the value from the device
is UP or DOWN. UpDownAdd can be attached to the active value for either one
of the sliders (or both) and the output directed to an active value that controls
whatever should be incremented by the slider. For example, in Figure 10.1, the
output is directed at MovingBoxSize which controls the size of the box, and
for a scroll bar, the output might be directed at the active value that controls the
scroll percent. The increment amount can be typed by the designer to tune the
device's behavior.

There is no need for a simulated device for the slider box since it can be
used directly. The actual buttons and sliders can be used at any time during the
design of the interface (there is no need to go into "run mode"). A special
process is forked which monitors the RS232 port when the designer specifies
that the slider will be used and this process is always active. If the slider box
was not available, however, it would be easy to supply a simulated device for
it.

The sliders and switches are always active, even while the mouse is moving. Therefore it is very easy to attach separate interactions to the various devices, and have them operate in parallel.

10.3. The Clock

Peridot supports a "centisecond" (1/100th second) clock. It has an active
value **Clock** composed of an integer that is incremented every 1/100th of
a second and a boolean that starts and stops it ticking.

One use of the clock is to control animations. The threshold notification
(section 8.6) can be used to cause an application procedure to be called every
time the clock increments by a certain amount. This procedure might set a different active value. As a special feature, the threshold notification checks to see
if the active value is **Clock** and if so, allows the designer to demonstrate
the amount of time to wait by pressing the real mouse's buttons. Alternatively,
the designer can type in the wait increment. Each time the threshold is passed,
the application procedure will be called, and it might toggle a boolean active
value to control blinking, or it might increment an active value attached to the x
position of some objects to achieve horizontal movement. More complex
movements could also be provided. For example, the rabbit in Figure 10.3 is
controlled by a procedure that increments its x every time, and sets the y to
(40*(ABS (SIN time))) which causes the rabbit to "hop." Of course, this

procedure is hand-coded in Lisp, but it is very simple, and the non-programmer designer can specify parameters for it and adjust the graphical presentation[2].

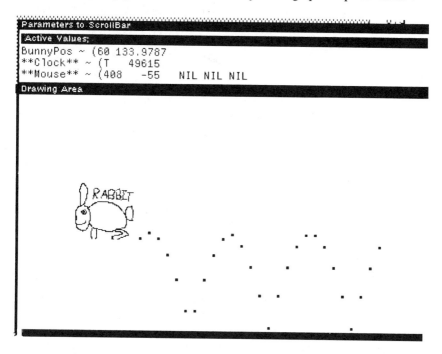

Figure 10.3.
The rabbit moves in a "hopping" fashion calculated by an application function attached to the clock.

Another use of the clock is to specify that an action should happen a certain period of time after some other action. For example, if the up arrow in the Macintosh scroll bar is pressed, the document scrolls up one line, and if the button is held down for about one second, the document starts scrolling up continuously until the button is released. To perform this in Peridot, the designer would make the button press on the arrow cause the clock to start ticking, and have a threshold notification cause another active value to be set later to start continuous scrolling. As discussed in section 9.10.2, this sequencing of one

---

[2] The extension to allow the designer to type in arithmetic expressions (section 8.10), would eliminate even this programming.

action after another cannot be done entirely by demonstration in Peridot and requires some application procedures. A sequencing mechanism that is demonstrational is an interesting extension that would help with this style of interface.

10.4. Extensions

10.4.1. Synchronization and Sequencing

As discussed above, a sequencing mechanism is needed. Closely related is a synchronization mechanism that would allow the application program to control when the different devices were active and insure that there are no conflicts in their use. Hill's ERS mechanism [Hill 87b] is very good for synchronization and also handles sequencing. It is a form of programming language, however, so it is not usable by non-programmers. On the other hand, synchronization in general is probably too complex for non-programmers to handle anyway, so this may be appropriate. It would be interesting, however, to investigate whether there are simpler techniques that are accessible to non-programmers and still powerful enough to handle the needs of user interfaces.

10.4.2. Other Input/Output Devices

It is very simple for an Interlisp programmer to add additional input devices to Peridot, once a device driver has been written. First, a name is selected for the active value that corresponds to the device. This active value will have a field for each data value that the device returns. A process would then be created that accepts events from the device and updates the active values appropriately. The 1109 computer which supports Peridot is very poor at handling RS232 and has no other ports for attaching input devices, which makes writing the device driver itself more complex. However, the active value mechanism in Peridot provides an appropriate and easy-to-connect-to interface for graphics, and should be considered in future systems. If a device has outputs, such as a light behind a button or an LED display connected with a slider, then an active value can be provided to control these outputs. The programmer can write a small routine that will be attached to the active value and cause the output to be updated appropriately. The non-programmer designer can then simply cause this active value to be set appropriately to update the outputs.

Simple devices are, obviously, the easiest to add. A knob or slider that had a limited range could be represented as an integer. A game joy stick that chooses between eight directions could be implemented as an active value that had values CENTER, N, NE, E, SE, S, SW, W or NW. A two-dimensional input device such as a tablet, touch tablet, or second mouse could be supported in a similar, straightforward manner, but additional mechanisms would probably be desirable, such as those provided for the primary mouse. It might be useful, for example, to be able to specify regions on the other device by demonstration and define different actions in different regions. The support for having different areas of touch tablets operate as different "virtual devices," discussed in [Buxton 85], could probably be provided in a demonstrational manner.

Some non-graphical input/output devices could even be attached to Peridot using the active value mechanism. For example, if a speech input device provided command codes or text strings, these could be put into an active value and the non-programmer designer could easily have them cause commands, change settings, supply parameters, etc. Similarly, a speech synthesizer could be driven by an active value, which the non-programmer designer could control.

10.4.3. The Clock

Some additional functionality would probably make the clock easier to use. For example, it might be helpful to allow the designer to move the mouse across the screen and calculate clock increments automatically to allow an object to move at that speed. Sequencing support would also help immensely, as discussed above.

10.5. Chapter Summary

Although Peridot only supports two input devices other than the mouse, this is sufficient to show that active values and demonstrational techniques can make it easy to handle multiple input devices operating at the same time. A few simple procedures provided by a programmer can be used by a non-programmer designer to create interesting interfaces with simple devices. Some extensions to Peridot, especially easier programming of active value updates and demonstrational sequencing, might allow the designer to use more input devices without any programming at all.

Chapter XI

Using Peridot-Created Procedures in Applications

11.1. Introduction

The features that have been described in the previous chapters make Peridot an excellent environment in which to prototype many types of highly interactive user interfaces. Peridot also aims to produce code that can be used in actual application programs, however. Therefore, designers are not necessarily just prototyping, they might be *implementing* the actual user interface code while designing. This chapter discusses how the code that Peridot creates is converted into procedures that applications can call. Peridot itself demonstrates that interfaces generated with the system can be used in actual applications, since it uses menus and other interfaces generated by Peridot (see Figures 3.1, 3.2, 3.6, 3.7, 3.11, 5.8, etc.).

While the designer is editing an interface, the interface is running "inside" Peridot. When the designer is happy with it, the interface can be written out so that it can run by itself "outside" Peridot. This is analogous to the mechanism for creating and editing files in a conventional text editor and then writing them out when finished[1].

When writing out a procedure, Peridot modifies the code somewhat so that the interface will be able to run outside of Peridot. In addition, the run time structures that are used when the procedure is running outside of Peridot are more efficient that those used while inside Peridot. This is because the back pointers and other information kept with objects to allow editing are not needed outside of Peridot.

11.2. User Interface for Writing Procedures

The user interface for writing out the Peridot-generated procedures is very simple; all of the interesting parts of this feature are in the implementation.

To write out a procedure, the designer gives the `Write-Procedure` Peridot command. The first step in designing an interface is to supply the name for

---

[1] Peridot currently does not support reading interfaces back in, as discussed in section 13.2.1.

the procedure, along with names and example values for the parameters and active values (as shown in Figure 3.15b). As a precaution, Peridot checks to see if a procedure by that name has already been defined and if so, asks the designer whether to overwrite the old definition of the procedure, abort the writing, or write the procedure with a different name. If the last option is chosen, then Peridot checks this new name to see if it has been defined previously, and gives the designer the same options. After the procedure is written, the designer can resume editing the interface and can write new versions at any time. If the designer tries to write out a procedure while an iteration or conditional is suspended, however, the writing is aborted because the interface is in an inconsistent state. The designer must either reinstantiate the iteration or conditional, or delete it.

When the designer gives the Exit command to leave Peridot, the system checks to see if the interface has been written out since it was last changed. If not, then the designer is queried as to whether to write out the procedure before exiting.

11.3. Implementation of Procedure Writing

The assignment of the code to a procedure name is very simple in Interlisp. Peridot generates the code for the interface in the correct form to be a procedure, and uses the Interlisp command (PUTD <name> <code>) which causes the code to be the function associated with the name. The function is then "marked" so that the Interlisp file system will recognize that it needs to be written to the disk.

The interesting part is that Peridot must modify the procedure before it is written out. This is required for two reasons. First, all of the names in Interlisp are global, and so the names for the objects when the procedure is run inside Peridot would conflict with the names for the objects used outside of Peridot. This would mean that the outside Peridot interaction could not be used at the same time as the inside Peridot interaction, which seems to be an unacceptable limitation. Therefore Peridot changes all of the names as the procedure is written out. The second reason that the procedure is modified is because the external version can use more efficient structures and mechanisms. Therefore, some of the embedded procedure calls that deal with inside structures (such as Field) must be changed to be procedures that know about the outside structures instead (RunField in this case).

11.3.1. Changing Object Names

When an attribute of an object depends on an attribute of another object, then the code for the first object contains references to the second object. For example, the code to create a white rectangle nested inside a black rectangle might be something like:

```
(CreateRectangle `WhiteRect0012
            0
            `(PLUS 5 (Field BlackRect0011 LEFT))
            `(PLUS 5 (Field BlackRect0011 BOTTOM))
            `(PLUS -10 (Field BlackRect0011 WIDTH))
            `(PLUS -10 (Field BlackRect0011 HEIGHT))
            `(INPUT . REPLACE))
```

The numbers appended to the end of the object names insure that each one is unique, as described in section 3.3.3.1. The objects created as a result of these operations exist within Peridot. When running outside Peridot, similar white and black rectangles will be needed, but the white rectangle outside Peridot should refer to the black rectangle outside Peridot, and not to the one inside Peridot. Therefore, Peridot adds a $ to all the names in the procedure. This changes the procedure to be:

```
(CreateRectangle `WhiteRect$0012
            0
            `(PLUS 5 (Field BlackRect$0011 LEFT))
            `(PLUS 5 (Field BlackRect$0011 BOTTOM))
            `(PLUS -10 (Field BlackRect$0011 WIDTH))
            `(PLUS -10 (Field BlackRect$0011 HEIGHT))
            `(INPUT . REPLACE))
```

Of course, the same operation is performed for generated names inside iterations and conditionals: `(Name `Iter0013 `A I)` becomes `(Name `Iter$0013 `A I)`. Fortunately, all the names have the same structure, so they can be easily found by looking at the atoms in the program.

11.3.2. Changing Function Names

Since the objects outside of Peridot have a different structure than the objects inside, the procedures that access this structure must be different[2]. Therefore functions, such as `Field`, are changed to their outside-Peridot equivalents. The final form for the procedure above would be:

---

[2] If Peridot had been constructed using a more complete object-oriented style, then this would probably not have been necessary, since the functions would be messages to the appropriate objects, and the objects would have different types inside and outside of Peridot.

```
(CreateRectangle `WhiteRect$0012
        0
        `(PLUS 5 (RunField BlackRect$0011 LEFT))
        `(PLUS 5 (RunField BlackRect$0011 BOTTOM))
        `(PLUS -10 (RunField BlackRect$0011 WIDTH))
        `(PLUS -10 (RunField BlackRect$0011 HEIGHT))
        `(INPUT . REPLACE))
```

Some other procedures that are changed are ReturnIterObjects, which returns a list of all the objects created by an iteration, and RunGetNameFor-SETActiveFromObj, which returns the iteration loop count and name for an object which is part of an iteration.

All of these are only used internally to Peridot, so there is no effect on application programs. Unfortunately, the SETActive procedure must also be different, since the structures it accesses are different. The external version, called RunSETActive, does not need to update the display of the active value (shown in the top window when inside Peridot). Therefore, application procedures that call SETActive have to be edited to call RunSETActive when they are used outside of Peridot.

11.3.3. Adding Extra Information

When the procedure is written out, some extra information is added to it so that the outside-Peridot procedure can be more efficient. This includes a list of which objects need to be changed when each active value is updated. Therefore, when the procedure is running, no searches of any kind are needed; the affected objects are simply redrawn when the active value changes.

Peridot also modifies the procedure to have three extra parameters: Window, WindowPosition, and ControlInfo. All graphics in Interlisp must be performed in windows, so at the top of the procedure, a call is added to create the window if it is passed in as NIL. At the end of the procedure, after all of the objects have been created, a call is added to draw all of the objects in the window and to begin running the interface. The ControlInfo parameter allows the application to specify some properties of the window. The next section discusses these extra parameters in detail.

11.4. The Window for Graphics

When inside Peridot, objects are obviously drawn in the Peridot drawing window (as in Figure 3.1). When outside Peridot, however, another window is needed in which to draw the graphics. This window is added as a parameter to the generated procedure. If the application supplies a window, then it will be used. If the application passes NIL, however, then a window will be automatically created at the position specified in the `WindowPosition` parameter. If `WindowPosition` is also `NIL`, then the end user places the window with the mouse.

An interesting issue is the placement of the graphics within the generated window. When the designer draws objects in Peridot, they have a fixed location with respect to the origin of the Peridot window. When the objects are later drawn in a window outside of Peridot, they would be in the same relative position with respect to the new window (see Figure 11.1a). This will typically not be correct, since the position in the Peridot window is usually arbitrary, and it is inconvenient to have to place the graphics at the lower left corner (the origin) of the Peridot window. Therefore, Peridot adjusts the origin of the created window so there will be no wasted space (Figure 11.1b).

(a)   (b)

Figure 11.1.
The graphics are placed at the same offset from the lower left corner in the created window as they were from the origin of the Peridot window, which leaves undesirable white space (a). Peridot fixes this by adjusting the origin of the created window (b).

If the application program supplies a window and if the position parameter is also non-`NIL`, then the `WindowPosition` is where the lower left corner of the graphics should go, and the positions of objects are adjusted accordingly. If the position parameter is NIL, then the objects are drawn with offsets in the new window exactly as the designer drew the objects in the Peridot window.

Another problem is calculating what size to make the generated window. Currently, its size is calculated to be just big enough to hold all of the graphics. Although this scheme usually calculates the correct size window, sometimes there are problems. The size of the window is calculated based on the initial value for all active values. When the active values change, the graphics might move in such a way as to require more room. For example, in Figure 11.2, the initial setting for CurrentColor was such that rectangles to show the current item are in the interior of the interface, and the window is just big enough to fit the background graphics. When CurrentColor is 1 or 8, however, the indicator is clipped because not enough room was left for it. Of course, this problem does not come up if the graphics that change are totally contained inside other graphics, which is usually the case (e.g. for conventional menus such as Figure 3.15). Of course, the designer could have provided an invisible rectangle big enough to fit over the entire picture. Other solutions to this problem are discussed in section 11.6.

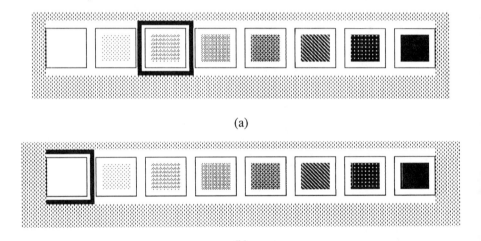

(a)

(b)

Figure 11.2.

The window for the interaction is just big enough for the background graphics (a), but when the active value changes to be 1 (b), the graphics are clipped because the window is not big enough.

Other automatic features provided by Peridot for use by the application are controlled using the parameter ControlInfo. These include whether the window will be a pop-up (and disappear when the interaction is complete) or permanent (stay around until explicitly removed), and whether the window background should be white or the picture that was underneath the window before it was created. This latter option is useful for pictures that are not rectangular, such as Figure 11.3 (all Interlisp-D windows must be rectangular).

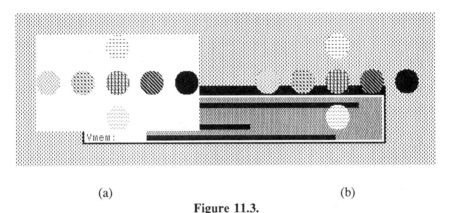

(a)   (b)

Figure 11.3.
A window erased to white (a) or set to the background picture (b) displaying the same interaction technique.

11.5. Outside Peridot Structures

The record structure for the objects used outside Peridot, which is shown in Figure 11.4, is similar to that used inside Peridot (Figure 3.14). The procedures for handling selection are missing, as well as the data for back references and the pointer from the object to the associated code. The fields that remain perform similar functions to the corresponding fields inside Peridot. The field names have been changed slightly to avoid name conflicts.

11.6. Extensions

Unfortunately, there are a number of problems with using the procedures created by Peridot in applications. Most of these deal with issues of modularization and separate name spaces. Interlisp-D does not provide modules or any other mechanism for preventing name conflicts, so, for example, the names of active values can conflict. In addition, the object names (e.g.

Field	Type	Usage
RMYNAME	LITATOM	The unique name given to this object; will contain a $
RMYTYPE	Enumerated Type	The type of the graphical primitive (one of Rectangle, Icon, Iteration, etc.)
RMYWINDOW	WINDOW	The window that this object is drawn in
RINSIDEPFN	FUNCTION	When passed a point, returns T if the point is inside this object
RDRAWFN	FUNCTION	Draws this object in its window
RERASEFN	FUNCTION	Erases this object
RDisplayedREGION	REGION numbers	Contains the numeric LEFT, BOTTOM, WIDTH and HEIGHT for this object if it is displayed
RSavedREGION	REGION expressions	Contains four expressions to calculate the DisplayedREGION field
RDrawFnc	Pair of Enumerated Types	Contains the Drawing Function to use when the object is drawn
RVAL	Anything	The current value (color, string, or bitmap) for this object
RVALReference	Expression	Expression to calculate VAL
RActiveP	BOOLEAN	Is this an active value?
ROtherInfo	Type-specific	Extra information needed by the type
RSubObjs	List of objects	If this object is an iteration or conditional, this lists the sub-objects
RRefIterVal	Pair of NUMBER, value	If a sub-object of an iteration or conditional, then the loop index and value for this object

Figure 11.4.

Fields for the object record used outside Peridot.

BlackRect$0011) for different instantiations of the *same* procedure will conflict, which means that it is illegal to use the same interaction technique more than once at the same time.

Solving these problems is clearly necessary for Peridot procedures to be used in real applications. However, solutions should not be difficult, especially if Peridot was reimplemented in a better structured environment which provides modules with separate name spaces (where the same procedure name can be linked to different routines based on explicit "import" and "export" facilities) such as in Common Lisp, Modula, or Ada. Perhaps even better would be to implement Peridot in a full object-oriented programming environment, such as Smalltalk. Lacking that, an indirect scheme could be used for naming objects, where the references would actually be indices into a list or array which holds pointers to the actual objects (in effect, creating separate symbol tables). This transformation could be done automatically when the procedure is written out so the designer would not be involved.

There is a similar problem with handling input devices. Interlisp-D does not provide a mechanism for allocating devices to windows. Unfortunately, this means, for example, that if two different interfaces both use the RS232 device, they will interfere with each other. This is true even if one of the interfaces is running inside of Peridot and one is running outside.

This problem could be easily solved by applying window management techniques. For example, the window which contained the mouse might be the only one that received RS232 and mouse events, or the devices might be explicitly allocated by the user or application program.

The size problem for created windows might be solved by having the designer or application program note the extreme values for active values that change and affect the picture size, and having the Peridot run-time calculate the size based on these. Alternatively, information about how much extra border area is needed could be explicitly specified.

A related problem deals with objects that can be dragged. If the designer does not provide a background area in which to drag the objects, then Peridot will not leave room for them to move. Usually, this will not be a problem since the application program will provide a window, or a background area will be provided, as in Figure 9.4. If all the objects are dragged together, and there are no other objects in the interface, then Peridot could automatically move the *window* for the interaction and leave the objects in the same relative place within the window. This is how icons, such as the simulated mouse, are moved in Interlisp. It would not be difficult to detect and handle this feature automatically in Peridot.

Another improvement would be to make the interactions run faster. Currently, objects being dragged stay almost with the mouse, and conditionals change very quickly. Unfortunately, there is a small but noticeable delay. It would be appropriate to expend some effort to speed up the outside-Peridot mechanisms so that all operations appear to occur ''instantaneously.'' This will probably not require any drastic changes, however.

Finally, the code produced by Peridot is not designed to be human-readable. Ideally, the code should never need to be read by people, since any changes should be made by reading the interface back into Peridot and editing it by demonstration[3]. It would be appropriate, however, for Peridot to generate comments and otherwise modify the code so it would be easier to read and

---

[3] Reading interfaces back in is not currently implemented in Peridot, however (see section 13.2.1).

modify, just in case this is ever necessary. A designer-readable representation for the expressions would clearly go a long way to solving this problem (section 13.2.6).

11.7. Chapter Summary

In addition to allowing the designer to prototype interfaces, Peridot also allows the interfaces to be written out as procedures that can be used by actual application programs. The implementation of writing out is complicated by a number of name-conflict problems, some of which have not been solved. These would be much easier to handle in an object-oriented environment or one that supported modules, but lacking that, solutions are available which would allow Peridot procedures to be used extensively in real application programs. Currently, the procedures can be used, as evidenced by their use in Peridot's own user interface, but some care is needed by the designer and application program to insure that no name conflicts arise.

Chapter XII
Visual Programming and
Example-Based Programming Aspects

12.1. Introduction

The previous chapters have presented all of Peridot's features from a functional viewpoint. This chapter takes a different view of the features and discusses the Visual Programming (VP) and Example-Based Programming (EBP) aspects. A number of VP and EBP systems were discussed in section 2.3. These systems have a number of problems and failures in common (summarized in [Myers 86a]), and this chapter discusses how Peridot addresses some of these.

In general, as discussed in section 1.5, Peridot uses these techniques successfully by limiting their domains. By carefully choosing what aspects of Visual Programming and Programming by Example to apply, Peridot avoids many of the problems with these techniques discussed in section 2.3.3.

12.2. Visual Programming

Section 1.1 defines "Visual Programming" (VP) as any system that allows the user to specify a program in a two (or more) dimensional fashion. Since Peridot allows the designer to create code by drawing pictures, it clearly qualifies as a Visual Programming system. Many previous Visual Programming systems have tried to use graphical techniques to support general-purpose programming, for example, using variants of flowcharts (e.g. [Glinert 84] [Pong 83 and 86] [Robillard 86]). These have mostly been unsuccessful because the representations have not been much more abstract than normal code and because textual code is much more compact. These systems often have trouble handling large programs or any "real-world" problems. Therefore, most of these systems have been limited to use by novice programmers. Not surprisingly, some of the systems expressly aimed at novice programmers have demonstrated some success. For example, Cunniff [86] reports that FPL helped novices learn to program.

Other Visual Programming systems have been designed for *non-*programmers, and some of these have been somewhat successful. Rehearsal World [Gould 84] allows non-programmer teachers to generate simulations of math problems, and OPAL [Musen 86] allows doctors to enter descriptions of cancer treatments. Peridot was also designed for non-programmers, and it, too, seems to be successful. The key to the success of these systems seems to be limiting the domain that the system is trying to address. Writing code in a general purpose language still seems to be the best way to provide full generality and power. However, when the user does not need this flexibility and the system can concentrate on providing a limited set of functions in an appropriate manner that is natural to the user, then Visual Programming systems can succeed.

In Peridot, the domain is creating graphical interfaces. This has proven to be an ideal candidate for Visual Programming since the result of the program (the user interface) is mostly graphical. Also, the majority of the operations that the designer wants to perform in Peridot have concrete and natural representations on the screen. Therefore, the representation of the program, which is the final graphical user interface, is readily understandable. The alternative Lisp-code representation of the program has not proven necessary for designers, since the graphical form contains sufficient information.

The iterations and conditionals in Peridot are more abstract and do not have graphical representations on the screen. This is not a problem, however, because the visible output graphics are naturally associated with the abstractions. In addition, it is generally not necessary for the designer to remember which graphics come from iterations and conditionals and which do not, since they all can be edited directly and the control structures are mostly created and maintained automatically by Peridot.

Mouse dependencies and application procedure attachments are even more abstract, and these do not have any direct visible representations. The designer must either exercise the interface or explicitly request that these be listed in order to know what has been created. This has not been a problem, however, because the design time is short enough, and the programs are small enough, that the designer does not forget what has been created.

One of the serious problems of many Visual Programming systems is that they cannot handle large programs due to a lack of modularization and the large screen area that is required for the visual representation of the program. In Peridot, this is not a problem since the visual representation is typically two to three times *smaller* than the code representation (measured by comparing the length of the picture to the length of the code printed in the same width window). In addition, Peridot creates parameterized procedures that can be combined into full interfaces, so that the designer can create interfaces out of small, modular, well-structured pieces.

In summary, on the problems with Visual Programming listed in section 2.3.3.1, Peridot addresses:

(1) Difficulty with large programs or large data: Peridot's pictures are smaller than normal code and are appropriately parameterized.

(2) Lack of functionality: Appendix A shows that Peridot can create a wide variety of interfaces, and this is the only domain that it is designed for.

(3) Inefficiency: Procedure generated by Peridot run acceptably fast, and Peridot uses its own Peridot-created procedures.

(4) Unstructured programs: Peridot creates appropriately parameterized procedures that can return values.

(5) Static representations of programs that are hard to understand: The picture of the interface is easy to create, but there is no good static representation of the code (see section 13.2.6).

(6) No place for comments: Not addressed.

12.3. Example-Based Programming

As explained in section 1.1, "Example-Based Programming" (EBP) refers to systems that allow the programmer to use examples of input and output data during the programming process. When the systems try to *infer* the program from the examples, then the systems are called "Programming *by* Example" (PBE). Systems without inferencing are called "Programming *with* Example" (PWE). Peridot requires the designer to give examples of values for parameters and active values, and uses the type of the examples to infer generalizations. In addition, Peridot infers control structures, how actions should depend on the mouse, and the relationships among graphical objects drawn on the screen. Therefore, Peridot is a Programming by Example system. However, it also has features in common with some PWE systems.

As with most Example-Based systems, Peridot allows the designer to use explicit specification when the example-based mechanisms do not work. For example, the designer can use the `ChangePropBySpec` command to explicitly define object-object relationships, and the `Iteration` command can be given for explicitly selected objects. Unlike previous systems, however, Peridot provides this option without reverting to a programming language. In Rehearsal World [Gould 84], Thinglab [Borning 79], and Smallstar [Halbert 81], the user must use a programming language when the example-based mechanisms do not work (Smalltalk is used for the first two and an invented language is used in Smallstar). Peridot does allow the escape into a programming language (using

active values) as a final option, of course, but at least there is an attempt to provide an explicit method which will work in most cases and that does not require
programming.

12.3.1. Programming-With-Example Aspects

Allowing the designer to work on example data while developing an interface with Peridot is a crucial component. Otherwise, the designer could not see
what the interface would look like. The examples allow the design process to
be concrete and direct, rather than abstract. The interface seems more like a
paint program, such as Apple MacDraw, rather than a programming system.
This feature depends primarily on the ability to refer to the example values for
parameters and active values. Since these references are specified explicitly by
the designer, this feature of Peridot does not depend on inferencing in order to
work.

12.3.2. Programming-By-Example Aspects: Plausible Inferencing

The inferencing aspects of Peridot are also important, however. Some
early PBE systems attempted to infer general programs and these were mostly
unsuccessful, as discussed in section 2.3. As with Visual Programming, the
systems that have had more limited domains have been more successful, such as
Editing by Example [Nix 85] for editing. Peridot limits inferencing to the
domain of graphical user interfaces, and the inferencing is reasonably successful, even though it uses very simple techniques. Another contributor to the success of Peridot in this area is that the programs being created deal with very
concrete objects, such as rectangles and strings, rather than abstract concepts,
which makes the inferencing easier for the system to perform and for the
designer to verify. The next sections discuss the various uses of inferencing in
Peridot.

12.3.2.1. How Examples are Used

Many PBE systems require the user to provide multiple examples in order
to generate code. In most cases Peridot infers code from single examples. This
is possible because the designer is required to explicitly give a command to
cause Peridot to perform the inferencing. Examples of this are conditionals and
mouse dependencies. For iterations, however, the designer is required to give
two examples, and Peridot can therefore usually infer the need for an iteration
without an explicit command from the user. If Peridot were extended so the
designer could demonstrate exceptions for iterations and the mouse, then this
would involve giving extra examples. These are sometimes called ''negative
examples'' since they show the system what *not* to do.

12.3.2.2. How Rules Are Used

The rules in Peridot are very simple; much simpler than those used in typical Artificial Intelligence (AI) systems. The goal was to see if simple mechanisms would be sufficient, which seems to be true. Some extensions to the rule mechanism discussed in section 4.6, such as best-fit rather than first-fit, would decrease the number of incorrect guesses, but this would still be a simple system. Much of the complications of true rule-based "Expert Systems," such as learning, explaining, and back-tracking, are simply not needed when there are only 50 rules.

12.3.2.3. Object-Object Relationships

As discussed in Chapter 4, Peridot infers how the various objects are related to each other. To do this, Peridot uses an extremely simple rule-based mechanism. Previous picture beautification systems, such as [Pavlidis 85], have had similar goals but have not used an explicit system for representing the relationships. One reason for Peridot's success is that the relationships of graphical objects in user interfaces is more limited than it would be in a general drawing package. Peridot incorporates only the relationships that are commonly used in user interfaces. If the designer wants other relationships, they can be explicitly specified or, if they occur frequently, a programmer can easily add them to the rule set. Another reason for Peridot's success is that it assumes that guesses will occasionally be wrong. Therefore, it always reports to the designer the guesses that it is planning to apply and allows the designer to confirm or prevent their application. This gives the designer confidence that the system is not mysteriously doing strange and possibly erroneous things. In addition, the results of the inferences are always immediately visible (the objects redraw themselves after every rule is applied), so the designer can view the results and see whether they were correct or not.

12.3.2.4. Variables vs. Constants

Some systems, such as [Bauer 78], attempt to infer from an example trace what should be variables and what should be constants in the program. To avoid this problem, Smallstar [Halbert 84] requires the user to edit a textual representation of the program to specify what are constants and what are variables. In this area, Peridot is more similar to Bauer's system because it automatically distinguishes constants from variables in iterations, conditionals, and object-object relationships. When an object depends on a parameter to the procedure or an active value, however, the designer must explicitly declare this.

For graphical objects, Peridot attempts to infer what attributes are constant and what attributes should depend on other objects, as discussed in the previous section. In iterations, Peridot compares each pair of objects and determines which attributes change and which are constant. For the attributes that change, Peridot only detects straightforward differences (section 6.4.2), such as depending on the iteration variable, changing as constants, or using the second relationship for all subsequent items. This, along with the fact that a very simple matching algorithm is used to identify which objects are in each group, makes this inferencing fairly straightforward. On the other hand, the designer is required to create objects in a particular way, or the iterations cannot be inferred, as discussed in the next section.

Even though the designer must specify that parameters and active value dependencies exist, Peridot automatically infers how they should be used. This inferencing is fairly simple, however, and is based mainly on the type of the parameter (list, string, number, etc.). Typically, there are only about eight choices from which Peridot chooses for this inference.

12.3.2.5. Control Structures

Like Bauer's system and unlike Smallstar, Peridot automatically infers when an iteration is appropriate. Again, the criterion for this in Peridot is very easy to understand. Systems such as Bauer's have a great deal of difficulty calculating how things change for each iteration, but Peridot's mechanism has been very successful. Again, this is due to the limited domain; graphical objects in user interfaces typically change in very simple ways in iterations. If Peridot detects that an iteration is plausible but it cannot calculate how to change the objects, the designer is notified. Clearly, the designer will have to be careful to create objects in the correct order so that Peridot will be able to create the iteration, but the copy command and other mechanisms promote this.

Peridot automatically infers conditionals when an object depends on the mouse. It is conceivable that Peridot could infer conditionals in some other cases also, for example, when a graphical object is drawn that depends on an iteration, as discussed in section 7.5. Peridot does infer how the conditional depends on the controlling parameter.

The situations under which mouse interactions occur are also a form of control structure. Peridot automatically infers when actions should happen based on the demonstration with the simulated mouse buttons, and where actions should happen based on the simulated mouse position. This information is converted into a test which is used to determine when the action should take place. Again, these inferences are very simple due to the very limited number of possibilities.

12.3.2.6. *Mouse Operations*

When a set of objects is defined to depend on the mouse (using the explicit MOUSEDependent command), Peridot infers when the interaction should happen, as described in the previous section, and also how the objects depend on the mouse and what should be done. Objects can depend on the mouse as conditionals, linear interpolations, or for dragging or size changing. The determination of which to use is generally defined by the previously specified dependencies of the objects themselves. For example, the designer must have explicitly set up a linear interpolation on the object for this option to be inferred.

12.3.2.7. *Exceptions*

One place that programming by example should be used, but is not currently, is to define exceptions to iterations and mouse interactions. The designer should be able to demonstrate an additional example and the system would notice that the example given is incompatible with the program that has already been inferred. It would then try to figure out what is different and how to tell when each of the different behaviors should happen. This possibility is discussed more fully in sections 6.5.2 and 9.10.3

12.3.2.8. *Other Possible Uses*

In addition to exceptions, there are a large number of other parts of Peridot where programming by example could be applied. When defining a mouse interaction, the designer could demonstrate whether the action should be continuous or discrete by moving objects around, rather than having this decision encoded in the button state. Similarly, the designer might demonstrate what operation should be performed when the mouse goes outside the objects.

Two other places where programming by example could be used instead of explicit specification are the criterion under which to call an application program (section 8.10), and how a mouse action should update a boolean conditional (section 3.2.2). It would be interesting to explore the possibility of making these and other parts of the Peridot user interface more demonstrational.

12.3.3. Example-Based Programming Summary

In summary, on the problems with Programming *with* Example systems listed in section 2.3.3.2, Peridot addresses:

(1) Lack of static representation: The interface running on example values is a partial static representation, but there are no others, except the normal Interlisp code.

(2) Problem with editing programs: Peridot allows full editing by demonstration.

(3) Problem with data description: Peridot requires the designer to explicitly specify the choice between having values be constant or depend on parameters or active values, and uses inferencing to guess other dependencies.

(4) Problem with control structure: Peridot supports only simple control structures that can be programmed by demonstration, but these are sufficient for the domain.

(5) Lack of functionality: Peridot uses Example-Based Programming for many aspects and explicit specification when this fails. Resorting to actual programming is also possible, but is rarely necessary.

(6) Avoiding the destruction of real data or other undesirable consequences: Not addressed since not applicable.

On the problems with Programming *by* Example systems listed in section 2.3.3.3, Peridot addresses:

(1) Hard to choose appropriate examples: The example values in Peridot are only used to define the *type* of the actual data, so the choice is much easier. Peridot always confirms with the designer the inferences made based on the types.

(2) Difficult to insure correct programs: Peridot always prints a message describing every inference and requires the designer to confirm its use. The results are always displayed or executable immediately. These techniques appear to mostly eliminate this problem.

12.4. Chapter Summary

In Peridot, Visual Programming allows the designer to use the appropriate graphical techniques to specify graphical entities. Example-based programming allows the designer to see the interface on example data as it is being developed, which is a critical feature of Peridot. The designer gives two examples for iterations and only one example in all other cases, to allow Peridot to generate the code. Inferencing helps to limit the number of options the designer must specify and helps to promote correct programs (since the designer is only asked about plausible options). A system similar to Peridot could be implemented without inferencing, but without either Visual Programming or Example-Based Programming, it would be a far different, and I believe significantly inferior, system.

Any system design is going to involve a set of compromises and decisions. Peridot uses Visual Programming and Programming by Example techniques in some places and not in others. Design decisions were based on an evaluation of what seemed to be easiest for the user interface designer, and what was feasible to implement with available technology. Where Visual Programming and Programming by Example have been applied in Peridot, they have generally been successful, which suggests that it is appropriate to investigate other areas in which to apply these techniques.

Chapter XIII

Future Work

13.1. Introduction

Although Peridot allows interfaces to be prototyped, edited, and used in actual application programs, it is clearly not ready to be a commercial product. There is a great deal that could be done to make the current Peridot system better, and the development of Peridot has suggested some new approaches and areas of research that might be profitably investigated in the future.

Extensions to the basic features of Peridot have been discussed in each of the previous chapters, and they will generally not be repeated here. This chapter takes a broader view and discusses more global changes. In addition, some ideas for future research are presented.

13.2. Additional Features for Peridot

This section lists some additional features that could easily be added to Peridot to make it more functional. These do not involve radical changes to Peridot's user interface or implementation.

13.2.1. Reading-In Interfaces

An important feature that is missing from Peridot is the ability to read interfaces back into Peridot after they have been written out. The interfaces can be used by applications, and they can be edited while they are being created. However, after the designer has exited Peridot, the interface cannot be edited again, unless it is re-entered from scratch. As discussed in section 11.2, the designer is free to continue editing after writing out an interface as long as Peridot is not exited. This would allow the designer to try out the interface in the application while saving the current Peridot session in case further editing is needed.

There is no question that any "real" system would require the ability to read in interfaces for further editing. This feature was not added to Peridot because it did not present any interesting research questions, and due to time constraints on Peridot's implementation.

Currently, the written versions of the procedures do not contain enough information to allow them to be read back in. For example, all of the back references are thrown away since they are not needed at run time. Peridot should generate another data structure that describes all of this information which would be written out with the executable procedure.

A designer might read in an interface for two reasons. First, the interface might need further editing. The second possibility is that the designer wants to incorporate the interface into a larger interface. For example, a scroll bar interaction might be used as part of a window interface. In this case, the interaction being read might not be editable, and only its externally available attributes, such as overall size and position, could be specified. The interaction would be treated as a single graphical object, and operations on it would be similar to those on rectangles, circles, etc. This would allow Peridot to perform some of the functions of "glue systems," as discussed in section 2.2.1.

13.2.2. Handling the Keyboard

Currently, Peridot will handle text output, but not keyboard input. It would be simple to add the keyboard as a giant button box (with an active value that has one boolean for every key) or a stream device (with an active value that has one element for the last key typed). This would allow special keys to be easily processed (e.g. STOP or Control-C), but would require a number of application procedures to be attached to the active value to process the keys so they could be used for text input. For example, some sort of editing of the characters would be desirable, so that the end user could type a string and use backspace, control-W (delete previous word), etc. to fix typing errors. It would be very interesting to investigate whether the types of editing allowed could be specified by demonstration, especially if editing the text characters using the mouse was supported.

Once an edited text input facility is provided, Peridot could be extended to handle various kinds of computer-based forms. New object-object inferencing rules could be added to support the kinds of rectangle and string relationships that are used in forms. The extension to iterations to handle two-dimensions would probably also be useful. The active value mechanism would allow application programs to deal with semantic error checking and semantic defaults. For example, when the active value for one field is set, an application program might be called to calculate the appropriate default value to be put into another field's active value. The display of the default would then be handled automatically. Of course, the application would be independent of the way the data in fields were entered and displayed. For example, the designer could use a graphical slider for a numeric field (or provide both a slider and text input which set the same active value so the user could choose which one to use) and the application would not be affected.

13.2.3. Specifying General Expressions Instead of Constants

In general, when Peridot requests a number from the designer, it would be appropriate to allow the designer to type an arbitrary expression instead. Even a non-programmer designer would probably know some arithmetic, so this would not necessarily violate the spirit of Peridot. The expressions might allow the designer to use two or more other objects, active values or parameters, although this would make it difficult to insure that there is always a one-pass evaluation order for the attributes. To provide a non-textual way to reference objects, the designer might select them and then select which attribute to use from a menu.

13.2.4. Top and Bottom Commands

Currently, there are no editing commands for changing the order of objects after they have been created. This severely limits the kinds of editing that can be performed, since there is no way to add a new object underneath (covered by) an old object. Two different features should probably be added. The first would allow an object to be selected before a new object is created, and then the new object would go just below (or above) the selected object in the drawing order. The second feature would allow an object to be selected and moved up or down in the drawing order, either by increments (e.g., move 3 places up), or to be before or after a selected object. Since the calculation order for attributes of objects can be either forwards or backwards, none of the attributes of any objects should need to be changed.

The one complication for this command is the hierarchical objects for iterations and conditionals. When editing these, all of the objects appear to be at the same level to the designer (the objects that are from the suspended iteration or conditional can be selected and edited just like all other objects). In order to maintain the illusion of a single, flat list of objects, the commands for changing drawing order would have to move the object in and out of the iterations and conditionals. If the designer attempted to move the object to be inside of a normal (un-suspended) conditional or iteration, the designer would be asked whether to jump across the entire conditional or iteration, or whether it should be suspended.

13.2.5. Better Integration of Features

In most cases, the various features of Peridot fit together very well and form a well-integrated system. Unfortunately, there are a few places where further work is needed. For example, the Copy command does not check to see how the objects being copied were created. The result of the copy is always a straight-line sequence of primitive "create" operations. If the objects being copied were part of an iteration or conditional, however, Peridot should probably copy the entire operation as a unit. This would not be easy, however, since the code in the iteration or conditional would have to be modified to insure that the new objects were displayed in the correct new place.

Similarly, an iteration over a linear interpolation, a mouse dependency over a conditional, and conditionals based on other conditionals probably should all be supported for consistency.

13.2.6. Designer-Readable Code Representation

Currently, the code generated by Peridot is in Interlisp-D. This is clearly unreadable for a non-programmer designer, but it is easier for Peridot. It turns out that the code has a very simple structure and it would probably be easy to generate a language that the designer could understand. This would help the designer verify that the system has inferred the correct generalizations and the correct graphical constraints. It is important to note that the designer would never be required to look at the code, and, most importantly, would never need to try to generate code by hand. Even if the designer tries to understand the code in order to verify interfaces, this is a long way from being required to type in correct programs. Of course, if desired, the designer could be allowed to edit the code directly, which would cause the display to be updated accordingly, as in Juno [Nelson 85]. This would probably be used primarily to adjust constants, rather than for adding new control structures as in Smallstar [Halbert 84]. Other advantages of a designer-readable code representation are discussed in section 4.6.7.

13.3. Implementation Changes

Most of the implementation changes are discussed in the previous chapters. The three main global improvements would be to use better data structures, to use a more object-oriented approach, and to change the way regions are represented.

13.3.1. Data Structures

Peridot uses the Interlisp list data structure for most of its internal data representation. This has some disadvantages. Most of the data in Peridot is fixed-length lists with particular types of data in each element, so a hierarchical record structure as in Pascal would have been very useful. Interlisp records are used to describe the graphical objects, but unfortunately, the record structures in Interlisp have proved inadequate for handling general Peridot data (see section

14.2.2.2). Most of the data structures in Peridot use both forward and backward links, and again the Interlisp mechanisms for dealing with these are inadequate. If Peridot were reimplemented in a structured language (section 13.4), many of these problems would be eliminated.

13.3.2. Data Abstraction Style

Peridot uses an object-oriented style to some extent, but there are far too many places that have knowledge about particular data structures. If a full data-abstraction or object-oriented style had been used, the design would have been a lot clearer and easier to modify. For example, there are many different procedures that deal with the editing of the generated code, and currently all of these know about the length of the primitive create statements. An object-oriented programming style would have made it much easier to add new parameters to these create statements (it was unreasonably difficult, for example, to add the multi-font capabilities for strings for this reason).

Another advantage of a fully object-oriented style would be that there would be more flexibility for designers to intermix types. Currently, for example, an iteration can be over icons or strings, but not both, even though they have virtually the same parameters and properties. If the create statement was object-oriented, it is conceivable that many such type restrictions could be relaxed.

13.3.3. Changing the Region Representation

Currently all regions in Peridot are represented by the lower-left corner and a width and height. This makes many object-object inferencing rules unsymmetric. For example, the rule for having one object connected to the bottom of another object is simple, but the rule for having one object connected to the top of another involves the bottoms and the heights of both objects. It might be simpler if regions were represented by opposite corners (although this would require rewriting vast quantities of code). The adding of straight lines to Peridot might be facilitated since lines are also most naturally represented as two points. On the other hand, strings and icons have fixed widths and heights, and so it is more natural to represent them with a corner and a size. If Peridot were being re-implemented, it would be interesting to investigate which approach was more natural overall, and whether the two approaches could be used together.

In addition, if objects were added that cannot be represented by rectangles, such as arbitrary polygons or curved lines, the basic structures would need to be changed.

13.4. Reimplementing Peridot in Another Language

Section 14.2 discusses the advantages and disadvantages of the Interlisp-D environment for the original creation of Peridot as a research project. This section discusses issues of re-implementing Peridot in another language.

The problems with data structures and data abstraction discussed above (section 13.3.1) would obviously be alleviated by using an object-oriented language like Smalltalk [Goldberg 83] or possibly even Lisp add-ons such as Loops [Stefik 83] or Flavors [Weinreb 80]. Using a structured language like Pascal would also help, however, and the data abstraction programming methodology could be used to better organize the program.

Since Peridot is basically a code generator, it benefited immensely from Interlisp's ability to generate code and then execute it. For example, all of the object-object relationships are created and calculated by CONSing up code and then executing it. If Peridot were reimplemented in a language that did not have a built in interpreter, this would clearly not be possible. In that case, an interpreter would have to be written. On the other hand, most of the code that Peridot creates and executes is composed of simple arithmetic expressions with variables and constants, and these would be particularly easy to write an interpreter for. If, in addition, a designer-readable code representation (section 13.2.6) was designed, then an interpreter would be needed anyway.

One important feature that would probably be sacrificed if Peridot was implemented in a compiled language is the ability to execute application procedures attached to active values while developing the interface. Currently, Peridot prompts the designer to type in the name of the procedure, and then simply EVALs a call to the procedure when appropriate. Most compiled languages do not support this dynamic linking so it would be impossible to call application programs until the interface was written out and compiled.

Based on an earlier version of this book, a student, Daniel Green at the University of Illinois at Urbana-Champaign, implemented a C version of Peridot on an Amiga called "C-Peridot" [Green 88]. Additional features in his version are colors, changing the drawing-order of objects, ellipses instead of circles, arbitrary arithmetic expressions for objects' attributes, and the ability to read in interfaces for further editing. C-Peridot does not support the Run-Procedure command or multiple clicking on mouse buttons, and active values, iterations, and input device handling are all a little less general than in the original Peridot. This implementation does prove that it is possible to create a program like Peridot in a conventional compiled environment.

13.5. "Productizing" Peridot

Obviously, Peridot is just a research prototype and is not appropriate for use by real designers for real projects. In addition to the extensions and bug fixes listed above and in previous chapters, a number of other changes would have to be made to make the system more complete. Peridot would have to be made more robust, with better error detection and recovery. For example, if the designer manages to create a recursive dependency among objects, this is duly reported, after which Peridot crashes and the interface must be re-created from scratch. There are a few other places where incorrect designer actions can cause Peridot to crash and these would have to be eliminated.

In addition, of course, Peridot would require an extensive manual and other training aids, help messages, and other user-friendly features such as "undo," so that designers would find it easier to use.

13.6. New Implementation Structure

Peridot was developed using experimental programming [Sheil 83], and its current implementation is not very well structured. If Peridot was to be used as a "real" UIMS, it should be completely reimplemented from scratch. This section provides some hints about what the new implementation structure might be.

As recommended in section 13.3.2, each graphical entity would be represented by an "object" in the object-oriented programming (Smalltalk) sense. The messages to this object would include those in Figure 3.14. In addition, there would be a set of messages to edit the attributes of the object. The graphical constraints would be stored with each object in a designer-readable form (section 13.2.6). Backward references would not be saved; they would be generated from the constraints when needed. Hopefully, the use of an object-oriented style would make the code conversion described in Chapter 11 unnecessary. The code generated should be runnable inside and outside Peridot without modification.

The graphical constraint inferencing would use a best-fit algorithm (section 4.6.2) and the rules and their ordering would be expressed in a designer-readable form (sections 4.6.3 and 4.6.4). The inferencing mechanism would be isolated from the rest of the system so it could be replaced with a different mechanism easily, and even turned on and off by the designer.

Editing operations would still be implemented as separate modules, as shown in the implementation overview of Figure 3.13. These operations should be easier to implement, however, because the actual data structure and code manipulation would be handled internally by the graphical objects.

The iteration and conditional control structures would also be implemented in a similar manner as currently, although they might be better integrated so that conditionals could act as exceptions for iterations. The general structure for active values also does not need major revision.

A new design for the mouse dependencies would require the most research. Making the basic mouse behaviors more explicit might make the design easier. Finding more direct ways to specify the behaviors (section 9.8) will have a large impact on future implementations of this part of the system.

13.7. Areas for Further Research

In addition to pointing out places where the current system could be improved, work on Peridot has uncovered many interesting areas for future research. In general, Peridot has demonstrated that Visual Programming, Programming by Example, Constraints and Plausible Inferencing can be successfully used in the construction of user interfaces. One important challenge is to find other domains in which these techniques can be applied.

13.7.1. Taxonomy of Interaction Techniques and Input Device Use

Work on inferring the mouse interactions clearly highlights the lack of a good taxonomy of possible ways a mouse or other input device can control a value (see section 15.2).

A closely related topic is the issue of handling input devices in general. It is clear that the input model used by PHIGS, GKS, CORE, etc. is not sufficient for modern interfaces, but no new models are being proposed [Myers 87b]. In addition to UIMSs, the efforts at creating new window manager standards (X, NeWS, and the X3H3.6 effort) are all being hurt by this deficiency in the field.

13.7.2. Abstract Behavior of Interactions

A closely related area is the identification of basic interaction behaviors, and how to use these to create a UIMS. Peridot supports conditionals, linear-interpolations, and unconstrained dragging and changing size as the basic behaviors, but it is clear that this is not comprehensive. Alternatively, it may be helpful to have a higher level description of behavior (c.g. menu, scroll bar) or lower level (locate, move, etc.) instead. Only by providing abstractions of the basic behaviors separate from their graphical representations is it possible to provide a system that provides adequate flexibility for creating different kinds of direct manipulation style interfaces.

13.7.3. Semantic Feedback

Another general issue that needs more research is the issue of handling semantic feedback in user interfaces [Myers prep]. Peridot provides semantic feedback through active values, but the calculation of the feedback has to be written in a conventional programming language. Other recent UIMSs, such as HIGGENS [Hudson 86] provide some support for the calculation of this feedback, but more work needs to be done. A recent UIMS workshop emphasized this as an important research area [Dance 87].

13.7.4. Application Output and Related Semantic Input

Some forms of semantic feedback are difficult to provide in Peridot. These include ones that require knowledge about the output that an application produces and any input events that are directly tied to that output. Peridot can handle some forms of output that most other UIMSs would consider to be solely the responsibility of the application. Examples include the square that the user can move around in Figure 10.1 and the logic gates in Figure 9.4. The interactions that Peridot supports on these objects include picking, moving, and changing size.

Unfortunately, there are many desired types of output and operations on that output that Peridot cannot handle. For example, in the logic simulator of Figure 9.4, Peridot might be easily extended to handle the placing of the logic gates. However, it would require a great deal of conventional coding to handle the placing of the wires between gates and for any editing operations on those wires available to the end user. A similar problem occurs for the end user selection operation in a text editor. Here, a block of text might be selected by dragging the mouse across it while a mouse button was held down. This cannot be handled by a system like Peridot without a great deal of application-supplied code. Other forms of input that require substantial knowledge of the semantics to process, such as gestural interfaces, also are not addressed by Peridot.

13.7.5. Sequencing in Direct Manipulation Interfaces

Initially it appears that direct manipulation interfaces have little need for tools to manage sequencing. This is because they have little syntax, and because existing syntax-based tools have been unable to handle direct manipulation style interfaces. The Peridot effort, however, shows that sequencing is still an important issue in these interfaces and cannot be ignored. One interaction follows another, and the various parts of a single interaction often happen in a particular order. New techniques for specifying sequencing for direct manipulation interfaces should be investigated. It would be especially beneficial if these techniques did not require programming knowledge. For example, a menu hierarchy, where each menu selection causes a different menu to appear, could be specified entirely by demonstration.

13.7.6. The Use of Inferencing in User Interfaces

Most systems that attempt to help the user through the use of inferencing or "intelligence" have been unsuccessful because the users perceive that the system is too often in error, and that it is difficult to detect and recover from these errors. Peridot demonstrates that this does not have to be the case. Although the sample size is obviously very small, the 10 designers who have used Peridot reported that the inferencing was helpful and not annoying. This is due to the careful design that assumed that the system would occasionally guess incorrectly.

The implication is that automatic inferencing would be beneficial in many other types of systems. An obvious example is in drawing packages where the "beautifying" properties of Peridot's inferencing can be directly applied. The automatic inferencing of iterations would be very useful for repetitive structures in many areas, for example, the placement of windows on a building in an architectural design program. Many other applications are also possible, even with the very simple and error-prone inferencing systems that are available today. Peridot's technique of asking questions after each inference might be successful in these other systems, but this will depend on two factors: how much work the user does in between inferences, and how much benefit the user perceives the inferencing providing. Clearly, as "expert systems" get better, there will be even more uses for intelligence in user interfaces.

13.7.7. The Use of Inferencing for Design Rules

One intriguing aspect of UIMSs where Peridot's rule-based inferencing might be applied is the evaluation of user interfaces. To the extent that user interface design rules can be codified, the system might apply them to check how "good" the interface was and propose ways to improve it. These rules might come from graphics design, cognitive psychology, ergonomics, etc. It appears, however, that most existing rules are too vague to be applied in this manner.

13.7.8. Example-Based Programming in Direct Manipulation Interfaces

A related topic is the application of Example-Based Programming techniques to allow end users to write programs in direct manipulation style interfaces. This is the capability that Smallstar [Halbert 84] provided in a non-inferencing manner, but it has never been used in a commercial system. One of the chief problems in direct manipulation systems is that the user has no way to create macros and program the interface to make common activities easier to specify. Example-Based Programming can allow the user to write programs by simply giving the commands normally while in "program mode." Some of the simple inferencing techniques in Peridot might be applied so the user does not need to learn a programming language for specifying control structures. For example, the system might be able to guess when an iteration is desired, and what changes in each cycle of the loop. Differentiating what should be constants and what should be variables is another important problem that might be handled automatically using techniques from Peridot.

13.7.9. Further Use of Active Values

Previous work has demonstrated that active values are very useful for attaching visual displays to simulations, both for monitoring and control (see section 2.4.2). Peridot demonstrates that active values are also useful in user interface construction. It seems clear that they would also be appropriate in many other areas. For example, one important problem with some program visualization systems that animate changes in data structures [Myers 86a] is that the code must usually be modified to insert calls to update the display when the data changes (e.g., in Balsa [Brown 84]). If the data were stored as active values, however, then no modification of the program code would be necessary.

13.8. Chapter Summary

There are a large number of features that could be added to Peridot to make it more functional, easier to use, easier to maintain, and faster. These include reading in previously created interfaces, handling text input, supporting general expressions instead of constants, commands for changing the drawing order, better integration of some features, a designer-readable representation of the generated program, and reimplementing Peridot using a data-abstraction style. Peridot could probably be reimplemented in a Pascal-like language fairly easily but an interpreter would be needed.

The research on Peridot has highlighted some areas that need further research, including classifying and handling interaction techniques and input devices in an abstract manner, semantic feedback, sequencing in direct manipulation interfaces, the use of inferencing in user interfaces, and the use of Example-Based Programming techniques for end user programming of direct manipulation interfaces.

Chapter XIV
Experience with Peridot

14.1. Introduction

This chapter discusses experience with implementing Peridot and experience with using Peridot

14.2. Experience with Implementing Peridot

Peridot was implemented in the Intermezzo version of the Interlisp-D [Xerox 83] Lisp system on the Xerox 1109 DandeTiger workstation. Peridot is comprised of about 450 procedures which require nearly 800K bytes of Interlisp source code, which takes over 300 paper pages to print out. The compiled binary for Peridot is about 360K bytes. This was clearly a rather large programming project, and this section discusses the appropriateness of the environment for implementing Peridot. In summary, the interpretive, multi-processing, multi-window nature of Interlisp made it ideal for this type of research programming, and, although there are many bugs and problems with Interlisp, I would not have traded it for the best-designed compiler-oriented environment.

14.2.1. Positive Aspects

Creating Peridot was very much a research effort, and the design for the system evolved significantly as the implementation progressed. Lisp is an ideal environment for this type of exploratory programming [Sheil 83]. Due to its interpretive nature, it is much easier to try out different possibilities quickly and see how they work.

The multi-window and multi-processing facilities in Interlisp are also crucial components. The ability to simultaneously edit the program in one window while executing it in another, and having the excellent source-level debugger running in a third window, greatly facilitated the development of the code. Usually, edits to the program would take effect immediately, without even requiring Peridot to be re-started. The windows and multiple processes are also used internally by Peridot. When running Peridot, many windows are used, and the generated procedures run outside Peridot in separate windows. Multi-processing is used to handle multiple input devices and to provide the animation which shows the current selection.

The fact that the language is interpreted also made the development of Peridot much faster. No time was wasted waiting for compilation, and any part of the system could be modified without concern about how much code would have to be recompiled as a result of the change (in contrast, if the system had been implemented in a language with strong typing, a change in a basic data structure would probably have required recompiling the entire system, which might have taken several hours). Also, when demonstration versions of Peridot were prepared, the program could be run through the Interlisp compiler. This generated efficient code so that it was rarely necessary to worry about performance during the development of Peridot.

One important function that Peridot performs is to generate code. Interlisp's built-in interpreter made this much easier because the generated code could be easily run inside of Peridot (by simply using EVAL). The simple form for Interlisp code made the code generation process much easier. EVAL was also important for allowing application-defined procedures to be called at design time, as discussed in section 13.4.

Other important features of the Interlisp-D environment were the support for graphics and the mouse. Peridot makes extensive use of the graphical output for drawing shaded rectangles, circles, etc., and the mouse is heavily used in Peridot. Also, the Interlisp facility that allows the mouse to be used when editing code and even when editing type-in was very helpful.

In addition, the MasterScope support tools in Interlisp-D were helpful when tracking the implications of changes to types and procedures. Finally, the ability in Interlisp to add new parameters to procedures without affecting previous callers (unspecified parameters use NIL) was very useful.

14.2.2. Negative Aspects

The Interlisp environment is very clearly the product of incremental development by a research group. The various features do not always work well together and there are many bugs. For example, if a procedure is being edited and that procedure hits a breakpoint, the code in the editor becomes detached from the system so that all subsequent edits are simply lost without a trace and without notification. In addition, the user interface of the Interlisp editor and window system has a number of annoying problems, and the documentation on the system is poor.

As mentioned above, the Interlisp system has fairly good performance, and the Peridot system runs at an acceptable speed. Unfortunately, the virtual memory system in Interlisp seems to be very poor, so as Peridot got larger, it was increasingly painful to try to do any editing or run the system interpretively.

The garbage collector in Interlisp runs about every four seconds, and all activity stops while it is operating, including objects being dragged by the mouse. This is very annoying when operating a real-time system like Peridot, and it significantly confused the non-programmers who used Peridot.

More importantly, however, are some problems with the Interlisp-D language itself, which are discussed below.

14.2.2.1. Comments

The Interlisp-D language actively discourages the use of comments. Comments are implemented as normal expressions that return values. This means that they can only go where it is legal to have an expression. It is impossible to comment the test part of an IF statement, for example, because the value of the comment will be used instead of the test. Also, the comments in the code shown throughout this book would be illegal in Interlisp. The result is that it is difficult to comment programs, and the Peridot code suffers from this.

14.2.2.2. Data Structures and Garbage Collection

The primary data structure in Interlisp is the list, with a primitive form of record also available. Whereas lists are useful for many kinds of operations, they are mostly a hindrance in Peridot. Almost all of the data structures use forward and backward links. For example, the object-object relationships, the active value references, and the connection between an object and the piece of code that created it, all required links in both directions. The natural way to encode this results in most lists being part of circular structures, which are not handled well by the printing routines or garbage collector in Interlisp. Peridot explicitly tries to break all of the cycles when de-allocating objects, but the garbage collector still does not seem to collect any of the Peridot structures[1]. It might have been easier to manually allocate and free data structures.

Another problem is that Peridot performs a great deal of data structure modification. All editing of graphic objects involves changing the internal list structures that represent the objects, so the lists were constantly being changed. In some cases, the lists themselves are modified (using RPLACA and RPLACD), and in other cases, new lists are generated. It was extremely difficult to keep

---

[1] The garbage collector uses reference counts which never get reset to zero for circular lists, as discussed in section 3.3.1.

track of whether a pointer referred to the "main" list so destructive modification could be used. Also, destructive modification occasionally changed too much (for example, it changed the Peridot implementation code itself). Again, it seems that explicitly managing the data might have been easier.

Finally, the lack of appropriate record structures was a hindrance, as described in section 13.3.1. It was often difficult to create, understand, and modify references to these lists.

14.2.2.3. Modularization

As discussed throughout this book, especially in section 11.6, Peridot suffers from the lack of any modularization mechanisms in Interlisp. Modularization would have been helpful to organize Peridot itself, and it would have made the code generation parts of Peridot much more straightforward and successful.

14.2.3. Implications for Future Projects

The experience with implementing Peridot suggests that future experimental, research programming projects would be well-advised to use an interpretive environment like Lisp or Smalltalk with a high-level debugger which is well-integrated with the rest of the system. Lots of support for the kinds of output desired (graphics in windows, in this case) would also be very useful. It is likely that a multi-paradigm environment [Hailpern 86], where lists, objects, and data structures all co-existed, would be very helpful. Even for a one-person project, the lack of appropriate modularization mechanisms (for separating procedures into modules with separate address spaces) is a distinct disadvantage. Other features that are desirable are efficient, fine-grain multi-processing, efficient execution, and, of course, a robust and reliable (i.e., bug-free) underlying system.

14.3. Experience with Using Peridot

In order to evaluate how easy Peridot is to use, 10 people used the system for about two hours each. Of these people, 5 were experienced programmers and 5 were non-programmers who had some experience using a mouse (for example, by using MacPaint on the Macintosh). The results of this experiment were very encouraging. After about 1½ hours of guided use of Peridot, but sometimes as little as 30 minutes, the subjects were able to create a menu unassisted. They generally took about 15 minutes to create this menu. Since there is no user's manual or on-line help for Peridot, it was necessary for me to guide the subjects through a few examples. The subjects created one or two menus in this manner, and then they were asked to create a menu by themselves. If they were interested, they then created a property sheet and a scroll bar with assistance. One subject (a programmer) was able to create a scroll bar of his own design after one practice try.

Not surprisingly, the non-programmers had more trouble with the initial specification of the interface (e.g., what the "parameters" should be and "example values" for those parameters). However, the actual *creation* of the interfaces was accomplished easily by the non-programmers. Therefore, one basic goal of Peridot has been fulfilled: non-programmers are able to create user interfaces with their own graphic design and their own specific behavior using Peridot.

14.3.1. The Need for Iterative Design

One result of having other people use Peridot is that a number of minor problems with Peridot's own user interface were uncovered. These did not involve any of the basic underlying concepts of Peridot, and were mostly small annoyances that I had just ignored. Unfortunately, they proved to be sufficiently bothersome that the first users found it very difficult to learn to use the system. Therefore, Peridot was iteratively modified after each subject to fix the problems that were found. After about the fifth subject, these types of problems had mostly been eliminated, and the subjects were able to learn and use the system without much trouble. This is an example of how important iterative design and rapid prototyping are for user interface design. In summary, the revisions that were required were:

- To make the prompt messages easier to understand. Many of the questions had poor wording or were ambiguous so that the subjects found them hard to interpret. Also, some of the messages were not precise about what would happen. For example, one message said "... centered at the top of ..." which was changed to "... centered horizontally and flush at the top of ...". Another example is the prompt for linear interpolations. Originally, the system asked about the "first" and then the "second" extreme value, but the subjects usually typed in the values backwards, so the order was reversed and the prompts changed to be "current" and "previous".

- To separate the displays of the various messages. The original designers found it very difficult to know where to start reading in the prompt window, since there was no separation between the old messages and the new message, and since messages are often multiple lines, as shown in Figure 14.1a. Therefore, a thin hair-line is drawn in the prompt

window between each message, as shown in Figure 14.1b. Also, COM-
MAND COMPLETED is printed when there are no more questions so the
designer knows that it is time to execute a new command.

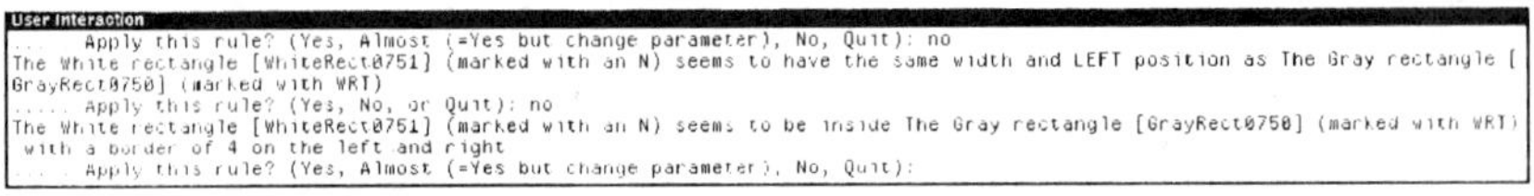

(a)

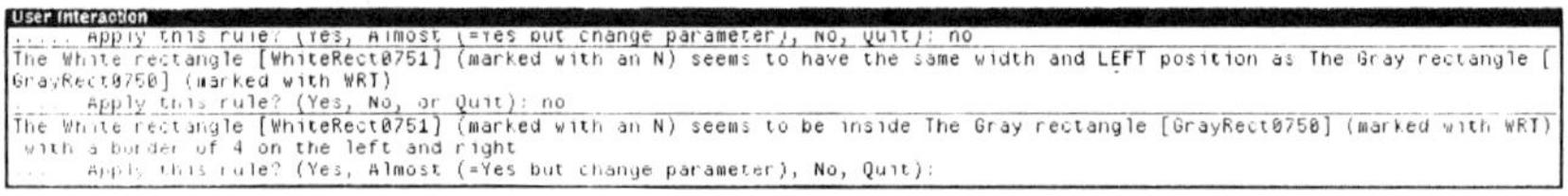

(b)
Figure 14.1.
The prompt window without (a) and with (b) separators.

- To provide an easier way to start Peridot. Originally, Peridot was
  invoked by constructing an Interlisp procedure call passing in a list of
  the parameters and active values, but this is clearly unacceptable for
  non-programmers. Therefore, the ability to press on the Peridot logo
  window and be prompted for the required information was added (as
  shown in the example of section 3.4). During this process, the subjects
  found it easier to specify the number of arguments first and then to type
  them in, rather than just typing the arguments and signaling completion
  with a blank line. Unfortunately, non-programmers still have problems
  with this process, since it requires some understanding of the difference
  between the *names* and *values* of parameters.

- To make the use of menus consistent. Originally, Peridot used the Interlisp menu package, which has submenus that appear when the cursor is
  slid out of the main menu on the right. Peridot used this sliding technique when a single submenu would result from the command. In some
  cases, however, Peridot would choose which submenu to use based on
  the type of the selected object. Here, Peridot would use pop-up submenus since the sliding type does not work if there can be different
  submenus. The original subjects were confused about whether to slide
  or press to obtain the desired submenu, so Peridot was changed to
  always use pop-up submenus.

- To provide menus for specifying more attributes of objects. Originally, a
  menu of colors appeared when a rectangle or circle was created, but the

designer had to type in the color value if the color was being edited. This was changed so that the same color menu is used in both places. One new option in this color menu brings up the shade editor (Figure 3.7) to make it easier to design new grey shades. Similarly, a new menu was added that listed a default set of icons that could be used, along with a call to the icon editor to create new icons.

- To alphabetize the commands in the main menu so that the designer could find the desired operation more easily. The commands were put in two groups, with the most common first, which also seemed to facilitate the searching.

- To add some new rules. As expected, the subjects created pictures in slightly different ways than I did, so some additional object-object rules were required. In all, 16 new rules were added, and most of these came from the initial few subjects.

- To remove the use of chording on the mouse buttons. Interlisp fakes a middle button by requiring the left and right buttons to be pressed at the same time, and this was used originally for de-selecting objects. Subjects found this difficult to use, so the right button is now used instead of the "middle" button. In addition, subjects seemed to assume that pressing the de-select button would de-select all the objects, rather than just the one pointed to, so now the right button de-selects all the objects if there is no object under the mouse.

- To increase the use of prompting. Subjects often forgot to select objects before giving commands. Rather than just printing an error message as was done originally, Peridot now prompts for an object to be selected.

- To prevent the execution of a command while another is in progress. Subjects occasionally would start another command while the previous command was still waiting for the answer to a question, which usually resulted in erroneous behavior. An explicit check was added to insure that this situation does not arise and Peridot beeps if a command is attempted before the previous is complete.

- To have better object names. Peridot originally used only the internal names (e.g. BlackRect0023) to refer to objects in the rules. Not surprisingly, the subjects found these hard to understand, even with the blinking arrows that show which objects are referred to. Therefore, Peridot was changed to produce messages like:

    the black rectangle [BlackRect0023] (marked with an N)

which, although longer, are much easier to understand. The internal name is still included since it is always unique and therefore occasionally useful for disambiguating similar objects.

- To rationalize the use of carriage-return. Normally, when Peridot asks a "yes" or "no" question, only y or n need to be typed, with no carriage-return. When a value is required, however, a return is needed to signify that the entire value has been typed. This confused many subjects, especially when the value typed was *, which signifies that the value comes from the selection. A partial fix would be to not require a return if the first character typed was a *, but this is apparently difficult to implement in Interlisp, so this problem has not been fixed.

14.3.2. Fundamental Implications

The changes discussed above are mostly cosmetic and none affect the basic underlying model for Peridot. The subjects liked creating interfaces using examples and the inferencing was generally very helpful. After the changes discussed in the previous section, there were almost always appropriate rules for all objects created by the subjects. As a result, there is high confidence that the rule set is now comprehensive enough to cover the set of interfaces that Peridot was designed to create. The only exception is that more rules are needed to make the size of rectangles be the sum of all objects inside (section 4.5). Except for this, the subjects were able to get *all* desired appearances and behaviors.

In general, the subjects were not bothered by having to answer all of the questions. On the contrary, they found it very helpful, and some subjects would have liked for the system to have prompted *more* often to suggest what to do next. The non-programmers did not seem to be intimidated by the questions; they read the messages and were willing to answer "no" if they seemed wrong. This is probably because they were somewhat computer-literate. Both the non-programmers and the experienced programmers found the labor-saving aspects of the rules (the automatic "beautifying" and the iterations) to be very helpful. In particular, the subjects seemed to be very impressed by the iterations; responses like "Oh, that's nice" and "Wow! Really smart" were typical.

In addition, the subjects seemed to enjoy using the system (some even called it "fun"), and it is interesting to note that the subjects always created different menus of their own design. The menus had different background graphics, different graphics to show the current choice, and different mouse operations to make that choice. The subjects also used different example values to design the interface.

Naturally, the subjects were less happy when Peridot guessed wrong, but this happened infrequently enough that the subjects were willing to accept this as part of the price to pay for the benefits. This positive attitude towards the system, coupled with the ability of even non-programmers to learn to use it in a short period of time, suggests that Peridot's basic model closely matches the subject's conceptual model of the problem domain and that it is appropriate for use in future systems.

14.4. Chapter Summary

The implementation effort to create Peridot was fairly large, and it was very helpful to have an experimental programming environment like Interlisp-D. Some specific features of the language and environment were helpful, and others were a hindrance, but overall the experience was positive.

In some informal tests, a few subjects used Peridot. In general, they were successful, especially after the changes recommended by the original few subjects were incorporated. Non-programmers were able to create menus of their own design fairly quickly, and all subjects said that they felt they were learning the system by the end of the two-hour trial. This demonstrates that Peridot is usable by non-programmers.

Chapter XV
Conclusions

15.1. Introduction

This chapter discusses the range of interfaces that Peridot can create, and the problems and successes of the system. In addition, the contributions of Peridot are reviewed.

15.2. Range of Peridot

All UIMSs are restricted in the forms of user interfaces that they can generate [Tanner 85]. Peridot is only aimed at graphical, highly-interactive interfaces that do not use the keyboard. Peridot does not help with textual command interfaces, text editing, form filling, or with the coding of the semantics of the application. Even after these restrictions, it is clear that Peridot cannot create every other kind of highly-interactive interface, and there are some other kinds of interfaces that it can handle. Therefore, an important question is: What is the range of interfaces that Peridot can create?

15.2.1. Formal Specification of Peridot's Range

Unfortunately, it is very difficult to answer this question in a formal way because there are no comprehensive taxonomies of existing interaction techniques, and new techniques are created all the time. In fact, one of Peridot's goals is to facilitate the creation of new techniques. A recent workshop at CHI+GI'87 [Nielson 87] failed to produce such a taxonomy, and this is clearly an important area for future research (see section 13.7.1).

Existing input classifications are too low level to say much about Peridot's capabilities. Foley [84b] discusses six fundamental "interaction tasks:" (1) *Select*—choose one or more from a set of alternatives (2) *Position*—place an object on an interactive display, (3) *Orient*—specify rotation in 2 or 3 dimensional space, (4) *Path*—specify a time sequence of positions or orientations, (5) *Quantify*—give the value of a measure, and (6) *Text*—type an edited string. Peridot can support all of these except text. Similarly, the proposed PHIGS graphics standard [PHIGS] has six input classes: locator, stroke, valuator, choice, pick and string, and Peridot can handle all but string. Each input class in PHIGS has three modes: (1) request mode—single value returned on a trigger, (2) sample mode—value returned immediately, and (3) event mode—

values returned in a continuous stream, and Peridot can also handle any of these.

15.2.2. Peridot's Range by Example

Due to this lack of a formal way to describe the range of Peridot, the best characterization is through examples. The next section discusses what Peridot can create now, section 15.2.2.2 lists examples of what it could create if it was extended slightly, section 15.2.2.3 discusses what could be added with some additional research, and section 15.2.2.4 discusses what a Peridot-style tool is probably not appropriate for. Finally, section 15.2.2.5 goes through some standard programs for the Apple Macintosh and shows what Peridot can and cannot handle.

15.2.2.1. What Peridot Can Create

Peridot supports three basic mouse behaviors that are used in typical interfaces: choosing among items, moving objects in a range, and modifying objects' size and position freely. The graphics that are associated with these behaviors is totally under the designer's control and can be created using rectangles, strings, circles, and static bitmap pictures, with other graphic primitives possible in the future. This allows the designer using Peridot to create menus of almost any form (with single or multiple items selected), light buttons, radio buttons, scroll bars and scroll areas of various forms, percent-done progress indicators, graphical sliders and potentiometers, and objects that can be dragged with the mouse. These actions can be triggered by single or multiple clicking of the mouse buttons over particular objects. This allows Peridot to create interfaces like those of the Apple Macintosh (section 15.2.2.5) and Sapphire Window Manager [Myers 84]. Appendix A shows examples of interfaces created using Peridot.

In addition, Peridot can support other input devices such as knobs, buttons, switches, one-dimensional sliders, and touch tablets. These can be used concurrently with the mouse and each other.

Peridot can also be used to create some kinds of dynamic pictures for business graphics and process control. For example, dynamic bar charts can be specified (Figure 6.3), as well as animations such as the hopping rabbit of Figure 10.3. This was an unintended application of Peridot, and it suggests that Peridot might be useful for creating systems to perform dynamic process viewing and control.

15.2.2.2. What Peridot Might Create with Small Extensions

If Peridot's implementation was enhanced slightly, other kinds of interfaces could also be handled. These would not require any important new design or research.

An interesting kind of menu that Peridot cannot handle is one when the indicator bar is stationary and the menu items themselves move up and down [Buxton 82].

Adding straight lines to Peridot (section 3.5) would allow Peridot to support gauges, dials, clocks, etc. These use rotating lines as markers, and therefore might also require the addition of another mouse behavior to handle rotation.

Another small addition would be to support clipping of graphics inside an arbitrary rectangle. This would allow Peridot to support the display of the picture inside the windows in Figures 5.7 and 9.7 without any application procedure at all.

Adding copying at run-time (section 9.3.8.5) would allow Peridot to handle some parts of many drawing applications for such things as PC board layout and architectural design.

15.2.2.3. What Peridot Might Create After New Research

The interfaces in this category would require new research into how to apply Peridot-style demonstrational techniques to new areas.

An important area would be to support text input (section 13.2.2). This would allow the designer to specify by demonstration what type of data was appropriate for various fields in a form, and what editing commands would be available on that input.

Another important area would be to support "gluing" of interaction techniques together to create full user interfaces (section 13.7.5). Whereas the physical placement of the interaction techniques may be easy to define demonstrationally, the sequencing aspects probably require more research.

15.2.2.4. Interfaces That Do Not Seem Appropriate

Whereas it is conceivable that almost any interface could be defined in a demonstrational manner, Peridot is successful because it concentrates on a specific class of interaction techniques which use well-understood mechanisms. Generalizing Peridot's techniques to open-ended areas such as application output graphics is likely to be very difficult because the problems of general Example Based Programming systems begin to appear (section 2.3.3). The system would not have enough knowledge to correctly interpret what the demonstration means if the range of the possible applications is too large.

Another class of interfaces that Peridot is not appropriate for are ones that are easier to specify using other techniques. An important example of this is probably textual command line interfaces. Here, syntax diagrams or BNFs seem more appropriate for specifying the available choices.

It is also probably not appropriate to try to handle those interfaces where the algorithms for handling the user input are not yet sufficiently understood so they can be separated from applications. The primary example of this is gestural interfaces, such as selecting objects by circling them with a mouse. Here, it seems that too much application knowledge is required to correctly interpret the gestures to allow them to be demonstrated in an application-independent way.

15.2.2.5. Interfaces in The Apple Macintosh

This sections discusses the Apple Macintosh user interface [Williams 84] and some of its standard programs. Each aspect of the interface is rated by which of the above categories it falls into based on whether Peridot can create it, as follows:

Now: Can be created by Peridot now (section 15.2.2.1),

Easy: Could be created by Peridot with a few extensions (section 15.2.2.2),

Research: Might be created by Peridot after some further research (section 15.2.2.3), or

N/A: Probably not appropriate to be created by Peridot (section 15.2.2.4).

Peridot can now create the horizontal menu at the top of the Macintosh screen, and the menus that "pull down" from them (see Figure 15.1) (*Now*). The connection from the top menu to the menu that appears would have to be provided by an application procedure, however (*Research*). If Peridot was extended to handle the keyboard as a large button box (no editing is needed), then the accelerators (e.g. "Command-G") could be handled (*Easy*).

Peridot can create the standard scroll bars used in most windows, where the line box follows the mouse (see Figure 9.5) (*Now*). The scroll bar used in

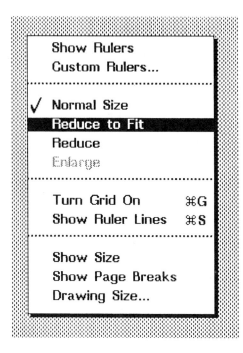

Figure 15.1.
A Macintosh-style menu produced by Peridot.

MacWrite has the main indicator follow the mouse and the line box stays behind. The indicator box always contains the correct page number. This could all also be handled by Peridot (*Now*), although an application procedure would clearly have to provide the page number to be displayed in the indicator.

The standard window icons for exiting and full-screen can be handled (see Figure 9.7) (*Now*), and the size and position controls can almost be handled (*Easy*). The problem here is that Peridot does not currently support changing size from the bottom right or moving from exactly the point where the mouse is pressed (see section 9.3.8.4).

For the special applications, Peridot can create the calculator and the control panel (*Now*), although clearly some application procedures would have to be written to perform the operations. For the keycaps panel, keyboard input as single characters would be needed (*Easy*), and two-dimensional iterations would be desirable (section 6.5.1) (*Easy*).

For MacPaint, Peridot can create all the menus around the drawing window (*Now*), although it might be easier to create some of these if Peridot had multi-line iterations (*Easy*). For the panel that appears when Save File or Read File is selected, Peridot can create the scrolling menu of file names (*Now*), although an application procedure would have to be written to calculate the new set of items in the menu after each scrolling operation (*Research*). The field that allows new file names to be typed cannot be handled (*Research*). Peridot is not appropriate for defining the operation in the main drawing window (*N/A*).

Similarly, for MacWrite, Peridot can support all menus and the "rulers" (*Now*), but it cannot support the text editing itself (*N/A*). For MacTerminal, Peridot could create the menus, the tab ruler and the keypad (*Now*), and it could support all of the dialogue boxes for various properties (*Now*), except for those fields that required text input (*Research*).

15.3. Problems with Peridot's Approach

There are a number of problems with the Peridot system and the approach it is based on. These are discussed in more detail in previous chapters and are summarized here.

The inferencing techniques used in Peridot are very simple. Especially with object-object relationships, the inferencing is occasionally incorrect on the first try. A more clever algorithm would probably help eliminate some of the incorrect guesses (section 4.6.2). A more basic problem is that Peridot can only infer relationships that it has rules for. While Peridot seems to incorporate most of the relationships used in current interfaces, the rules might not apply if the designer invents a new graphical style. Even for the current style of interfaces, it is not uncommon for the designer to have to resort to explicit specification which can be awkward. Some better methods for changing the rule ordering and extending the rule set would be appropriate (discussed in sections 4.6.3 and 4.6.4).

No matter how many rules are added, there will clearly not be a rule for every possible situation, so the system will work best if the designer is careful to create the interface so that the rules will work. With the current rule set, for example, there are more rules for objects below and to the right of previous objects, so it is better to build pictures left to right and top to bottom, which is the natural way for most English-language user interfaces. It takes some experience with the system in order to learn these "tricks" so that the designer can work most effectively.

Another major problem with Peridot's approach is that the mouse behaviors that it can support are hard-wired and these do not cover every possible type of interaction that might be desired. Each supported behavior has its own mechanism, parameters, and implementation. It would be fairly difficult to add new behaviors or to change the way the current ones work. Similarly, there is no general mechanism for specifying or programming the behaviors of other input devices. The solution to this problem awaits more research into the classification of interaction behaviors.

While the rule-based inferencing of graphical constraints does not limit the kinds and styles of interfaces that can be created, the hard-wired mouse behaviors do limit the styles somewhat.

15.4. Successes of Peridot

Peridot successfully achieves the goals listed in section 1.4. It can create direct manipulation interfaces that use the mouse and/or other input devices. The lowest-level interaction techniques themselves can be created, and active values can be used to supply semantic feedback, semantic error checking and semantic defaults that can be used in inner loops of mouse tracking and other input device handling. Multiple interaction techniques can be available at the same time, allowing the end user to choose which one to use, and they can also be operating at the same time, allowing the designer to use multiple input devices concurrently. The ability to create the interaction techniques in the Macintosh Toolbox demonstrates that Peridot has sufficient power and functionality to be usable and practical.

The interface to Peridot is easy to use, and both the presentation (graphic displays) and actions (based on input devices) can be demonstrated completely without using conventional programming. Automatic inferencing is used to eliminate some effort for the designer, and all graphics and interactions can be easily edited. The interface is visible and executable at all times so changes are immediately apparent. The success of the non-programmers that have used Peridot demonstrates that Peridot is easier to use than programming language approaches, and that it would be accessible to non-programmer user interface specialists.

In addition, even programmers will appreciate using Peridot to define the graphical parts of interaction techniques. It is always much easier to use appropriate tools, and a graphical tool like Peridot can make defining and editing pictures an interesting and creative process, rather than a difficult and tedious task.

One reason is that Peridot significantly shortens the time to create user interfaces. For the interfaces that Peridot is designed to best create, e.g. menus, scroll bars, light buttons, etc., it appears to be around 5000% faster (a factor of 50 times faster) to use Peridot rather than coding the interface by hand.

These numbers came from a small, informal experiment, where a number of expert programmers were asked to implement the menu of the example of Figure 3.15. The programmers used their own graphics hardware in whatever manner was fastest (as long as the result looked exactly like Figure 3.15n). Some wrote the menu from scratch, and others modified existing code. The results are shown in Figure 15.2. Although the particular times are not meaningful by themselves due to the small sample, the overall trend is clear. The average and median times are around 3 hours, which is significantly longer than the time to create the interface in Peridot (4 minutes). Editing changes are similarly much faster.

Who	Language	Computer	OS	From Scratch?	Time (mins)	Time (hrs)
me	Peridot	--	--	yes	4.0	0.0666
novice	Peridot	--	--	yes	15.5	0.2583
me	Interlisp-D	Xerox 1109	Intermezzo	yes	50.0	0.8333
<A>	Pascal	Atari 1040 with Ram Disk	GEM	yes	90.0	1.5
<B>	C	IRIS	UNIX system 5	yes	120.0	2.0
<B>	C	IRIS	UNIX system 5	no	180.0	3.0
<C>	ZetaLisp	Symbolics 3600	Symbolics V6.0	no	195.0	3.25
<D>	C Manx Aztec V3.20a	Commodore Amiga	Kickstart/ Workbench V1.2	yes	500.0	8.3333

Figure 15.2.
Times to implement the menu of Figure 3.15 in Peridot and by hand in various languages on various computers. The novice using Peridot had only 1½ hours practice with the system.

In addition, Peridot creates reasonably efficient code so that the resulting interfaces can be used with actual application programs. Therefore, the professional UI designer is both designing *and implementing* the interface. This is demonstrated by the ability of Peridot to use Peridot-created procedures for its own user interface.

The success of the C language version of Peridot system [Green 88] demonstrates that the ideas in Peridot can be successfully translated into conventional, compiled environments, and do not depend on any special properties of Interlisp-D.

15.5. Peridot's Place in User Interface Development

Figure 2.1 gives an overall structure for User Interface Management Systems (UIMSs). Peridot chiefly performs the interaction-technique builder function in this diagram (along with the associated run-time support, of course). If Peridot was extended to allow interactions to be read back in, it could also supply some of the system glue functionality. The major components of UIMSs that Peridot does not provide are support for sequencing, also called syntax or dialogue control, and support for analysis of the user interface. A future system might be able to use ideas from Peridot and user interface design guidelines to attempt to provide some automatic analysis of user interfaces (discussed in section 13.7.7).

15.6. Review of Contributions

Peridot shows that it is possible to have a non-programmer create dynamic, graphical, highly interactive, direct manipulation user interfaces. To the best of our knowledge, it is the first system to allow the dynamic, interactive behavior of the interfaces to be specified in a demonstrational manner without programming. In addition, it demonstrates that Visual Programming, Programming by Example, Graphical and Data Constraints, and Plausible Inferencing can be efficiently and effectively applied to computer systems.

Peridot supports *extremely rapid prototyping* since it takes very little time to create interaction techniques from scratch or to edit existing interfaces. Due to the use of example values for parameters and active values, the interface is visible and executable by the designer at all times. In addition, when editing interfaces, the changes are also immediately visible and executable. This makes it much easier to develop interfaces and understand how they work. The procedures that Peridot generates for the interfaces are efficient enough so that they can be used by actual application programs. This means that the designer is not merely prototyping; the actual interfaces are being implemented.

The procedures being created can have parameters, just like procedures normally found in interaction technique libraries. As far as we know, Peridot is the first system to provide this capability.

The interactions that Peridot supports are all based on three primitive mouse behaviors: choice, changing in a range, and changing freely. These behaviors can be associated with arbitrary graphical feedback and can be triggered by a variety of mouse actions. Previous research has failed to identify a canonical set of primitive behaviors that underly *all* interaction techniques, but Peridot's success here suggests that this might be possible.

Peridot demonstrates that graphical constraints can be automatically inferred using a simple form of plausible inference, and that this will be helpful to users and appreciated by them, since it has the beneficial side effect of automatically "beautifying" the pictures. The constraints in Peridot are very limited, so they can be implemented very efficiently. They are still highly useful, however, and they are sufficient for use in actual systems.

The powerful mechanism of active values with data constraints allows the interfaces to take advantage of fine grain control in which applications can provide semantic feedback, semantic error checking and semantic defaults in an efficient manner that still insulates the application from details of the graphic presentation and input techniques in use. Peridot also supports coarse-grain control, in which applications are not called until there is a substantial amount of work to be done. These mechanisms allow the use of application (internal) control, UIMS (external) control, or parallel (mixed) control.

Peridot supports concurrency for output and input. Application programs can have multiple processes updating output objects at the same time, and multiple input devices can be active at the same time, for example, one in each hand.

In addition, Peridot promotes structured design and creates well structured code. The designer creates functions with (optional) parameters and return values for each interaction technique and these can be combined in a modular fashion. In addition, calls to application procedures from within Peridot are appropriately parameterized.

15.7. Summary

Peridot successfully demonstrates that it is possible to program a large variety of mouse and other input device interactions by demonstration. Peridot can create user interfaces like those of state-of-the-art, easy-to-use graphical programs, such the Apple Macintosh, window managers, and other direct manipulation systems, including Peridot's own user interface. Both the presentation (layout) and interaction (behavior) of these direct manipulation interfaces can be created in an extremely natural, direct manipulation manner without conventional programming. Peridot may even be simple enough so that end users could use it to modify their user interfaces.

The use of active values supports multi-processing and makes the linking to application programs straightforward, fast and natural, and supports semantic feedback easily. Plausible inferencing is used to free the designer from having to specify most of the properties of objects. Constant feedback through queries, and continuously making the results of actions visible, helps to insure that all inferences are correct. Interfaces created with Peridot can be tried out immediately (with or without the application program), and the code generated is efficient enough to be used in actual end applications.

This is achieved by applying ideas from Visual Programming, Programming by Example, Constraints, and Plausible Inferencing, which demonstrates that these techniques are practical and useful.

Peridot clearly supports extremely rapid prototyping of dynamic user interfaces. By providing the ability to use explicit specification and demonstrational methods, Peridot allows the designer to use the most appropriate techniques for creating the user interfaces. The novel use of demonstrational (programming-by-example) methods makes a large class of previously hard-to-create interaction techniques easy to design, implement, and modify. In addition, Peridot makes it easy to investigate many new techniques that have never been used before, which may help designers discover the next generation of exciting user interfaces.

Some Interfaces Created Using Peridot

A.1. Introduction

This appendix contains pictures and short descriptions of some of the interfaces created using Peridot. Many of these pictures have appeared earlier in this book, but they are repeated here so that this appendix will give an idea of the range of interfaces that Peridot can create.

A.2. Menus and Property Sheets

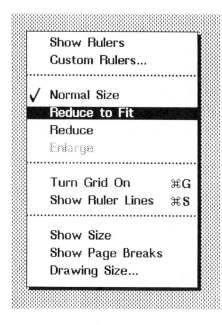

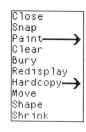

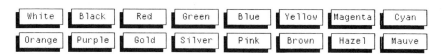

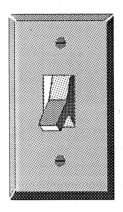 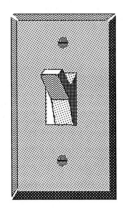

Bold
Italic
StrikeThrough
Underline
Superscript
Inverted

New South Wales
Victoria
South Australia
Western Australia
Queensland
Tasmania

ACT
Northern Territory

Rectangle
Circle
Ellipse
Line
Spline
Text
Polygon

(●) Bold

(●) Italic

( ) StrikeThrough

(●) Underline

( ) Superscript

( ) Inverted

[ ] Bold

[✓] Italic

[✓] StrikeThrough

[ ] Underline

[ ] Superscript

[✓] Inverted

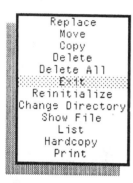

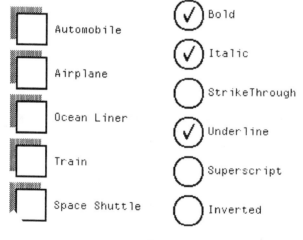

Automobile

Airplane

Ocean Liner

Train

Space Shuttle

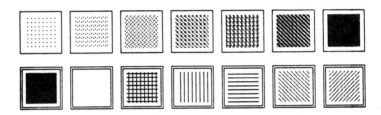

A.3. Number Pads

A.4. Scroll Bars and Sliders

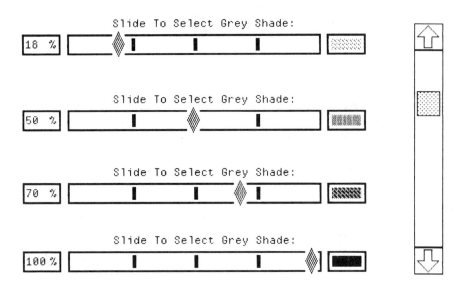

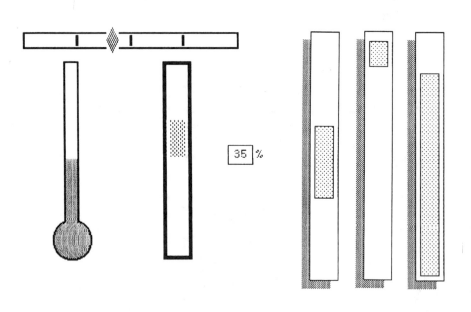

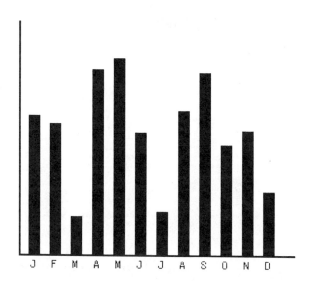

A.5. Larger-level Interfaces

A.5.1. Peridot's User Interface

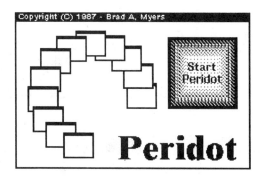

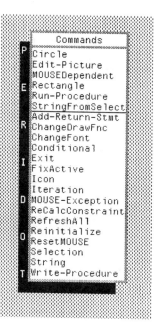

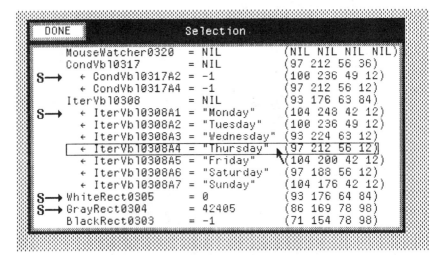

  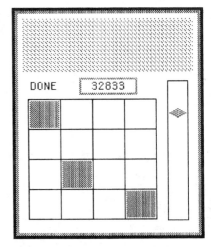

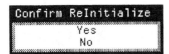

A.5.2. Scrolling Windows

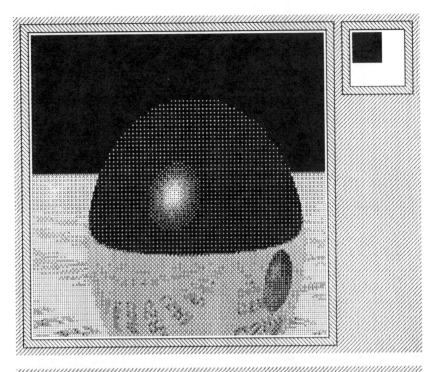

A.5.3. Multiple Input Devices

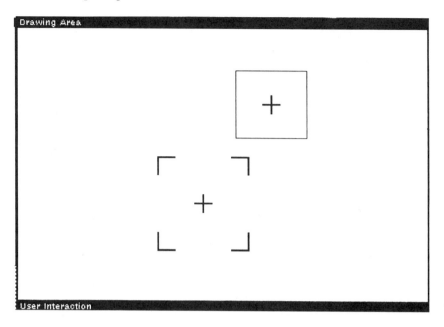

A.5.4. Animation

Appendix B
Comparison with Hill's Sassafras System

B.1. Introduction

This appendix is a joint effort with Ralph Hill, and also appears as Appendix H in his PhD dissertation [Hill 87b]. It presents brief and parallel summaries of Sassafras and Peridot, with a comparison of their major features. Since both UIMSs were developed at approximately the same time on the same hardware at the University of Toronto, it seems appropriate to provide an in-depth comparison. Sassafras was discussed briefly in section 2.2.3.2, and other articles about Sassafras are [Hill 87a] [Hill 87c].

B.2. Sassafras

Sassafras is a prototype UIMS based on Event-Response Language (ERL) and the Local Event Broadcast Method (LEBM). In general, this section discusses ERL and LEBM rather than Sassafras because the designs of ERL and LEBM are the important parts of Sassafras, and Sassafras itself is only a crude prototype.

B.2.1. UIMS Components Addressed

In the structure presented in section 2.2.1, ERL provides the dialogue specification language and can also be used to specify the application interface. ERL is a language for specifying the syntax of user interfaces that builds on the low-level interaction techniques in the interaction technique library.

LEBM provides the run-time structure of a user interface. It connects together the pieces of the user interface, and allows them to communicate and synchronize.

B.2.2. Goals

ERL and LEBM were designed as the key components of a UIMS to support concurrent dialogues. Specifically, they were designed to support concurrency, communication and synchronization in the user interface. They were not intended to greatly simplify user interface specification, but were designed to support a wide range of user interface styles (wider than supported by existing systems) and be efficiently implementable. They were not intended to

- 241 -

provide all of the functionality required in a user interface; in particular, development of the interaction modules and graphical output are not supported.

B.2.3. Dialogue Specification Technique

ERL is a textual language for specifying the syntax of human-computer dialogues. ERL is based on a form of language recognition automata that is formally equivalent in power to finite state machines, but has a radically different structure. This different structure makes ERL suitable for the specification of concurrent dialogues.

B.2.4. Communication with Application Routines

LEBM allows ERL modules to communicate and synchronize with the application routines using a form of asynchronous message passing. This same technique is used to communicate with the interaction modules. It supports two-way exchange of information and synchronization, and allows the application routines to run asynchronously as another process. The design of the communication mechanism allows it to be implemented in simple sequential code, making the implementation efficient.

B.2.5. Method for Handling Concurrency

Sassafras deals with concurrency at two levels. ERL allows fine grain concurrency control, and provides simple primitives that can be used to implement forks, joins and semaphores. These constructs have proven to be sufficient in practice. Their simplicity allows them to be efficiently implemented and easily learned.

A coarser grain of concurrency support is provided by LEBM. It allows the modules of the user interface to execute in parallel, and communicate and synchronize via message passing. This can be implemented in a single process, with the implementation of LEBM providing the scheduling of the execution of the modules.

B.2.6. Constructing a User Interface

When constructing a user interface with Sassafras, ERL is used to specify the syntactic level of the dialogue. ERL specifications make use of the interaction techniques (from the library) as low-level input routines, and builds higher level interfaces from them. LEBM is used to connect the various components of the interface together.

Interface construction consists of writing the dialogue specification in ERL, selecting the interaction techniques that are to be used from the library, writing the application routines (in some appropriate language) and then telling the implementation of LEBM about all components of the user interface.

B.2.7. Changing a User Interface

Sassafras allows the user interface implementor to suspend the execution of a user interface, alter the ERL specification, and then resume execution from the point of suspension, but running the changed specification. This allows changes to be quickly added, and tested in the context that inspired them. It is not possible to change all aspects of the user interface, but many changes that have a great impact on the user interface can be quickly installed this way.

More complex changes may require changes to the application routines, or may require that the user interface be stopped and re-initialized so that new interaction modules may be linked in.

B.2.8. Visual Aspects of the User Interface

ERL and LEBM explicitly do not address graphical output or feedback. These must be provided by the interaction modules or application routines.

B.2.9. Intended Users

ERL and LEBM are intended to be used by a user interface designer or implementor who has some basic knowledge of programming (approximately high school or first year university level programming). They are not suitable for use by true non-programmers.

B.3. Peridot

Peridot can create graphical, highly interactive, direct manipulation interfaces. Peridot stands for Programming by Example for Real-time Interface Design Obviating Typing and is implemented in Interlisp-D on a Xerox Dande-Tiger (1109) workstation. The central approach of Peridot is to allow the user interface designer to design and implement direct manipulation user interfaces in a direct manipulation manner. The designer does not need to do any programming in the conventional sense since all commands and actions are given graphically. The general strategy of Peridot is to allow the designer to *draw* the screen display that the end user will see, and then to *perform* actions just as the end user would, such as moving a mouse or pressing its buttons or hitting keyboard keys. The results are immediately visible and executable on the screen and can be edited easily. The designer gives examples of typical values for parameters and actions and Peridot automatically guesses (or *infers*) the general case.

B.3.1. UIMS Components Addressed

In the structure presented in section 2.2.1, Peridot is mainly aimed at creating the Interaction Modules.

B.3.2. Goals

The goals of Peridot are that:

1) interaction techniques for direct manipulation interfaces should be supported,

2) multiple interaction techniques should be *available* at the same time (giving the end user a choice for the next operation),

3) multiple interaction techniques should be *operational* at the same time (allowing the end user to use two different techniques in parallel—e.g. one with each hand),

4) semantic feedback, semantic error checking, and semantic defaults controlled by the application program should be provided, and

5) the system should be easy to use for the designer and require little or no training (in particular, the designer should not have to write programs),

6) the interface should be visible at all times as it is developed and changes should be immediately apparent,

7) the *behavior* of the interface should also be created in a direct manipulation manner and it should run in real time (points 6 and 7 provide for extremely rapid prototyping),

8) the time to prototype an interface should be significantly shorter than for programming by hand. This will make Peridot desirable for use by programmers as well as non-programmers.

9) the system should create run-time code that is efficient enough for use in actual application programs.

B.3.3. Dialogue Specification Technique

Peridot does not really incorporate the notion of a "dialogue" in the conventional sense. However, at a low level, the sequence of actions that the end user must perform is specified by the designer by *demonstrating* those actions on an example of the type of pictures that the end user will see.

B.3.4. Communication with Application Routines

If the application is in control, then Peridot can be used to create a library of routines that the application can simply call as conventional procedures. Alternatively, if the user interface is in control, then Peridot uses "active values" to attach application programs to user interfaces[1]. Active values are variables that can have arbitrary values of any type, and whenever they are set, either by the application program or by input devices, all pictures that depend on them are immediately updated. In addition, any active value can have one or more procedures attached to it which are called whenever the value is set or changed. Active values can be implemented with a variety of techniques including direct procedure calls, remote procedure calls, synchronous or asynchronous message passing, monitors, etc.

B.3.5. Method for Handling Concurrency

Peridot allows multiple active values to be updated at the same time, possibly by different input devices, so it is easy to provide concurrency. It is up to the application program, however, to schedule when the various active values are enabled and deal with any synchronization issues. This is based on the assumption that the concurrency needed for user interfaces is usually very straightforward and it is rare for multiple processes or devices to conflict. Therefore, elaborate synchronization mechanisms are not needed.

B.3.6. Constructing a User Interface

The designer first draws a picture using Peridot to demonstrate what the user interface should look like and then demonstrates the interaction using the input devices. Finally, the designer attaches any required application procedures to active values.

---

[1] Active values are also used internally to connect input devices to graphics.

B.3.7. Changing a User Interface
A user interface can be modified at any time in Peridot and the effects immediately seen or experimented with. No "compile" phase is required.

B.3.8. Visual Aspects of the User Interface
Peridot focuses on handling graphical input, output, and feedback.

B.3.9. Intended Users
Peridot is intended to be used by user interface designers with no programming knowledge. For example, professional graphic designers might use Peridot to define a system's overall look.

B.4. Comparison of Major Features of Peridot and Sassafras
Sassafras and Peridot have similar goals. They both:

- aim to make the job of specifying highly interactive, graphical, direct manipulation interfaces easier,

- provide for rapid prototyping,

- allow multiple interaction techniques to be available and operational at the same time,

- support semantic feedback, semantic error checking, and semantic defaults controlled by the application program.

This section discusses these points, and the complementary aspects of Peridot and Sassafras, in more detail.

B.4.1. Ease of Specification
Both Sassafras and Peridot try to simplify the specification and implementation of user interfaces. This is achieved by providing tools that are designed to support specific tasks within the larger problem of user interface design and specification, rather than by trying to provide general purpose tools or programming languages. Peridot is aimed at the low level interaction techniques and Sassafras is aimed at the intermediate control level. Since the interaction techniques may be designed by a graphic designer who is not a programmer, Peridot allows the interaction techniques to be specified by drawing pictures and demonstrating the desired behavior. Sassafras is aimed at the higher level control structures and provides a simple, flexible and appropriate mechanism designed for this task. Although this mechanism is based on a textual specification that resembles traditional programming languages, it is much simpler and better suited to the implementation of user interfaces than general purpose programming languages.

B.4.2. Prototyping Support

Both Peridot and Sassafras support rapid prototyping by providing tools specifically designed to implement user interfaces and by allowing user interface designs to be rapidly altered and executed. To support rapid modification of user interfaces Peridot supports *continuous editing* (where the user can alter the user interface while it is running) and Sassafras supports *suspended time editing* (where the execution is suspended while the editing is in progress). Continuous editing is superior to suspended time editing in that there is no need to start and stop the editor to install each change. Due to the nature of ERL specifications, however, it would be difficult to construct a continuous editing system for Sassafras that could guarantee that the ERL specification is always executable. Nevertheless, both continuous editing and suspended time editing are major improvements over the editing support in most existing UIMSs, which require that the user interface be terminated and restarted after each change.

B.4.3. Multiple Simultaneous Interaction Techniques

In order to allow multiple interaction techniques to be simultaneously available and operational, both Sassafras and Peridot make efforts to improve support for concurrency and communication in user interfaces. Their approaches, however, are quite different. Peridot allows concurrency and communication through its active values but assumes that the concurrency will be simple and that any required synchronization mechanisms can be provided by the application routines.

In Sassafras, concurrency and synchronization are explicitly supported on two levels. ERL provides fine grain concurrency and synchronization within the syntactic level specification. LEBM supports concurrency on a larger scale, allowing the various pieces of the user interface to execute in parallel. Communication and synchronization among these modules is supported by LEBM's event passing mechanism.

As far as we know, no previously existing UIMS supported concurrency in the user interface, yet concurrency makes the implementation of many user interface features easier. Thus, both Peridot and Sassafras are major steps forward in this area.

B.4.4. Communication with the Application

Both active values (in Peridot) and event passing (in Sassafras) are major advances over other existing communication mechanisms, as they allow two-way communication between interface components. Without two-way communication, it is difficult to support user interface features that depend on the state of the application program, for example, context dependent defaults or range limits, and error checking in the user interface.

Most existing UIMSs emphasize one-way communication, and therefore inhibit the implementation of some useful user interface features.

B.4.5. Complimentary Aspects

Peridot and Sassafras are complimentary in that each emphasizes a different level of dialogue specification, and combined, they cover most of the parts of user interfaces. With some modifications to the communications mechanisms of either Peridot or Sassafras (or both), they could be used together to create sophisticated, complete interfaces. Peridot could be used to develop interaction techniques and other user interface components involving simple interaction, and Sassafras could be used as a higher level tool to assemble these pieces.

B.5. Summary

One of the primary goals of a UIMS is to make the creation of user interfaces easier. To do this, tools should be used that are well matched to the various tasks that are part of the UI creation task. For example, a graphical tool should be used to specify the graphic look and placement of interaction techniques, and, since Peridot is intended to handle those aspects, it is designed as an extended drawing package. On the other hand, the connection to the application program, and especially synchronization problems, are more abstract. Therefore a more indirect approach, such as the event-response system of Sassafras, is appropriate.

These two differing approaches are well matched to the skills of the expected UI designers using the two systems. The designer using Peridot is responsible for the look and feel of UI and should be a graphic artist or UI specialist who will not necessarily be a programmer. Therefore Peridot does not require the use of programming. On the other hand, the designer using Sassafras is responsible for the overall structure of the interactive system and will need to have a deeper and more informed understanding of operation of the computer, its processes, and the implementation of the specific application. Therefore, it is appropriate to require this person to have some programming skills.

Peridot Commands

The following are the commands, in alphabetical order, that the designer can use to operate Peridot:

Add-Return-Stmt

One active value should be selected. Allows the designer to select when the interface should exit based on the setting or changing of the active value. Discussed in section 8.7.

ChangeDrawFnc

Allows the default Drawing Function to be changed. All subsequent graphic objects will use the new drawing function specified. Discussed in section 3.2.3.

ChangeFont

Allows the default font to be changed. All subsequent strings will use the new font specified. Discussed in section 3.2.3.

ChangePropByFunctionalCombination

Subcommand of EditPicture. Allows the designer to specify that an attribute of a graphical object should be the maximum, minimum, sum, etc. of two demonstrated values for that attribute. One object should be selected, and this command saves the current attributes of the object. Then the designer uses other commands to edit the object, and this command is given again. Discussed in section 5.7

ChangePropByLinearInterp

Subcommand of EditPicture. Allows the designer to specify that graphical objects should vary between two extremes. One object should be selected, and this command saves the current attributes of the object. Then the designer uses other commands to edit the object to the other extreme, and then this command is given again. Discussed in section 5.6

ChangePropByMouse   Subcommand of EditPicture. One or more of the selected object's attributes can be changed using the mouse. Discussed in section 5.4.

ChangePropBySpec   Subcommand of EditPicture. One or more of the selected object's attributes can be changed either by typing a new constant value, or by selecting another graphical object, parameter, or active value that the attribute should depend on. Discussed in section 5.5.

Circle   Initiates the drawing of a new circle object. The designer is prompted to choose a color for the inside of the circle, and then to place and size the circle with the mouse. Discussed in section 3.2.3.

Conditional   One or more objects should be selected. Transforms those objects to be conditional. The designer is prompted to select a parameter or active value that the conditional should depend on. Conditionals can be used to cause the graphical objects to blink on and off in place or to be displayed relative to one or more out of an iteration. Discussed in Chapter 7.

CopyAll   Subcommand of EditPicture. One or more objects should be selected. Creates new objects that are the same as the original objects, except that they can be in a different place. The designer is prompted for whether the LEFT, BOTTOM or both should change in the copies. Discussed in section 5.3.

Delete-Interactions   Subcommand of FixActive. If an active value is selected, then lists all the interactions that depend on that active value, and asks for each one whether it should be deleted. If nothing is selected, then lists and asks about all the interactions. Discussed in section 9.6.

Deselect-All

Subcommand of Selection. De-selects any objects selected. If nothing is selected, then does nothing. Discussed in section 3.2.4.

Deselect-In-Box

Subcommand of Selection. Allows the designer to draw a rectangular region with the mouse, and all the objects within the region will be de-selected. Discussed in section 3.2.4.

Edit-Picture

Brings up a sub-menu containing the editing commands.

EraseSelection

Subcommand of EditPicture. Causes the selected objects to be erased. Discussed in section 5.2.

Exit

Prompts for confirmation, and then exits Peridot. If the interface has not been written out using the Write-Procedure command, then asks if the procedure should be written before exiting.

FixActive

Brings up a sub-menu containing the commands for manipulating active values.

Icon

Initiates the drawing of a new icon object. The designer is prompted to choose the name of the bitmap to use as the icon, and then to place the icon with the mouse. Discussed in section 3.2.3.

Iteration

Makes all of the selected objects be part of an iteration, either based on a list or for some integer number of times. If nothing is selected, then searches for a suspended iteration and re-instantiates it. Discussed in Chapter 6.

MOUSEDependent

Causes the selected objects to be mouse dependent. If there is no selection, then uses the object directly under the simulated mouse. The objects will change based on the mouse in various ways depending on the type of the objects. Discussed in Chapter 9.

MOUSE-Exception   The selected object should be a part of a conditional. Causes a mouse interaction to have an exception so that it will not operate when the mouse is over any of the values of the conditional. Discussed in section 9.5.

ReCalcConstraint   Causes the object-object relationships for the selected object to be recalculated. Runs the same rules as if the object were newly created. Discussed in section 5.8.

Rect   Initiates the drawing of a new rectangle object. The designer is prompted to choose a color for the inside of the rectangle, and then to place and size the rectangle with the mouse. Discussed in section 3.2.3.

RefreshAll   Causes all of the objects to be erased and redrawn in order. Also refreshes the code display window, if it is in use.

Reinitialize   Prompts for confirmation, and then deletes all the objects so a new interface can be created (with the same parameters and active values).

ResetMOUSE   Causes the simulated mouse to return to its "home" under the Peridot menu. Also clears the simulated mouse button history used for demonstrating multiple clicks. Discussed in section 9.3.6.

Run-Procedure   Causes Peridot to go into "run mode" where the real mouse can be used to execute the interface. No Peridot commands can be given while in run mode. Run mode is exited by hitting the keyboard key labeled "Stop," or when the interface exits. Discussed in section 9.4.

SelectByName

Subcommand of Selection. Pops up a menu of all the objects in drawing order and allows the designer to pick objects to be selected and de-selected. Each object is listed with its name, current value and DisplayedREGION. When the menu appears, the objects originally selected are marked. The designer can turn selection on and off for any objects. Discussed in section 3.2.4.

Select-In-Box

Subcommand of Selection. Allows the designer to draw a rectangular region with the mouse, and all the objects within the region will be selected. Discussed in section 3.2.4.

Selection

Brings up a sub-menu containing the commands for selection.

Selection<-Mouse

Subcommand of Selection. Causes the object that is underneath the simulated mouse to become selected.

SetActiveValue

Subcommand of FixActive. A single active value should be selected. If the active value is a list, then one of its elements can be selected instead. Allows the designer to type a new value for the active value. Discussed in section 8.4.

Show-Interactions

Subcommand of FixActive. If an active value is selected, then lists all the interactions that depend on the active value. If nothing is selected, then lists all the interactions. Discussed in section 9.10.4.

SpecifyApplicationHandling

Subcommand of FixActive. Allows the designer to attach any procedure to an active value. An active value should be selected before giving the command, and the designer will be prompted to select when the application procedure should be called, what procedure to use, an optional extra parameter to the procedure, and, optionally, another active value to set with the result. Discussed in section 8.6.

SpecifyOutOfRangeHandling

Subcommand of FixActive. Allows the designer to specify out-of-range handling for an active value. An active value should be selected before giving the command, and the designer will be prompted to select what type of range handling should be used and what should be done to the value if it is out of range. Discussed in section 8.5.

String

Initiates the drawing of a new string object. The designer is prompted to select or type the new string to use, and then to place the string with the mouse. Discussed in section 3.2.3.

StringFromSelect

Same as String, except assumes that the string to use will come from a parameter or active value, which should have been previously selected. Discussed in section 3.2.3.

Write-Procedure

Writes out the procedure to the name typed by the designer. Checks to see if the procedure will overwrite a previous definition, and if so allows a new name to be typed. Discussed in section 11.2.

Object-Object Rules Used in Peridot

D.1. Introduction

Peridot uses rule-based inferencing in four different places: (1) inferring object-object relationships (section 4.2), (2) inferring when iterations should occur (section 6.2), (3) inferring how a conditional should depend on an active value (section 7.2), and (4) inferring how the mouse should set an active value (section 9.3.3). This appendix lists all the rules used for object-object inferencing. The rules used for the other inferences are listed in the sections which discuss them.

D.2. Object-Object Rules

D.2.1. Rectangles with respect to Rectangles

Rule Name	Specifies	Description
Rect-same	all	Two rectangles have identical size and position
Rect-same-size-with-same-offset	all	Rectangles are same size, and the position of one is offset from the other by the same amount in x and y
Rect-same-size-with-diff-offset	all	Rectangles are same size, and the position of one is offset from the other by different amounts in x and y
Rect-sub-region-equal	all	Rectangle nested inside another with the same size border all around
Rect-super-region-equal	all	Rectangle nested outside another with the same size border all around
Rect-sub-region-title	all	Rectangle nested inside another with the same size border all around except at top
Rect-super-region-title	all	Rectangle nested outside another with the same size border all around except at top
Rect-flush-right	all	Rectangles are the same size, and second is to the right of the first
Rect-flush-bottom	all	Rectangles are the same size, and second is directly below the first
Rect-same-size	WIDTH HEIGHT	Rectangles are the same size

Rectangles with respect to Rectangles, cont.

Rule Name	Specifies	Description
Rect-same-width-left	LEFT WIDTH	Rectangles have the same width and left
Rect-centered-X	LEFT WIDTH	Rectangle centered horizontally inside another rectangle, with equal offsets on the left and right
Rect-centered-Y	BOTTOM HEIGHT	Rectangle centered vertically inside another rectangle, with equal offsets on the top and bottom
Rect-Flush-Bottom	BOTTOM	Rectangle's bottom has small offset from the bottom of other rectangle
Rect-Flush-Top	BOTTOM	Rectangle's top has small offset from the top of other rectangle
Rect-Attached-Top	HEIGHT	Rectangle's top has small offset from the bottom of other rectangle
Rect-Flush-Top-Height	HEIGHT	Rectangle's top has small offset from the top of other rectangle
Rect-Flush-Left	LEFT	Rectangle's left has small offset from the left of other rectangle
Rect-Flush-Right	LEFT	Rectangle's right has small offset from the right of other rectangle
Rect-Sub-Width	WIDTH	Rectangle's width is close to the width of other rectangle
Rect-Sub-Height	HEIGHT	Rectangle's height is close to the height of other rectangle

D.2.2. Strings, Icons and Circles with respect to Strings and Icons

Rule Name	Specifies	Description
String-Flush-Below-Centered	all	String or icon centered flush below the other string or icon
String-Flush-Below-Left	all	String or icon aligned at the left and flush below the other string or icon
String-Flush-Below-Right	all	String or icon aligned at the right and flush below the other string or icon
String-Offset-Below-Centered	all	String or icon centered below the other string or icon, offset by a constant
String-Offset-Below-Right-Offset	all	String or icon aligned at the right and offset below the other string or icon
String-Offset-Below-Left-Offset	all	String or icon aligned at the left and offset below the other string or icon
String-Left	all	String or icon directly to the left of the other string or icon
String-Right	all	String or icon directly to the right of the other string or icon

D.2.3. Strings, Icons, and Circles with respect to Rectangles or Circles

NOTE: These rules are used for strings, icons, or circles with respect to rectangles, and for strings and icons with respect to circles. In the rules, "source" refers to the object that will depend on the "destination" object. For example, for strings, icons, or circles with respect to rectangles, the source is the string, icon, or circle, and the destination is the rectangle. Clearly, for strings and icons, the LEFT BOTTOM in the "Specifies" field are all the properties for those objects; for circles, the DIAMETER field is not specified by the rules.

Rule Name	Specifies	Description
String-Centered	LEFT BOTTOM	Source centered inside destination
String-Centered-At-Top-Of-Rect	LEFT BOTTOM	Source inside destination, centered horizontally, and flush at the top
String-Left-At-Top-Of-Rect	LEFT BOTTOM	Source inside destination at the left and top
String-Right-At-Top-Of-Rect	LEFT BOTTOM	Source inside destination right-flushed at top
String-Centered-Offset	LEFT BOTTOM	Source inside destination centered horizontally, offset from top
String-Centered-On-Right	LEFT BOTTOM	Source outside destination centered vertically and offset horizontally to the right
String-Centered-On-Left	LEFT BOTTOM	Source outside destination centered vertically and offset horizontally to the left
String-Left-Offset-Top-Offset	LEFT BOTTOM	Source inside destination offset by constants from the top, left
String-Right-Offset-Top-Offset	LEFT BOTTOM	Source inside destination offset by constants from the top, right
Icon-Outside-Top-Left	LEFT BOTTOM	Source outside destination at the top, left
Icon-Outside-Bot-Left	LEFT BOTTOM	Source outside destination at the bottom, left
Icon-Outside-Top-Right	LEFT BOTTOM	Source outside destination at the top, right
Icon-Outside-Bot-Right	LEFT BOTTOM	Source outside destination at the bottom, right

D.2.4. Rectangles with respect to Strings and Icons

Rule Name	Specifies	Description
Rect-Same-Size-as-String	all	Rectangle same size as string or icon
Rect-Offset-around-String	WIDTH HEIGHT	Rectangle has constant offset all around string or icon
Rect-Height-Y-at-String	BOTTOM HEIGHT	Rectangle has same y position and height as string, but some other width and x
Rect-Centered-around-String	LEFT BOTTOM	Rectangle centered around string or icon

D.2.5. Circles with respect to Circles

Rule Name	Specifies	Description
Circle-Centered-in-Circle	LEFT BOTTOM	Circle centered inside another

D.2.6. Rectangles with respect to Many

Rule Name	Specifies	Description
Rect-Sum-of-Stacked-Iteration	all	Rectangle same size the sum of a vertical iteration of strings

References

[Ae 86] Tadashi Ae, Masafumi Yamashita, Wagner Chiepa Cunha, and Hroshi Matsumoto. "Visual User-Interface of A Programming System: MOPS-2," *IEEE Computer Society Workshop on Visual Languages*. IEEE CS Order No. 722. Dallas, Texas. June 25-27, 1986. pp. 44-53.

[Ahuja 86] Sudhir Ahuja, Nicholas Carriero, and David Gelernter. "Linda and Friends," *IEEE Computer*. Vol. 19, no. 6, June, 1986. pp. 62-71.

[Albizuri-Romero 84] Miren B. Albizuri-Romero. "GRASE--A Graphical Syntax-Directed Editor for Structured Programming," *SIGPLAN Notices*. Vol. 19, no. 2, Feb. 1984. pp. 28-37.

[Amanatides 83] John Amanatides. *DPAC: A Dynamic Graphics Package for a Real-Time Raster Device*. Master of Science Thesis. Department of Computer Science, University of Toronto, Toronto, Ontario, Canada. January 1983.

[Anderson 85] Nancy S. Anderson and Judith Reitman Olson, eds. *Methods for Designing Software to Fit Human Needs and Capabilities*, Proceedings of the Workshop on Software Human Factors. 1985: National Academy Press, Washington, D.C. 34 pages.

[Apple 85] Apple Computer, Inc. *Inside Macintosh*. Addison-Wesley, 1985.

[Attardi 82] Giuseppe Attardi and Maria Simi. "Extending the Power of Programming by Example," *SIGOA Conference on Office Information Systems*, Philadelphia, PA, Jun. 21-23, 1982. pp. 52-66.

[Baecker 81] Ron Baecker. *Sorting out Sorting*. 16mm color, sound film, 25 minutes. Dynamics Graphics Project, Computer Systems Research Institute, University of Toronto, Toronto, Ontario, Canada. 1981. Presented at ACM SIGGRAPH'81. Dallas, TX. Aug. 1981.

[Bauer 78] Michael Anthony Bauer. *A Basis for the Acquisition of Procedures*. PhD Thesis, Department of Computer Science, University of Toronto. 1978. 310 pages.

[Bergman 76] S. Bergman and A. Kaufman. "BGRAPH2: A Real-Time Graphics Language with Modular Objects and Implicit Dynamics," *Computer Graphics*. Vol. 10, no. 2, Summer, 1976. pp. 133-138.

[Bewley 83] William L. Bewley, Teresa L. Roberts, David Schroit, William L. Verplank. "Human Factors Testing in the Design of Xerox's 8010 'Star' Office Workstation," *Proceedings SIGCHI'83: Human Factors in Computing Systems*. Dec. 12-15, 1983. Boston, Mass. pp. 72-77.

[Bier 86] Eric Allan Bier and Maureen C. Stone. "Snap-Dragging," *Computer Graphics: SIGGRAPH '86 Conference Proceedings.* Vol. 20, no. 4, August 18-22, 1986. Dallas, Texas. pp. 233-240.

[Biermann 76a] Alan W. Biermann. "Approaches to Automatic Programming," *Advances in Computers*, Morris Rubinoff and Marshall C. Yovitz, eds. Vol. 15. New York: Academic Press, 1976. pp. 1-63.

[Biermann 76b] Alan W. Biermann and Ramachandran Krishnaswamy. "Constructing Programs from Example Computations," *IEEE Transactions on Software Engineering.* Vol. SE-2, no. 3. Sept. 1976. pp. 141-153.

[Boies 85] S.J. Boies, J.D. Gould, S. Levy, J.T. Richards, and J.W. Schoonard. "The 1984 Olympic Message System—A Case Study in System Design," *IBM Research Report.* RC-11138. 1985.

[Borning 79] Alan Borning. *Thinglab--A Constraint-Oriented Simulation Laboratory.* Xerox Palo Alto Research Center Technical Report SSL-79-3. July, 1979. 100 pages.

[Borning 81] Alan Borning. "The Programming Language Aspects of Thinglab; a Constraint-Oriented Simulation Laboratory," *Transactions on Programming Language and Systems.* Vol. 3, no. 4, Oct. 1981. pp. 353-387.

[Borning 86] Alan Borning. "Defining Constraints Graphically," *Human Factors in Computing Systems: Proceedings SIGCHI'86.* Boston, MA. Apr. 13-17, 1986.

[Brown 84] Marc H. Brown and Robert Sedgewick. "A System for Algorithm Animation," *Computer Graphics: SIGGRAPH'84 Conference Proceedings.* Minneapolis, Minn. Vol. 18, no. 3, July 23-27, 1984. pp. 177-186.

[Buneman 79] O.P. Buneman and E.K. Clemons, "Efficiently Monitoring Relational Databases," *ACM Transactions on Database Systems.* Vol. 4, no. 3. Sept. 1979. pp. 368-382.

[Buxton 80] William A. S. Buxton and R. Sniderman. "Iteration in the Design of the Human-Computer Interface," *Proceedings: 13th Annual Meeting, Human Factors Association of Canada.* pp. 72-81.

[Buxton 82] William Buxton. "An Informal Study of Selection Positioning Tasks," *Graphics Interface, '82,* Toronto, Ontario, May 17-21, 1982. pp. 323-328.

[Buxton 83] W. Buxton, M.R. Lamb, D. Sherman, and K.C. Smith. "Towards a Comprehensive User Interface Management System," *Computer Graphics: SIGGRAPH'83 Conference Proceedings.* Detroit, Mich. Vol. 17, no. 3. July 25-29, 1983. pp. 35-42.

[Buxton 85] William Buxton, Ralph Hill, and Peter Rowley. "Issues and Techniques in Touch-Sensitive Tablet Input," *Computer Graphics: SIGGRAPH'85 Conference Proceedings*. San Francisco, CA. Vol. 19, no. 3. July 22-26, 1985. pp. 215-224.

[Buxton 86] William Buxton and Brad Myers. "A Study in Two-Handed Input," *Proceedings SIGCHI'86: Human Factors in Computing Systems*. Boston, MA. April 13-17, 1986. pp. 321-326.

[Cardelli 85] Luca Cardelli and Rob Pike. "Squeak: A Language for Communicating with Mice," *Computer Graphics: SIGGRAPH'85 Conference Proceedings*. San Francisco, CA. Vol. 19, no. 3. July 22-26, 1985. pp. 199-204.

[Charniak 85] Eugene Charniak and Drew McDermott. *An Introduction to Artificial Intelligence*. Reading, MA: Addison-Wesley Publishing Company, 1985.

[Christensen 68] Carlos Christensen. "An Example of the Manipulation of Directed Graphs in the AMBIT/G Programming Language," in *Interactive Systems for Experimental Applied Mathematics*, Melvin Klerer and Juris Reinfelds, eds. New York: Academic Press, 1968. pp. 423-435.

[Christensen 71] Carlos Christensen. "An Introduction to AMBIT/L, A Diagramatic Language for List Processing," *Proceedings of the 2nd Symposium on Symbolic and Algebraic Manipulation*. Los Angeles, CA. Mar. 23-25, 1971. pp. 248-260.

[Cunniff 86] Nancy Cunniff, Robert P. Taylor, and John B. Black. "Does Programming Language Affect the Type of Conceptual Bugs in Beginners' Programs? A Comparison of FPL and Pascal," *Proceedings SIGCHI'86: Human Factors in Computing Systems*. Boston, MA. April 13-17, 1986. pp. 175-182.

[Dance 87] John R. Dance, Tamar E. Granor, Ralph D. Hill, Scott E. Hudson, Jon Meads, Brad A. Myers, and Andrew Schulert. "Report on the Runtime Structure of UIMS-Supported Applications," *Proceedings ACM SIGGRAPH Workshop on Software Tools for User Interface Development*. to appear in *Computer Graphics*, 1987.

[Desain 86] Peter Desain. "Graphical Programming in Computer Music," *Proceedings of the International Computer Music Conference*. Royal Conservatory, The Hague, Netherlands. Oct. 20-24, 1986. pp. 161-166.

[Duisberg 86] Robert A. Duisberg. "Animated Graphical Interfaces using Temporal Constraints," *Proceedings SIGCHI'86: Human Factors in Computing Systems*. Boston, MA. April 13-17, 1986. pp. 131-136.

[Ellis 69] T.O. Ellis, J.F. Heafner and W.L. Sibley. *The Grail Project: An Experiment in Man-Machine Communication.* RAND Report RM-5999-Arpa. 1969.

[Foley 84a] James D. Foley. "Managing the Design of User-Computer Interfaces," *Proceedings of the Fifth Annual NCGA Conference and Exposition.* Anaheim, CA. Vol. II. May 13-17, 1984. pp. 436-451.

[Foley 84b] James D. Foley, Victor L. Wallace, and Peggy Chan. "The Human Factors of Computer Graphics Interaction Techniques," *IEEE CG&A.* Vol. 4, no. 11, Nov. 1984. pp. 13-48.

[Foley 86] James D. Foley and Charles F. McMath. "Dynamic Process Visualization," *IEEE Computer Graphics and Applications.* Vol. 6, no. 2. March, 1986. pp. 16-25.

[Fox 86] Mark Fox. Carnegie Group, Inc. Pittsburgh, PA. private communication.

[Glinert 84] Ephraim P. Glinert and Steven L. Tanimoto. "Pict: An Interactive Graphical Programming Environment," *IEEE Computer.* Vol. 17, no. 11, Nov. 1984. pp. 7-25.

[Goldberg 83] Adele Goldberg and Dave Robson. *Smalltalk-80: The Language and Its Implementation.* Reading, MA: Addison-Wesley Publishing Company, 1983.

[Good 84] Michael D. Good, John A. Whiteside, Dennis R. Wilson, and Sandra J. Jones. "Building a User-Derived Interface," *CACM.* Vol. 27, no. 10. Oct. 1984. pp. 1032-1043.

[Gould 84] Laura Gould and William Finzer. *Programming by Rehearsal.* Xerox Palo Alto Research Center Technical Report SCL-84-1. May, 1984. 133 pages. A short version appears in *Byte.* Vol. 9, no. 6. June, 1984.

[Grafton 85] Robert B. Grafton and Tadao Ichikawa, eds. *IEEE Computer*, Special Issue on Visual Programming. Vol. 18, no. 8, Aug. 1985.

[Granor 86] Tamar Ezekiel Granor. *A User Interface Management Systems Generator.* PhD Thesis. Department of Computer and Information Science, University of Pennsylvania. Philadelphia, PA. Technical Report MS-CIS-86-42 Graphics Lab 12. May, 1986. 158 pages.

[Green 88] Daniel Martin Green. *C-Peridot: a C Language Implementation of Peridot.* Master's Thesis. Department of Computer Science, University of Illinois at Urbana-Champaign. 1988.

[Hailpern 86] Brent Hailpern. "Multi-Paradigm Languages and Environments," *IEEE Software*, (Special Issue on Multi-Paradigm Environments). Vol. 3, no. 1, Jan, 1986. pp. 6-9.

[Halbert 81] Daniel C. Halbert. *An Example of Programming by Example.* Masters of Science Thesis. Computer Science Division, Dept. of EE&CS, University of California, Berkeley and Xerox Corporation Office Products Division, Palo Alto, CA. June, 1981. 55 pages.

[Halbert 84] Daniel C. Halbert. *Programming by Example.* PhD Thesis. Computer Science Division, Dept. of EE&CS, University of California, Berkeley. 1984. Also: Xerox Office Systems Division, Systems Development Department, TR OSD-T8402, December, 1984. 83 pages.

[Hayes 85] Philip J. Hayes, Pedro A. Szekely, and Richard A. Lerner. "Design Alternatives for User Interface Management Systems Based on Experience with COUSIN," *Proceedings SIGCHI'85: Human Factors in Computing Systems.* San Francisco, CA. April 14-18, 1985. pp. 169-175.

[Helfman 87] Janathan Helfman. "Panther: A Tabular User-Interface Specification System," *Proceedings SIGCHI+GI'87: Human Factors in Computing Systems.* Toronto, Ont., Canada. April 5-9, 1987. pp. 279-284.

[Henderson 86] D. Austin Henderson, Jr. "The Trillium User Interface Design Environment," *Proceedings SIGCHI'86: Human Factors in Computing Systems.* Boston, MA. April 13-17, 1986. pp. 221-227.

[Hill 87a] Ralph D. Hill. "Event-Response Systems — A Technique for Specifying Multi-Threaded Dialogues," *Proceedings SIGCHI+GI'87: Human Factors in Computing Systems.* Toronto, Ont., Canada. April 5-9, 1987. pp. 241-248.

[Hill 87b] Ralph D. Hill. *Supporting Concurrency, Communication and Synchronization in Human-Computer Interaction.* PhD Thesis. Department of Computer Science, University of Toronto. Toronto, Ontario, Canada, M5S 1A4. January, 1987. 206 pages.

[Hill 87c] Ralph D. Hill. "Supporting Concurrency, Communication and Synchronization in Human-Computer Interaction—The Sassafras UIMS," to appear in *ACM Trans. on Graphics* special issue on User Interface Software. 1987.

[Honeywell 85] Honeywell Process Control Division. *Work Cell Operator Station.* Fort Washington, PA. 1985.

[Hudson 86] Scott E. Hudson and Roger King. "A Generator of Direct Manipulation Office Systems," *ACM Transactions on Office Systems.* Vol. 4, no. 2, April 1986. pp. 132-163.

[Hutchins 86] Edwin L. Hutchins, James D. Hollan, and Donald A. Norman. "Direct Manipulation Interfaces," *User Centered System Design*, Donald A. Norman and Stephen W. Draper, eds. Hillsdale, New Jersey: Lawrence Erlbaum Associates, 1986. pp. 87-124.

[IEEE 86] *IEEE Computer Society Workshop on Visual Languages*. IEEE CS Order No. 722. Dallas, Texas. June 25-27, 1986. 179 pages.

[Jacob 83] Robert J.K. Jacob. "Executable Specifications for a Human-Computer Interface," *Human Factors in Computing Systems: Proceedings SIGCHI'83*. Boston, MA. Dec. 12-15, 1983. pp. 28-34.

[Jacob 84] Robert J.K. Jacob. "An Executable Specification Technique for Describing Human-Computer Interaction," in *Advances in Human-Computer Interaction*, H.R. Hartson, ed. Ablex Publishing Co. 1984. 39 pages.

[Jacob 85] Robert J.K. Jacob. "A State Transition Diagram Language for Visual Programming," *IEEE Computer*. Vol. 18, no. 8. Aug. 1985. pp. 51-59.

[Kasik 82] David J. Kasik. "A User-Interface Management System," *Computer Graphics: SIGGRAPH'82 Conference Procedings*. Boston, MA. Vol. 16, no. 3 . July 26-30, 1982. pp. 99-106.

[Lieberman 82] Henry Lieberman. "Constructing Graphical User Interfaces by Example," *Graphics Interface, '82*, Toronto, Ontario, May 17-21, 1982. pp. 295-302.

[Mason 83] R.E.A. Mason and T.T. Carey. "Prototyping Interactive Information Systems," *Communications of the ACM*. Vol. 26, no. 5. May, 1983. pp. 347-354.

[Mittal 86] Sanjay Mittal, Clive L. Dym, and Mahesh Morjaria. "Pride: An Expert System for the Design of Paper Handling Systems," *IEEE Computer*. Vol. 19, no. 7, July, 1986. pp. 102-114.

[Morgan 83] C. Morgan, G. Williams, and P. Lemmons. "An Interview with Wayne Rosing, Bruce Daniels, and Larry Tesler," *Byte*. Vol. 8, no. 2, February, 1983. pp. 90-114.

[Morse 84] Alan C. Morse. "A System For Embedding Data Displays in Graphical Contexts," Intelligent Software Systems, Inc. and Visual Intelligence Corp., technical report 84-7-1. Amherst, Mass. July, 1984.

[Musen 86] Mark A. Musen, Lawrence M. Fagen, and Edward H. Shortliffe. "Graphical Specification of Procedural Knowledge for an Expert System," *IEEE Computer Society Workshop on Visual Languages*. IEEE CS Order No. 722. Dallas, Texas. June 25-27, 1986. pp. 167-178.

[Myers 80] Brad A. Myers. *Displaying Data Structures for Interactive Debugging*. Xerox Palo Alto Research Center Technical Report CSL-80-7. June, 1980. 97 pages.

[Myers 83] Brad A. Myers. "Incense: A System for Displaying Data Structures," *Computer Graphics: SIGGRAPH '83 Conference Proceedings*. Vol. 17, no. 3. July 1983. pp. 115-125.

[Myers 84] Brad A. Myers. "The User Interface for Sapphire," *IEEE Computer Graphics and Applications*. Vol. 4, no. 12. Dec. 1984. pp. 13-23.

[Myers 85] Brad A. Myers. "The Importance of Percent-Done Progress Indicators for Computer-Human Interfaces," *Proceedings SIGCHI'85: Human Factors in Computing Systems*. San Francisco, CA, April 14-18, 1985. pp. 11-17.

[Myers 86a] Brad A. Myers. "Visual Programming, Programming by Example, and Program Visualization; A Taxonomy," *Proceedings SIGCHI'86: Human Factors in Computing Systems*. Boston, MA. April 13-17, 1986. pp. 59-66.

[Myers 86b] Brad A. Myers and William Buxton. "Creating Highly Interactive and Graphical User Interfaces by Demonstration," *Computer Graphics: SIGGRAPH'86 Conference Proceedings*. Vol. 20, no. 4, August 18-22, 1986. Dallas, Texas. pp. 249-258.

[Myers 87a] Brad A. Myers. "Creating Dynamic Interaction Techniques by Demonstration," *Proceedings SIGCHI+GI'87: Human Factors in Computing Systems*. Toronto, Ont., Canada. April 5-9, 1987. pp. 271-278.

[Myers 87b] Brad A. Myers. "Gaining General Acceptance for UIMSs," *Proceedings ACM SIGGRAPH Workshop on Software Tools for User Interface Development*. to appear in *Computer Graphics*, 1987.

[Myers 87c] Brad A. Myers. *Creating User Interfaces by Demonstration: The Peridot User Interface Management Systems*. 15 minute Videotape. Dynamic Graphics Project, Computer Systems Research Institute, University of Toronto, Toronto, Ontario, Canada, M5S 1A4.

[Myers prep] Brad A. Myers. "The Issue of Semantic Feedback." In preparation.

[Nassi 73] I. Nassi and B. Shneiderman. "Flowchart Techniques for Structured Programming," *SIGPLAN Notices*. Vol. 8, no. 8, Aug. 1973. pp. 12-26.

[Nelson 85] Greg Nelson. "Juno, a Constraint-Based Graphics System," *Computer Graphics: SIGGRAPH'85 Conference Proceedings*. San Francisco, CA. Vol. 19, no. 3. July 22-26, 1985. pp. 235-243.

[Newman 68] William M. Newman. "A System for Interactive Graphical Programming," *Proceedings of the AFIPS Spring Joint Computer Conference.* 1968. pp. 47-54.

[Nielson 87] Jakob Nielson. "Classification of Dialogue Techniques," workshop at SIGCHI+GI'87 conference. Toronto, Ont., Canada. April 5-9, 1987. Summary to appear in *SIGCHI Bulletin.*

[Nix 86] Robert P. Nix. "Editing by Example," *ACM Transactions on Programming Languages and Systems.* Vol. 7, no. 4. Oct. 1985. pp. 600-621.

[Olsen 83] Dan R. Olsen, Jr. and Elizabeth P. Dempsey. "Syngraph: A Graphical User Interface Generator," *Computer Graphics: SIGGRAPH'83 Conference Proceedings.* Detroit, Mich. Vol. 17, no. 3. July 25-29, 1983. pp. 43-50.

[Olsen 84] Dan R. Olsen, Jr., William Buxton, Roger Ehrich, David J. Kasik, James R. Rhyne, and John Sibert. "A Context for User Interface Management," *IEEE Computer Graphics and Applications.* Vol. 4, no. 2. Dec. 1984. pp. 33-42.

[Olsen 85a] Dan R. Olsen, Jr., Elisabeth P. Dempsey, and Roy Rogge. "Input-Output Linkage in a User Interface Management System," *Computer Graphics: SIGGRAPH'85 Conference Proceedings.* San Francisco, CA. Vol. 19, no. 3. July 22-26, 1985. pp. 225-234.

[Olsen 85b] Dan R. Olsen, Jr. *Automatic Generation of Efficient Display Algorithms.* Brigham Young University, Computer Science Department, Technical Report, 1985. 22 pages.

[Olsen 87] Dan R. Olsen, Jr. "Larger Issues in User Interface Management," *Proceedings ACM SIGGRAPH Workshop on Software Tools for User Interface Development.* to appear in *Computer Graphics,* 1987.

[Pavlidis 85] Theo Pavlidis and Christopher J. Van Wyk. "An Automatic Beautifier for Drawings and Illustrations," *Computer Graphics: SIGGRAPH'85 Conference Proceedings.* San Francisco, CA. Vol. 19, no. 3. July 22-26, 1985. pp. 225-234.

[Pfaff 85] Gunther R. Pfaff, ed. *User Interface Management Systems.* Berlin: Springer-Verlag, 1985. 224 pages.

[PHIGS] *Draft Proposal American National Standard for the Functional Specification of the Programmer's Hierarchical Interactive Graphics Standard (PHIGS).* American National Standards Committee: X3H3/84-40.

[Pietrzykowski 83] Thomas Pietrzykowski, Stanislaw Matwin, and Tomasz Muldner. "The Programming Language PROGRAPH: Yet Another Application of Graphics," *Graphics Interface'83*, Edmonton, Alberta. May 9-13, 1983. pp. 143-145.

[Pietrzykowski 84] T. Pietrzykowski and S. Matwin. *PROGRAPH: A Preliminary Report.* University of Ottawa Technical Report TR-84-07. April, 1984. 91 pages.

[Pong 83] M.C. Pong and N. Ng. "Pigs--A System for Programming with Interactive Graphical Support," *Software--Practice and Experience.* Vol. 13, no. 9. Sept. 1983. pp. 847-855.

[Pong 86] Man-Chi Pong. "A Graphical Language for Concurrent Programming," *IEEE Computer Society Workshop on Visual Languages.* IEEE CS Order No. 722. Dallas, Texas. June 25-27, 1986. pp. 26-33.

[Ramamoorthy 87] C.V. Ramamoorthy, Shashi Shekhar, and Vijay Garg. "Software Development Support for AI Programs," *IEEE Computer.* Vol. 20, no. 1, Jan, 1987. pp. 30-40.

[Robillard 86] Pierre N. Robillard. "Schematic Pseudocode for Program Constructs and its Computer Automation by SchemaCode," *CACM.* Vol. 29, no. 11. Nov. 1986. pp. 1072-1089.

[Rovner 69] P.D. Rovner and D.A. Henderson, Jr. "On the Implementation of AMBIT/G: A Graphical Programming Language," *Proceedings of the International Joint Conference on Artificial Intelligence.* Washington, D.C. May 7-9, 1969. pp. 9-20.

[Schmucker 86] Kurt J. Schmucker. "MacApp: An Application Framework," *Byte*, August 1986. pp. 189-193.

[Schulert 85] Andrew J. Schulert, George T. Rogers, and James A. Hamilton. "ADM—A Dialogue Manager," *Proceedings SIGCHI'85: Human Factors in Computing Systems.* San Francisco, CA, April 14-18, 1985. pp. 177-183.

[Shaw 75] David E. Shaw, William R. Swartout, and C. Cordell Green. "Inferring Lisp Programs from Examples," *Fourth International Joint Conference on Artificial Intelligence.* Tbilisi, USSR. Sept. 3-8, 1975. Vol. 1. pp. 260-267.

[Sheil 83] Beau Sheil. "Power Tools for Programmers," *Datamation.* Vol. 29, no. 2. Feb. 1983. pp. 131-144.

[Shneiderman 83] Ben Shneiderman. "Direct Manipulation: A Step Beyond Programming Languages," *IEEE Computer.* Vol. 16, no. 8. Aug. 1983. pp. 57-69.

[Shneiderman 86] Ben Shneiderman. "Seven Plus or Minus Two Central Issues in Human-Computer Interfaces," *Proceedings SIGCHI'86: Human Factors in Computing Systems.* (closing plenary address) Boston, MA. April 13-17, 1986. pp. 343-349.

[Shu 85] Nan C. Shu. "FORMAL: A Forms-Oriented Visual-Directed Application Development System," *IEEE Computer.* Vol. 18, no. 8, Aug. 1985. pp. 38-49.

[Sibert 86] John L. Sibert, William D. Hurley, and Teresa W. Bleser. "An Object-Oriented User Interface Management System," *Computer Graphics: SIGGRAPH '86 Conference Proceedings.* Vol. 20, no. 4, August 18-22, 1986. Dallas, Texas. pp. 259-268.

[Smith 77] David Canfield Smith. *Pygmalion: A Computer Program to Model and Stimulate Creative Thought.* Basel, Stuttgart: Birkhauser, 1977. 187 pages.

[Smith 82] David Canfield Smith, Charles Irby, Ralph Kimball, Bill Verplank, and Erik Harslem. "Designing the Star User Interface," *Byte Magazine,* April 1982, pp. 242-282.

[Smith 86] Randall B. Smith. "The Alternate Reality Kit," *IEEE Computer Society Workshop on Visual Languages.* IEEE CS Order No. 722. Dallas, Texas. June 25-27, 1986. pp. 99-106.

[Smith 87] Randall B. Smith. "Experiences with the Alternate Reality Kit: An Example of the Tension Between Literalism and Magic," *Proceedings SIGCHI+GI'87: Human Factors in Computing Systems.* Toronto, Ont., Canada. April 5-9, 1987. pp. 61-67.

[Stefik 83] Mark Stefik, Daniel G. Bobrow, Sanjay Mittal, and Lynn Conway. "Knowledge Programming in Loops: Report on an Experimental Course," *The AI Magazine.* Vol. 4, no. 3, Fall, 1983. pp. 3-13.

[Stefik 86] Mark Stefik, Daniel G. Bobrow, and Kenneth M. Kahn. "Integrating Access-Oriented Programming into a Multi-Paradigm Environment," *IEEE Software.* Vol. 3, no. 1, Jan, 1986. pp. 10-18.

[Stevens 83] Albert Stevens, Bruce Roberts, and Larry Stead, "The Use of A Sophisticated Graphics Interface in Computer Assisted Instruction," *IEEE Computer Graphics and Applications.* Vol. 3, no. 2. March/April, 1983. pp. 25-31.

[Sutherland 63] Ivan E. Sutherland. "SketchPad: A Man-Machine Graphical Communication System," *AFIPS Spring Joint Computer Conference.* Vol. 23. 1963. pp. 329-346.

[Sutherland 66] William R. Sutherland. *On-line Graphical Specification of Computer Procedures*. MIT PhD Thesis. Lincoln Labs Report TR-405. 1966.

[Sutton 78] Jimmy A. Sutton and Ralph H. Sprague, Jr. *A Study of Display Generation and Management in Interactive Business Applications*. IBM Research Report RJ2392. Nov. 9, 1978. 20 pages.

[Swartout 82] W. Swartout and R. Balzer. "The Inevitable Intertwining of Specification and Implementation," *Communications of the ACM*. Vol. 25, no. 7. 1982. pp. 438-440.

[Tanner 85] Peter P. Tanner and William A.S. Buxton. "Some Issues in Future User Interface Management System (UIMS) Development," in *User Interface Management Systems*, Gunther R. Pfaff, ed. Berlin: Springer-Verlag, 1985. pp. 67-79.

[Tanner 86] Peter P. Tanner, S.A. MacKay, D.A. Stewart, and M. Wein. "A Multitasking Switchboard Approach to User Interface Management," *Computer Graphics: SIGGRAPH'86 Conference Proceedings*. Vol. 20, no. 4, August 18-22, 1986. Dallas, Texas. pp. 241-248.

[Taylor 86] Thomas H. Taylor and Robert P. Burton. "An Icon-Based Graphical Editor," *Computer Graphics World*. Vol. 9, no. 10. Oct, 1986. pp. 77-82.

[Tesler 81] Larry Tesler, "The Smalltalk Environment," *Byte*. Vol. 6, no. 8, Aug., 1981, pp. 90-147.

[Thomas 83] James J. Thomas and Griffith Hamlin, eds. "Graphical Input Interaction Technique (GIIT) Workshop Summary." ACM/SIGGRAPH, Seattle, WA. June 2-4, 1982. in *Computer Graphics*. Vol. 17, no. 1. Jan. 1983. pp. 5-30.

[Wasserman 82] A.I. Wasserman and D.T. Shewmake. "Rapid Prototyping of Interactive Information Systems," *ACM Software Engineering Notes*. Vol. 7, no. 5. pp. 171-180.

[Weinreb 80] D. Weinreb and D. Moon. *Flavors: Message Passing in the Lisp Machine*. MIT AI Laboratory Memo No. 602. 1980.

[Weinreb 81] D. Weinreb and D. Moon. *Introduction to Using the Window System*. Symbolics, Inc. 1981.

[Williams 83] Gregg Williams. "The Lisa Computer System," *Byte Magazine*, February 1983, pp. 33-50.

[Williams 84] Gregg Williams. "The Apple Macintosh Computer," *Byte Magazine*. Vol. 9, no. 2, February 1984. pp. 30-54.

[Wong 82] Peter C.S. Wong and Eric R. Reid. "Flair--User Interface Dialogue Design Tool," *Computer Graphics: SIGGRAPH'82 Conference Proceedings*. Boston, MA. Vol. 16, no. 3 . July 26-30, 1982. pp. 87-98.

[Xerox 83] Xerox Corporation. *Interlisp Reference Manual*. Pasadena, CA. October, 1983.

[Yoshimoto 86] I. Yoshimoto, N. Monden, M. Hirakawa, M. Tanaka, and T. Ichikawa. "Interactive Iconic Programming Facility in HI-VISUAL," *IEEE Computer Society Workshop on Visual Languages*. IEEE CS Order No. 722. Dallas, Texas. June 25-27, 1986. pp. 34-41.

[Zloof 77] Moshe M. Zloof and S. Peter de Jong. "The System for Business Automation (SBA): Programming Language," *CACM*. Vol. 20, no. 6, June, 1977. pp. 385-396.

[Zloof 81] Moshe M. Zloof. "QBE/OBE: A Language for Office and Business Automation," *IEEE Computer*. Vol. 14, no. 5, May, 1981. pp. 13-22.

Index

Perspectives in Computing

Volumes 1–12 were published as **Notes and Reports in Computer Science and Applied Mathematics.**

DATE DUE	St-Raymond	
1		
2 8 OCT 1992		
0 5 FEV. 2001		
3 1 AOUT 2005		

Bibliofiche 297B